'A book for those of us who didn't have the fairy tale. It's important to know that even though things don't always go to plan it doesn't mean you aren't a superhero or a power mum in your own right. A must-read for all of those muddling through.'

Paloma Faith

'Amazing. This book is proof that although Laura's mind was her undoing, it is also an incredible asset that is going to help so many people.'

Clemmie Telford, @clemmie_telford

'This book is a comfort to women recovering who read it and realise that all their crazy mad-ass thoughts were the illness and not themselves.'

Fiona Telford, postpartum psychosis survivor

'Laura's raw, honest book gets to the core of postpartum psychosis. She has emerged with a greater understanding of self, with deeper compassion for those who suffer from mental illness, and with a determination to combat stigma and ignorance by speaking out. I hope this book will give women and their families confidence that the brain and body will heal. And I hope it will encourage other women to speak out.'

Dr Jessica Heron, CEO, Action on Postpartum Psychosis

'This book will bring hope to many women and their partners who have struggled with their mental health during this already nerve-wracking and overwhelming time.'

Becca Maberly, @amotherplace

'An incredibly powerful book. Brave, brilliant and so, so important.'

Jessie Ware

'Raw, powerful, visceral: this book has so much to offer to anyone who reads it, whether they be a pregnant woman, new mother, partner, midwife, or someone recovering from mental illness. It is so important on so many levels to hear experiences like Laura's to widen our understanding of these issues and how they can affect us'.

Isabelle Bourton, midwife

'Every maternity nurse must read this book. Laura has taught me what no course could have taught me.'

'The Maternity Nurse'

'I absolutely loved this book. It's so honest, I related to the rawness of it all. There was so much I could identify with.'

Helen Grimes, postpartum psychosis survivor

'Unfiltered and inspiring. I felt like I was right there on the journey with Laura and I felt privileged she shared it.'

Rosey Adams, @pndandme

'A seminal work which will help people worldwide who identify with Laura's experience.'

Karen Levi, psychotherapist

'I cried, laughed and cried again. It's therapeutic to read. This book will help to raise awareness and help people understand what it's like to go through this, to see light at the end of the tunnel and know you won't always feel like this.'

Jessie Hunt, postpartum psychosis survivor

'This book will save lives. Laura is completely honest about her experiences and shows incredible insight into her thoughts and feelings at that time. A must-read for everybody.'

Mia Vaughan, @cigarettesandcalpol

'An important book and I have no doubt it will have a significant impact.'

Dr Chi-Chi Obuaya, psychiatrist

What Have I Done?

An honest memoir about surviving postnatal mental illness

LAURA DOCKRILL

◼ SQUARE PEG

1 3 5 7 9 10 8 6 4 2

Square Peg, an imprint of Vintage
20 Vauxhall Bridge Road,
London SW1V 2SA

Square Peg is part of the Penguin Random House group of companies
whose addresses can be found at global.penguinrandomhouse.com

First published by Square Peg in 2020

Penguin.co.uk/vintage

A CIP catalogue record for this book is available from the British Library

ISBN 9781529110210

Typeset in 11.5/17.5pt Adobe Garamond by Jouve (UK), Milton Keynes
Printed and bound in Great Britain by Clays Ltd, Elcograf, S.p.A.

Penguin Random House is committed to a sustainable future
for our business, our readers and our planet. This book is made
from Forest Stewardship Council® certified paper.

For Hugo and Jet

The events described here are based on memories of my experiences. The identifying features of some people and places have been changed in order to protect the privacy. Any similarities are purely coincidental.

Author's Note

I *very nearly* didn't write this book.

It scares me to death. Revisiting the messy pain of what happened. It's a lot of 'what the FUCK was all that about?' But also a lot of holding onto myself, thinking, 'Wow. That was close.' I've seen something I can't un-see. Trauma can make you fragile and vulnerable, and shame can stalk you in its wake. You become a sort of mental health police officer, trying to identify and assess the slightest thing that might trigger your symptoms, troubleshooting your days so as to not upset your delicate equilibrium. Writing about my postpartum psychosis is like stepping into a field full of landmines with a blindfold on.

Perhaps your first year of motherhood was what you expected, but it certainly wasn't for me. Having a baby almost ruined my life. I soon realised that I am not alone. So many women have related to some degree. Many mums feel they pushed their personalities out of their bodies along with their baby, they feel lost, and are trying to somehow put their old selves back together.

And nobody warns us.

The story of motherhood goes well beyond mine, from miscarriage, child-loss, termination for medical reasons (TFMR), adoption, surrogacy, parents unable to conceive, IVF – there are many different paths to becoming a mother. I recognise I am lucky. To be able to *have* a child is lucky, and I want to acknowledge that I write this from the vantage point of privilege. I am not trying to play the violin here, but I want to use my position of being a 'middle-class, healthy, white woman' – with a supportive partner and family close by living in the UK where the health-care system is exceptional compared to most parts of the world and pregnancy and birth are generally safe – to help bring attention to postnatal mental health. And what even *makes* you a mother anyway? It is not found alone inside the simple act of carrying and birthing a child, I can tell you that. It took me *ages* to understand that I was a mum – in fact, it's something I'm still trying to understand.

There is a stigma surrounding postnatal mental health. There is silence. I am telling my version of events to add my voice to the wider conversation that needs to grow around women's health experiences.

To get better, I needed everything from medication, a psychiatrist, a psychotherapist, midwives, the NHS and lots of support from my family and friends. My partner Hugo says if he could share one piece of advice from our experience, it is this: speak up. Talk about what you're experiencing. A lot of the problem with any mental health illness is about finding the vocabulary to articulate what you are going through. So trust your loved ones and talk to them – they know you better than anybody, they know who you are.

This book might contain 'triggers' that could be sensitive to some readers. As I have said, landmines are everywhere! I had never experienced any kind of mental-health issue or illness up until the birth of my son so I know as well as anyone that it can happen to anybody and it does not discriminate. You are not immune from mental illness. The spectrum is vast and kaleidoscopic and we are all on it.

If you find some of this book hard to read then please ask for help, there is no weakness in taking responsibility for your health.

The bravest thing a person can do is ask for help.

Prologue

I t was my first Mother's Day.

I woke up alone and confused in starched white sheets in a bed that wasn't mine. The room was office-y with a 'homely' touch, kind of Premier Inn-meets-hospital-ward. Cream walls and a navy-blue carpet. A sink. A mirror. A wardrobe. A desk. A chair. A TV. A small chest of drawers. A bathroom. A framed photograph of a hot air balloon floating up above fields in a blue sky.

There was no Hugo.

The door to the room was ajar. An eye peered in, watching me. I didn't recognise the face it belonged to.

I was bleeding, my scar was raw and sore and my boobs were full of milk.

Is this a hell hotel? Have I done something really terrible? I feel like I have. Is this a posh prison? An asylum?

It was as though I'd been returned to the world from a blackout – like I'd been on a serious bender for the past month and this was the 'What the hell did I do last night?' moment, times a million. I felt like I needed to contact everybody in my phone in that 'apologise to everybody for everything I've ever done' panicked dread. But before I knew it, all the feelings that I'd been fighting against came flooding back. After a few sweet hours of sedated sleep, all my racing, looping, intrusive thoughts surged back and all I could do was lie there, looking at the ceiling, and say, 'Oh no. Oh God. Oh God. Oh God.'

Because I knew I had to kill myself.

And I really didn't want to.

Even if I did, it seemed, there was no way of doing so. This room was kill-yourself-proof. The triple glazed window was jammed shut with industrial-scale locks. The TV was screwed to the wall. All cables were tied up: my phone charger; the lamp. It was like waking up at the start of some wretched zombie film in which I was the main character.

I looked at the captive electrical wires and thought, *Ha! Joke's on you, guys. I wasn't even gonna do it that way anyway.*

And that was why I was here, in this place, being watched, because I was having thoughts like that.

In fact, I'm pretty sure that somebody had sat in the room with me that night and watched me sleep. As in, that person's only job was to sit there in the darkness, watching me. I had definitely asked somebody to sit with me because I was terrified of myself. And I wanted to feel safe.

A nurse came into my room. I knew she was a nurse because she was wearing a nurse outfit. I couldn't bring myself to look at her. I felt like a child. No, like a wild animal that had been snatched from the veld and unloaded from some dark shipping container at a zoo. *This is your life now.*

'Would you like some breakfast, Laura?' I had zero appetite but I asked for scrambled eggs on toast because that's what I'd been eating at the hospital and it reminded me of home. I was so desperate to feel anything that reminded me of who I am – or who I was.

I said thank you, though. I had to be polite. I had to work *with* this place.

The scrambled eggs arrived on a beige lightweight wooden tray with a plastic knife and fork. I felt weak, slow and extremely numb. I crawled towards the chair, the duvet wrapped around my head. My hands were trembling. I didn't want the nurse to see my face because I was ashamed. Guilty. Disgusted. Ugly. Transparent. I felt sick for even eating, like I didn't deserve the food. The eggs went down my throat like lumps of clay.

A month before I had been the happiest I'd ever been, and now I was a shell. Suicidal. Another nurse came in to give me tablets. I was scared, but the Laura bit of me almost wanted to laugh. This couldn't be real. It was a cliché of a nightmare: you wake up in a psychiatric ward with no clue how you ended up there, a kind nurse gently coaxing, 'Time to take *your* pills, *insert name here*.'

Oh. God. Oh God. Oh God.

What had I done?

I had a baby.

And then I went mad.

I

If childbirth and motherhood are the most natural, universal, common things in the world, the things that women have been doing since the beginning of time, then why does nobody tell us that there's a good chance that you might not feel like yourself after you have a baby? That you might even lose your head? That you might not ever come back?

We are all too conscious of the physical changes and pain of pregnancy and childbirth – I mean, from late childhood, we women have been in pain (some of us wrapped in shame too) since we started bleeding monthly as young girls. It's no secret. But what about our minds?

As one of my friends said recently, 'The birth of your baby is also the death of yourself.'

I wanted to snog her for her honesty.

On 3 March 2018, about three weeks after my son was born, I posted a photo of me up on social media. I'm in a restaurant, smiling, with my bright pink lipstick on, proudly holding a celebratory glass of champagne. The caption read, 'Guess what, world? . . . I'm a MUM!'

That photo was a complete lie. And I knew it was. I was pretending to be myself. Lying *to* myself. It doesn't show how terrified I am. Of the whole world. Of the slightest noise that made me jump. Of myself and my baby and of what I might do. It doesn't show that, secretly, I want to get on a train to somewhere far, far away with Hugo, and never come back.

Six days after I posted that photo I was admitted to a psychiatric unit.

3

It's not easy to admit that the worst time of your life was when your baby was born.

We've all seen them. The Instagram post of Mum in her cool leopard-print leggings and Nike Air Max, red lips smiling. Are those *painted* nails? Boy, has she got it together! Smugly poised at a laptop, earning the bacon with a plump seven-month baby swaddled in its hippy wrap (which, BTW, are a complete nightmare) sucking on her breast. The caption: 'It's simply doing everything I did before, just this time with a baby'.

Or there's the New Mum at her Cross Fit class using baby as a deadweight, and another burpee-ing her way around the swings in the playground while her six-week-old baby watches on from a car seat, frowning all concerned, like: 'Are you OK, Mum?'

Or the one of New Mum having champagne and cake with the girls. Another doing 'date night' two weeks before her six-week check, like, 'Yes, we *still have* sex!' Mum is fitting back into her clothes; Mum is making papier-mâché piggy banks; drinking enough water; shaving her armpits; reading a bedtime story; going to a gig; playing peekaboo. Mum is keeping up with her favourite TV shows; reading the Booker longlist; being a good friend; making a healthy yet tasty cost-effective-probably-vegan meal; recycling; giving baby massage; sterilising. Mum is getting rid of her pregnancy knickers when they are the only knickers she truly likes; doing her taxes; walking the dog; donating to charity; freezing bananas; learning Japanese because why not? . . . Oh look! Mum is abseiling down the Shard and *still* finding the time to express and write a blog about the whole experience.

Yes. Some mums can do it all. And are really good at it. But why do we feel like we *have* to do it all? Social media doesn't help, because guess what guys: SOCIAL MEDIA SOMETIMES LIES . . . How do I know? Because I am guilty of it. Sorry about that.

But sometimes, if you look closely at those seemingly ordinary photographs the reality is there, plain for all to see. Behind the powder-pink babygrows and bug-eyed soft toys often lurks a scene of domestic horror, scented by washing powder and underscored by a terrifying lullaby: the frantic struggling confusion of, 'What the hell do I do with this *thing* that *really needs me?*' and 'How the hell do I take care of it when I can't even take care of *myself*?'

Who am I? Where did I go? Why the fuck did nobody tell me that this is what it's like?

But no time for that. The baby needs you. The baby needs *you*. Not your mum or grandma or Janice from number 97. *You*.

And what do you do if you just cannot be found at all? What if you are lost?

I think back to being on the Tube when I was pregnant, proudly wearing my 'Baby on Board' badge. I would smile at mums on the train with babies in buggies and they would never smile back. I once watched a woman carrying her pram down the out-of-service escalators at Victoria Station and she said to me, 'They're better in than out.' Now I know why.

Now, I patrol around the park like the 'Postpartum Police', looking into the eyes of every parent and surveying their behaviour.

'Yes, I can see the baby is fine. But *how are you?*'

4

When we were fourteen, Hugo and I were best friends. We met sometime over the summer stretch of school holidays on Wandsworth Common and spent long hot, lazy days lying on the grass, sharing Ribenas and beers, or jumping on our friends' massive trampoline. We spent most of our time making each other laugh. In the evenings, we spoke on the phone and made each other mixtapes. We moved like inseparable Geminis, sat back to back like the Kappa logo.

He came to my mum and stepdad's wedding and I went to his mum's funeral. We held hands as we walked back to his house afterwards. Hugo was the most beautiful person I'd ever met; seeing him in so much pain was almost too much to bear, but there was nothing I could do to make it better. Hugo grieved gracefully and silently. We spent hours on his bed listening to music, eating easy-peelers and stroking his cat Curly. We wrote each other letters.

We would joke about getting married if we couldn't find anybody else (we didn't want to find anybody else) and have babies. We chose our babies' names. Made designs of our future house. We got drunk.

We snogged each other's friends. We accidentally fell in love but never said a word to each other about it. It never happened and when we were twenty, we fell apart.

Ten years on and we were reunited. We found each other again in two whirlwinds that seemed to spin together. We were in love. Boy, proper love. We had ten years' worth of catching up to do. We stayed up all night drinking and dancing, singing, reading to each other, watching every film we loved, eating at every restaurant we liked, telling each other stupid story after stupid story. We filled in the gaps, explained ourselves, laughing and kissing. It was ridiculous *and* reasonable. We became nocturnal. Adrenalin burned through our veins as we walked through the city in the evenings, play-fought, met each other's friends and drank and talked more. We ran in the park in the dark and ate dinner at 3 a.m. Then we would sleep in the day with our faces touching.

We fell through a trap door in the world. Nobody could find us. Hugo would play guitar and I'd read him poems. Yes, gross. It *was* grossly romantic and full on. We shared clothes. We shared a toothbrush, we thought the same thoughts, cared about the same things, laughed at the same stuff. We got our hair cut the same way! This was it. It was as though I'd been walking around in one pair of shoes my whole life and then suddenly putting another pair on and going, 'Oh-h-h-h! *That's* what shoes are *meant* to feel like.' We just fit.

We were starting again and didn't have much. We slept on a borrowed bed. We didn't have a TV. We sat on my best friend's old sofa and used an ironing board with two garden chairs as a makeshift dining table and we were so, so happy.

Six months and one holiday to Morocco later, I fell pregnant.

I know this seems extremely premature, but it didn't scare me one bit. It was the right thing. No, it was the *best* thing that could have ever happened.

If Hugo and I hadn't known each other for so long I don't think we would have survived what happened next.

We still share the same toothbrush.

5

My pregnancy was a dream. I felt proud and excited, beautiful and strong, enormously creative and productive.

I was prepared to be as unprepared as I could be. I didn't overdo it on the reading or research but I knew enough to not be completely surprised. We didn't go and buy the whole floor of John Lewis. I didn't want a baby shower. I didn't make a birth plan because although they are reassuring, essential and empowering for many couples, for me, it was like writing a guide to the Land of Anxiety. I had read enough to know that the birth rarely goes as you think or hope. So, we remained open-minded, trusted our instinct and just took care of ourselves until the time came.

We saved money so we could take time off to enjoy the baby once he came. I saw my friends. I relaxed properly for the first time in my life and I felt so precious and important and *necessary*. Every day I felt purposeful, deliberate and delighted; it was as if I walked around surrounded by this special Saturn-like ring of protection. Nothing could harm me. I couldn't get a cold. Friends couldn't fall out with me. Murderers didn't exist. Bad things didn't happen. I felt like nothing could touch me and when I felt him wriggling under my skin I couldn't wait to meet him.

The first time we 'met' him at the scan, we couldn't find him. The sonographer chased him around my bare belly trying to catch glimpses of our tiny baby. It was like tracking Bigfoot – we never got close enough to take a photograph. I suddenly recognised that this was a real actual human with a life of his own.

The sonographer tried again, this time an internal scan, and suddenly there he was. A little black-and-white pixelated prawn from another planet. And his heart. *Loud*. The nurse even said it herself, 'Wow! He has a strong heartbeat.' He was surrounded by a cave of sponge-like mass. I mean the poor thing's face was pressed flat against the stuff.

'What's that?' I asked.

'Err . . . are you constipated by chance?' The nurse blushed red.

'Oh . . .' And I went even redder.

Funny how the big things you imagine in life, like seeing your first baby scan, are never quite how you picture them.

I used to hate the dark, now I would look forward to waking up in the middle of the night, just me and my bump. Bowls of porridge with maple syrup. Peanut butter and bagels and watching TV, then softly creeping back into bed. Snuggling down in my nest. Blankets and socks. Hugo, arm slumped around my growing belly.

It was the first time in my life I felt like I was good at something. Like I wasn't being a fraud or winging it or asking for permission or convincing somebody that I was able to or waiting to be *found out,* because I knew this was *my* experience. Nobody could tell me how to do it because my body was doing it for me.

I look back at that naive me sitting on the sofa eating her bowls of cereal and I want to hug her. It makes me cry just thinking about it, because that pregnant me really had *no* idea of what was about to come her way.

6

There is a huge expectation of expectant mothers. You feel like you are born with a special seed-like thing in the pit of your stomach that will blossom once you become pregnant: nature will take over your body and your maternal instinct will kick into gear. You trust that you will *know* what to do.

I imagined this Mother Nature version of me who'd waft about barefoot in flowing skirts and arms jangling with bracelets, my long mermaidy hair studded with flowers picked from my lawn. I'd wear anklets, maybe even a toe ring. I'd hang out my washing on a line with real wooden pegs. I'd become like one of those renaissance pieces of art: fecund and blissful, stretched across a swamp of silk, my 'babe', a naked chubby cherub, suckling from my breast. Of course, I'd suddenly be able to bake perfect bread and boil fluffy rice every time. I'd shout at people in shops and have them listen to my complaints, because I am *a mother*.

I would be an *inspiration*.

And when I heard those other mums that say they found it hard or couldn't cope, I'd think, *Hah, you found it hard but you are just not* me. *For I was born to do this. I am up there with Florence Night-ingale and Mother Goose and Aunt Bessie. My skin is a Cath Kidston print. I will boss this.* After all, I was ten years older than my mum was when she had me. I'd be fine!

I promise that I wasn't being all white-picket-fence about it. I was being realistic. I *kind*-of-*ish* knew what to expect. My friends had kids. I had always made extra money from babysitting, I'd done a lot of nanny jobs and used to work at a children's play centre. I have a younger brother and sister. I write children's books for a living. I was under no illusion that this wasn't going to be tough.

I was pre-warned. And then there was all the third-party advice. You might get piles. They might shave your fanny hair in the hos-pital. A 'natural' birth is so much more conducive to bonding than one in which medical intervention is necessary, *yes, yes, I'm going to have a natural birth, with just gas and air, yes, yes, of course.* You might poo during labour. Your fanny gets wrecked. People told Hugo, 'Don't go down the goal end, mate; it's like watching your favourite pub burn down.'

Oh ha. Ha. Ha.

Get all your sleep in at once, Laura, because you'll get *none* once the baby arrives.

Remember to sleep when the baby sleeps. Breast is best. Don't ever bring your baby into your bed, you'll be making a rod for your own back, Laura. They should be in their own room from six months, if not earlier. You will have no time to yourself. You and your partner will fight. The baby won't stop crying. Your nipples will hurt. Your boobs will never be the same again. Wave goodbye to your jeans.

Anxiety-inducing statements flew at me from every angle. People *love* to give advice, they can't help themselves. It's well intentioned but all it's doing is notching you higher and higher up the anxiety rollercoaster of motherhood making your drop even scarier . . . *crank, crank, crank* . . .

Childbirth and raising a child became not an experience but a *threat* that the slightest bad decision would negatively impact our child's future.

The size of my bump was compared to everybody's and anybody's; someone would tell me that his partner's grandmother heroically gave birth to her triplets all by herself in the middle of a cornfield without any pain relief and had to bite all three umbilical cords off with her teeth.

Panic set in. What would everybody think if *I* needed an intervention? How can I get all my sleep in at once? That's a coma, surely? Am I moving too much? Not enough? Should I be working, *still*? Did I accidentally eat raw eggs in that mayonnaise? Did I use the wrong bubble bath? Is bubble bath safe during pregnancy? How hot was my bath anyway? Do we have a room thermometer? What does a rod for your back even mean?

I began to wonder if I was up to this, so I tried my best to be as prepared as unprepared can be.

7

Ever since I first found out I was pregnant, I've thought about my mum a lot.

My sister and I don't have many memories of her growing up. Our memories are mostly of our dad. Those I do have of my mum are forever shifting and impossible to capture; they are like glancing Super 8 flashes in my mind that blur and blend like ink in water, like feathers. I see disco-light glimpses of long blonde tangled hair surrounded by a roaring blitz of colour. She's a firework with a cackling dirty laugh.

I remember a ferocious, electric woman with a fiery tongue and a wild imagination – and amazing boobs. Someone who was strong and powerful. Who kept up with my friends' dads' boisterous jokes and bravado. She was interested in *everything*. She liked ghost trains and magic tricks, car-boot sales, animals and insects, spicy food, pints of beer and conversation. She was known for being quick-witted, impossible to out-do, confident, hilarious, generous, outrageous, grotesque and competitive.

We adored her. But she was not a *mum* mum, and I struggled with that when I was little. She worked for most of my childhood. And hard too. She was a free thinker and impossible for anybody to jar and label. I felt like I was always running behind, trying to catch up with this butterfly of a person, just so I could get a closer look. But I never ever could. I would watch her from the back seat in the car, doing her make-up in the pull-down mirror, and think, *Who are you*?

I wanted so badly to understand her. I wanted *normal*. My name sewn into my school jumper by *her*; packed lunches made by *her* hands; for *her* to pick me up from school. I wanted her to own a first-aid box and for her to put bandages on my knee and kiss it better; to mark my height on the doorframe; to read me bedtime stories; to plait my hair and hum me a song. But she wasn't that kind of woman. She didn't teach us about periods or sex but taught us how to cook curry and chilli, how to be a feminist by simply being one herself, how to be creative, the art of conversation, about morals and principles, how to stick up for ourselves, how to be bold and to celebrate our individuality.

Later, in my early twenties, when I found out that she had suffered from postnatal depression with her youngest, my little brother Hector, it somehow didn't surprise me. It made sense and filled in the gaps of my childhood. But to this day I feel like a detective trying to put together the clues of my enigma of a mother, because she is a beautiful complicated mystery. And one of a kind.

I remember bits: my mum lying in bed in a darkened room, a lot. I remember that my dad (my parents have since separated) would take care of us, almost like a single dad. He'd make endless cups of tea and ask us to carry them down the hall to her. I would carefully balance the mug, not wanting to spill a drop. That bright magical mum of mine was now distant and her edges frayed. I remember her

20

often on the phone, crying, in her dirty dressing gown. She would play computer games for hours on end. I remember her once screaming, tearing her pyjamas off like a wrestler, the buttons flying in the air. The neighbours taking care of us, a lot. And I remember that she and Hector had this incredible bond. He slept in her bed until he was about seven.

She loved us with a tough love that I used to resent but now I know she was like a lioness. It has made us resilient. I used to blame her and resent her for working so much but now I know that it's because she wanted to give us a better life. She was the breadwinner and Dad was the carer. She wanted to inspire us, but also, maybe, she wanted to survive – she worked because it was something she was good at.

Once, over dinner, I remember telling my mum that I didn't have many memories of her from when I was young and she got upset. This was before I'd become a mum myself and I didn't realise how hurtful that was for her to hear. I didn't want to tell her that the only proof I had of her being there was from photographs. She said that she didn't enjoy us as kids, but loves us now as adults, we are her friends. And really we are. It's now I know that she's the best.

But Mum doesn't see herself as a hero; she barely talks about what happened to her after Hector was born. It wasn't until I was ill myself that so many people told me just how bad Mum's postnatal depression was. That she would crawl on all fours down the hallway. That there wasn't a minute that went by when she wasn't trapped inside her own head. And my poor mum was undiagnosed. She suffered like that for a whole year with two daughters already to care for, little money and no family nearby. She says she remembers coming out of the darkness and getting her hair cut for the first time and thinking,

Oh my God, I don't feel anxious, I don't feel depressed. I can't believe it. And that was it. It was gone.

I asked my dad what it was like. He said, 'I don't remember, I've blocked it out. But she wasn't Jaine.'

There is *some* faint biological link that suggests postnatal depression can be hereditary. What's interesting is that my mum is adopted. She prides herself on this fact, saying that it's the best thing that ever happened to her because it made her who she is. We used to joke that her birth parents were a T-Rex and a shark. She never met her mum and that didn't seem to affect her. We can't trace back to see if my biological grandmother had postnatal depression (or if she actually was a T-Rex).

Mum didn't have a strong bond with her adopted mother either. She had no imprint of a maternal figure, no traditional template of motherhood, and was unorthodox in her approach. But . . . could that have something to do with my mum's adoption? Did my mum's biological mother have postnatal depression? Could that even be why she was adopted in the first place?

8

E arly on in my pregnancy, I told the midwife that my mum had suffered from postnatal depression. She didn't seem worried.

I said, 'I'm scared to push the baby out.'

The midwife reassured me, 'Trust me, at forty weeks you will be desperate to get this baby out of you!'

All was good. I was healthy. I weed, aiming awkwardly and messily, into the clear plastic cup she gave me with the screw top lid. My blood was drawn and tested. Mine was a regular low-risk pregnancy. There was no reason why anything should go wrong. There was no reason why there would be a complication.

But as my pregnancy progressed my blood pressure increased. It continued to rise to the point that every time that Velcro strap went around my arm, I started to get anxious. I began to dread the midwife appointments purely for this reason.

As I approached forty weeks, people kept telling me that my belly looked *unusually* small. They didn't seem to believe that I was almost full term. I told my midwife that I was worried, but she measured me and said that everything was absolutely normal: my bump was completely healthy.

She *was* concerned, however, about my ever-increasing blood pressure, and told me to go to the hospital to be checked out.

'Get a snack though,' she said. 'It could be a long wait.'

It *was* a long wait for Hugo and me in the hospital corridor. We met a cute two-year-old girl who covered Hugo's hand in stickers and we felt giddy about the little friend in my tummy who we'd get to meet very soon. The girl's heavily pregnant mum smiled at us wearily from across the waiting area, grateful we were entertaining her toddler. I love watching Hugo with kids. He's natural, funny, warm and gentle. And although the two-year-old couldn't yet talk, they seemed to have found a common language. I felt happy seeing them together. I'd already made one good decision as a mum: choosing Hugo to be the dad.

I couldn't help staring at the other women waiting alongside us in the corridor, oddly jealous of their swollen stomachs, breasts up by their chins, hands on lower back all teapot like, breathing deep and waddling. I didn't look like that. I reminded myself that everybody is different. I was overthinking it, surely?

I was plugged into a monitor. Our heartbeats – my baby's and my own – were galloping like wild horses. The nurse encouraged me to 'relax' (they all said that – as if!). Hugo went to get us a drink from the hospital shop, leaving me alone, just me and my baby's beating heart. Saying '*Hi.*'

It was a beautiful day in London. I watched the sparkling river, the people tiny below. The sun kissed my stomach through the window. Everything seemed to calm. The horses stopped galloping. Our hearts settled. The nurse reassured us that everything was normal. And we went home.

At forty weeks all was good. Although I was full term, it isn't uncommon for first babies to be overdue. My mum was almost three weeks post term with me.

The doctor offered to give me a 'stretch and sweep' but by this point I'd have said 'Yes' to anything to get my baby out safely, so they pulled a curtain around a bed and down went my dotty leggings.

A stretch and sweep is not as perky as it sounds – do not be fooled by your obstetrician's chirpy cheeky-chappy bob's-your-uncle chimney-cleaner routine. It's when your doctor lubes you up and with her fingers attempts to separate the amniotic sac, which has the baby inside, from the cervix to encourage the first movements of labour. It's uncomfortable, intrusive and 'worse than a smear-test' painful.

The doctor apologised. 'Sorry, my hands are quite small.'

Was I already having intervention? Was I already having an 'unnatural birth' by letting a doctor finger me? I tried to block the whole thing out. And breathed.

That would be the first of five stretch and sweeps.

9

M y mum was so excited and supportive. She bought a posh pram and a fancy car seat and sent me a box of crisp white baby vests. She bought a real wool hat and the sweetest grey baby-grow with white stars on it to bring him home in. She said, 'The most painful thing about having a baby isn't the labour but the bit when they bulldoze your heart down with a truck of love, it's unbearable.'

One day the doorbell rang and it was boxes and boxes of nappies, a big tub of Sudocrem and wipes. Mum texted me to say, 'We couldn't always afford nappies when you were a baby, and I never want you to have to worry about that.'

She also sent me the biggest bag of table salt that you've ever seen and told me that I should bathe in it after I'd had the baby. Still, to this day, she's the *only* person that has ever suggested that. I know she is a bit of a witch doctor but isn't 'salt on the wound' a thing that you *don't* want?

I kept the salt anyway. For oven chips.

It was Valentine's Day and I was bouncing on a giant pink yoga ball and watching *The Office*. I was nearly two weeks over my expected delivery date and hadn't slept much.

26

I had an unexpected call from one of my friends' mums informing me that I *could* orgasm in labour. 'OK,' I said. 'I'll look into that.' And put the kettle on instead.

I had begun to nest, not because I felt compelled to go into pre-birth prep overdrive, but because I felt like I should be feeling that much-vaunted urge. I had an inner voice (don't worry not in *that* way . . . yet) in the back of my head sounding like some pumped-up football coach, reminding me that I'd have no time to myself once the baby was here. I made endless batches of vegetarian shepherd's pie and macaroni cheese for the freezer, de-scaled the kettle, cleaned the oven (which I'd never done before in my life), packed and re-packed my hospital bag.

Hugo had assembled the cot, bought us a TV, painted the baby's room, bought a tumble drier *and* a microwave, he'd rehearsed fitting the car seat in the back, his eager 'Baby on Board' badge stuck on the rear window, and now all there was left to do was get all that sleep in and wait. But I didn't exactly know what I was waiting for.

My body was well versed in Braxton Hicks and false alarms so I guessed my labour would start for real with the theatre of my waters breaking – that surprising splatter of clear liquid that smacks the floor alerting you that IT IS TIME. No one wants that to happen in the supermarket or to soak the seats of your friend's car, so I stayed at home, convincing myself that every twinge and belly rumble was a contraction.

I spent hours on pregnancy forums, gleaning what was useful from the endless feeds proffering free advice about preparing for labour, researching all the signs. 'Sprouting feathers out of your bum and clucking?' *Ah yes: labour symptom!*

I solemnly tried to follow the bossy gospel of Dos and Don'ts. It's

'EAT, EAT, EAT like you've never eaten before – for the energy, eating encourages the baby to move about!' And then it's 'DON'T, DON'T, DON'T eat anything at all because it will make you nauseous and you'll poo yourself when you push.'

Next it's 'Take a hot bath and relax: it's the last bath you'll ever have in peace, so enjoy', but then it's 'DON'T you DARE take a bath – what are you trying to do? Boil the baby? Poach your foetus?'

Then it's 'Dab this cloth with essential oils to help you to relax.' But one click away and it's 'WHAT ARE YOU, A WITCH? Put that smelly rag down and eat a bowl of ice cream, you hippy weirdo!'

I started to think that it was maybe just a whole lot of fuss.

I was doing all of the things I could to bring on labour – more of those wretched stretch and sweeps, spicy curry and beer, herbal teas, reflexology, essential oils, bouncing on the ball, pregnancy yoga, swimming, snogging (apparently it brings on the labour hormones?). Hugo had been giving me perineal massages with sunflower oil (look it up – boy, it's no joke) and he even shaved my fanny hairs. What a guy.

And when the squirmy, snotty, squid-like famous 'plug' plopped out, I thought, *Oh God. It's happening.*

But it didn't. Nothing happened.

My midwife suggested we go to the hospital to have a pessary inserted – a tampon-y thing containing hormones to encourage labour. It sounded fine and not too intrusive. I'd come home afterwards and hoped it worked its magic overnight. I'd sleep on a towel just in case I wet the bed with the impressive tidal wave of my waters breaking.

We called the labour ward to arrange to come in for the pessary, but they said they were unusually busy because 'It's Valentine's Day and everybody wants to have their baby on Valentine's Day.' (Eyeball roll.)

Yes, I get that you're busy, I thought, *but is everyone else two weeks over their due date, or is it just because they want a Valentine's baby? It's hardly the same as booking a hotel in Paris.*

We kept being told to call back later and the waiting was making us nervous. I really didn't feel *ready* to give birth. I didn't feel flustered or tired or heavy and my nose hadn't 'bloated' or any of the things they said I would feel on the pregnancy forums.

We finally got a call from the hospital to say they were ready for us. We didn't bother washing up and switched the lights off. We took the hospital bag *just in case*, threw it in the boot of the car and jumped in.

'I hope we don't lose our parking space,' Hugo said as we drove off. 'I parked it by the front door, you know, in case we suddenly have to rush out if you go into labour during the night.'

We wouldn't come home until five days later.

We waited, once again, in the long corridor of pregnant mums although this time it was emptier. It was getting late and the atmosphere was that of a busy day coming to an end. It felt so dark. 'Maybe it needs to be dark for the newborns' precious baby eyes to adjust?' I thought.

There was a note of exhaustion in the midwives' voices. What was such a big deal to us was for them just another day at work, which was deflating and reassuring at the same time. (I like to see a relaxed, almost tired nurse the same way I like to see a nonchalant air stewardess on an aeroplane during turbulence.)

Eventually, the midwife greeted us. 'Sorry we're so busy today, it's just that everybody wants to have a Valentine's baby.' She shook her head. 'I don't celebrate Valentine's Day, to be honest.'

Neither do we.

'You're lucky you've got a room,' she said as she led us through to a ward.

I looked to Hugo.

'I don't think we need a room,' I said. 'We're just here for the pessary induction.'

The room she brought us to was a good size but dark purple and a bit sad. It had a bed. A mini sticky-leather sofa. A bathroom. And a clear plastic basin for a newborn. Where was the birthing pool, the soft lighting and the casually strewn birthing balls and beanbags?

It wasn't that I'd planned my birth too much but I didn't want it to be like *this*. I would try gas and air. I wasn't against pain relief – if I needed it I would take it. I'd imagined a water birth because my friends had 'enjoyed' it and apparently if you poo when you're pushing they can catch it and scoop it out with a fishing net. I had brought a bikini top but I was also quite up for rolling around naked like a hippo in a lake.

I wasn't ready to give birth. I didn't feel even faintly under the weather, instead, I felt like I could maybe go nightclubbing. The midwife was suddenly nowhere to be seen.

'I'll go and find her,' Hugo said and left me alone on the tiny sofa. Before I knew it, I was having my first ever panic attack.

In the later catalogue of panic attacks, it was a tame one, I think, but at that point, I hadn't anything to compare it with. My heart was drumming and my face was red and an angry rash had appeared all over my chest. I found it hard to breathe. I was trying to grab oxygen, like a fish gasping at the surface of its tank.

I went to the bathroom and splashed water on my face and the inside of my wrists as a friend had once told me to do when I needed to sober up at a party.

It didn't work. Adrenalin continued to shoot its powerful volts through my blood.

Hugo came back. 'A midwife is coming now. Are you OK?' My face was soaking wet and flustered. Furious bees were buzzing around under my skin.

'Yep!' I practically sang, not wanting to worry him.

Another midwife arrived with that bloody anxiety-inflaming blood pressure machine again and I was burbling, 'Not now. It will be too high; I'm having a heart attack.'

I looked at the empty plastic dish cot.

How on earth am I going to fill that thing with a baby?

The midwife had said that at forty weeks, I'd be desperate to get the baby out. Now the idea of giving birth felt as impossible as being told to regurgitate a lung. How? I mean physically HOW was I going to push a baby *out of there*?

My blood pressure reading was alarmingly high.

'Relax,' she smiled. 'Lovely view of London you have here. Enjoy it.'

I looked out of the window. The Thames was black shimmering tar. A wave of sequins. A night sky. The Houses of Parliament, tall and proud, like on the news. Grand and gold, its little windows, glimmering as if lit by candles, like something out of a fairy tale. I might have been able to enjoy the view a little more if I was in a fancy posh hotel with Hugo, lounging in a fluffy white dressing gown, watching telly and eating room service. This circumstance wasn't really summoning up the emotion of 'enjoyment' for me.

'Just wait here and *your* midwife will be along shortly,' she said as she left.

It was like waiting for a blind date to turn up.

Please be a good one, please be a good one.

I thought of the photograph of my birthday in the same hospital thirty years before. My mum holding me, smiling, bleach-blonde punky hair, beautiful and relieved. My dad, a Joe Strummer look-alike, leaning over with his eighties' haircut and chiselled jawline. Teary. Overwhelmed. They looked *so* cool. Mighty Big Ben behind us in all its glory, setting the tone for the scene, a bellowing welcoming giant looking down on us, dressed all smart for the occasion. Mum and Dad had managed to get out of Chichester, they had rewritten the script: I was a 'Londoner'. My dad had told me that as soon as they got home they had gin and tonics and celebrated. I couldn't wait for that. I was going to have Tanqueray in a heavy glass with ice and lime and posh Fever-Tree tonic, and a massive bowl of smoked almonds.

And then she entered. Midwife Number Three. The midwife of dreams.

She looked like a baker. A chef in a Victorian household. She had bright red cheeks and a warm voice, both matter-of-fact and comforting. She soothed me, plumping the pillows behind my head, telling me that she'd done this job for as long as she could remember. That it was always as *special*. As *emotional*. As *joyous*. She'd had many babies herself. 'Mind you, they're all grown up now,' she said.

I felt my chest soften. The horses of my heart quieted down.

Then she asked, 'Right, can I get you something to eat?'

'No, no, I'm just here for the pessary induction,' I said, once again. 'I'll eat at home.'

'Home? Oh, there's no point in you going home! You're two weeks overdue, my love. I think it's time we got this baby out!'

I immediately felt trapped.

'We might head down to get the hospital bag from the car?' I said. What I meant was, 'May I please have permission to run away?'

32

'Good idea,' Midwife Number Three said. 'You never know, it might get baby moving!'

I felt like 'baby' couldn't be further from budging. It was like he'd been sucked up the chute of my body like a tiny Augustus Gloop in *Charlie and the Chocolate Factory* or, chimpanzee-like, he was hiding high up in the lofty reaches of my ribcage, legs clinging to my organs.

We walked down the corridor; I was trembling but I held it down and tried to act normal. I cracked a few jokes, tried to stay upbeat and positive. I heard a woman screaming, a ghastly violent shredding sound. Hugo and I both laughed – in terror.

We tried to busy ourselves on the ground floor but it was deadly quiet and most of the shops were closed. We bought a magazine each. I got something on cooking to take my mind off things. I also got energy food. Raw nuts, a banana, some dark chocolate. Oooh, and Jaffa Cakes because my dad always says footballers eat them. Hugo got chewing gum.

We went out to the car, which was waiting nicely for us in the most expensive car park in the world. We decided to sit in the car for a bit. We turned the engine on and listened to the radio, trying to normalise ourselves with the soft glow of the lights and the heating on. We read our magazines and I ate the Jaffa cakes.

I wished we could drive away.

We nervously headed back inside to the ward and returned to our little dark-purple room. Hugo was invited to 'make himself a bed' with what he could on the leather sofa.

The midwife asked me to wee inside a pot. I managed to fill it but drenched my hand in the process. As I twisted the cap on I saw a wormy line floating in the jar.

There was protein in my urine. Not a good sign.

Midwife Number Three gave me *another* stretch and sweep, and this time Hugo nearly fainted. I felt his hand weaken in my grasp. The colour had leeched from his face and he stepped back. I felt powerless. I couldn't take care of him.

Then she inserted the pessary with a cheery, 'Fingers crossed this makes something happen!'

How was this little tampon going to bring on contractions?

She also decided to wire me up to a heart-rate monitor, again, to measure both my and the baby's heart and she gave me some frankincense on a tissue to inhale. I remembered the woman in the health shop saying that frankincense is 'grounding'.

'Well, frankincense, now is your time to shine,' I muttered.

Once again, I could hear our two hearts pounding but this time it wasn't comforting. It was more like the theme tune to a shark attack.

An alarm suddenly went off and it was panic stations. The heart-rate printer was out of paper. A fluster of midwives impressively rushed in, restocked the printer and the shark attack resumed.

But Midwife Number Three said that our baby's heart rate had momentarily fallen off the scale; he could be pulling on the umbilical cord.

'Is that normal?' I asked.

'It's OK, he recovered very quickly. Nothing to worry about, my love.' She squeezed my foot. She dimmed the lights, then said, 'Now I suggest getting some rest. You're about to run a marathon.'

Hugo was tossing and turning on the couch in the gloom and I felt really scared. I'd never been to hospital before, not properly. Could I just change my mind and have the baby at home? Could I leave? Or was that illegal?

I hugged my belly and let the sky turn from navy-blue to pink. My back ached. It was early on a Thursday morning and London was waking up. I felt a slight cramping but nothing more than that. The packet of raw nuts had split in my bag and were now scattered all over the floor. I got up to wee, my bare feet on the cold lino, and saw the pessary lying helpless in my knickers and before I could catch it to shove it back up, it plopped, like a dead mouse, into the toilet. I rang the buzzer for assistance.

A new midwife arrived: Midwife Number Four. Where was the farmer's wife? 'My pessary came out during the night. It's just fallen into the toilet,' I told her.

'OK. Don't worry. It happens. Can I make you some toast?'

I couldn't face the toast. Neither could Hugo, who now looked as though he was about to gag. I tried a small bite and then the diarrhoea kicked in. Big time.

Midwife Number Five arrived. She was quite cool-looking; dyed blonde hair, piercings. She was funny, the sort of person you'd want to go to the pub with. I told her about the diarrhoea and she cracked up laughing. She said it was normal and to go ahead and poo as much as I wanted. I liked Midwife Number Five. But then she checked the heart-monitor reading and didn't like what she saw.

'Well, your blood pressure is so high, Laura, you're showing up small, you're two weeks overdue and there's protein in your urine. Your baby is struggling to keep up. Has anybody mentioned pre-eclampsia to you?' she said.

I wasn't entirely sure what preeclampsia was, but, basically, it's a pregnancy complication with all of the above symptoms.

'How did nobody spot this?' She frowned. 'Did you not have more than two scans? You should have been a high-risk pregnancy.'

And before we knew it, Hugo and I were taken to the high-risk ward.

'The view isn't as nice but it's closer to the doctors' station,' Midwife Number Five explained.

Suddenly, things started to feel very scary. The room got a bit busier and I couldn't stop pooing. They stripped me down, removed my huge M&S knickers and wrapped me in a hospital gown.

I looked at my dissected hospital bag spilling its guts on the floor. The lavender spray, headband, water mist, iPod speaker, bikini top all felt a bit ambitious and foolish now.

I had a feeling I wouldn't be needing any of that.

A male doctor arrived, busy and assertive. I heard him say that there was no point in doing another scan, and there was also no point in inserting another pessary because they cost £33. (Good to know in case I ever wanted to buy one.)

I was definitely 'high risk'. Thank God for Midwife Number Five, then she dropped the bomb.

'I'm really sorry, my shift has finished,' she said.

NO!!!

'But great meeting you and good luck!'

Where was Midwife Number Three? Who was scheduling this rota?!

And we were then introduced to *our* midwife: Midwife Number Six.

Midwife Number Six was small and angry, not the sort of person you could picture kissing your sweaty head, screaming, 'YOU DID IT!'

Do a good job of resentfully slamming your shots of Patron down at a bar at one in the morning?

Probably. Yes.

She *couldn't* be my cheerleader. She didn't want to be either. My baby burrowed even further into my body.

I remembered the advice: 'If you don't like the approach of your midwife you must say so. This is *your* experience. They will not be offended: just because that midwife is not right for you, it doesn't mean they won't be the right midwife for somebody else.'

'Please find that other midwife, please phone our normal midwife, please get any single person you can find on the street. But not this woman. Please,' I frantically whispered at Hugo beneath the din of the busy room.

Hugo got to it straight away, but I could see that the ward was understaffed and over-run.

Midwife Number Six looked at me with deep-black onyx eyes. She could tell I was trying to trade her in.

We were not working together, there was no team spirit. We were opponents in a boxing ring and she had the upper-hand.

I needed to poo. Again. *Oh God.* It was even worse with my bum all exposed in the gaping hospital gown. I kept telling myself, 'They've seen it all before.'

Coming back from the toilet, I felt mild contractions. Like period pains, grumbling low and deep. My legs quaked. My knees were like pancake batter. I held on tight to the bars of the bed as another contraction followed fast on the last.

Oh God, oh God. And these are going to get WORSE?

A vice was cranking me apart. My hip bones were widening, like a piece of machinery. I was metamorphosing like a Transformer, but softer, like a Gremlin!

I managed to get on the bed again and Midwife Number Six aggressively stuck her fingers up me and told me I was only one centimetre dilated.

HOW?

She asked me if I remembered my waters breaking.

'No!' I replied. I was excited for that bit. But they could have? It wasn't *impossible*. In the shower? On the toilet? In the bath?

Midwife Number Six was unimpressed. 'You *don't* even know if your waters broke or not?'

She rolled her eyes. It was a trick question and I had failed!

Please get me a new midwife.

I needed to go to the bathroom, again. I asked Hugo to make some phone calls. I could tell he hated it in here and he hadn't eaten properly in a while. Also, the smell of my poo was becoming overpowering – it was so hot on the ward and I was stinking out the whole room. I was embarrassed.

I had an odd temptation to tell everybody to leave me alone so I could get on with it by myself: a primal urge to get naked on all fours and roar like a beastly rhino, sweating and screaming as wee and poo and blood and spit and snot and foul-mouthed expletives howled out of me as I pushed out my little baby.

I totally understood why pregnant cats retreat to a cosy airing cupboard and do it alone.

'We're going to try to break your waters,' Midwife Number Six said, snapping on a rubber glove.

Please, not with your fingers, I thought.

Midwife Number Six produced what can only be described as a huge crochet hook. It looked like that thing they used to pull the brains out through the nostrils in Ancient Egypt.

OK . . . PLEASE DO IT WITH YOUR FINGERS.

The pain was unreal. I yelped, flying up and off the bed. 'Stop, please stop. Can I have some pain relief for this?'

Just as I realised how grateful I was that Hugo wasn't there to witness this, he returned.

'You weren't gone long,' I said, trying not to sound annoyed. 'They're *just* breaking my waters!' I explained, almost *delighted*, trying to keep the enthusiasm up and seem brave.

'You might want to try the gas and air first?' Midwife Number Six suggested. 'It takes a few tries to get it right.'

I'd never taken drugs in my life. I get a buzz from loose tea leaves. I took a drag. My voice immediately grew low and slow and I felt trippy and dozy.

I hated it already. But I tried to go with the feeling.

'Share the wealth!' Hugo grinned cheekily, making light of the situation. I smiled, a glimmer of normality in this otherwise surreal experience. I passed the mouthpiece to him and my hand felt weightless and floating, like lifting an empty Coke can when you expect it to be full.

'Whoa, it's strong,' he said, surprised. He considered the gas and air and then looked back at me.

'It's strange at first but you'll get used to it,' Midwife Number Six told me like I was the class geek trying my first cigarette with her after school. 'You ready?'

I drew a deep breath on the gas and air, biting down on the mouthpiece as she inserted the crochet hook. I can't remember exactly how it unfolded, but then I was naked, legs apart, shrieking up and off the bed in an exorcism-like levitation, being restrained by two other midwives, convulsing, screaming. (I promise, I am not a wet blanket when it comes to pain, I once broke my wrist and didn't realise for three days until my hand basically slid off the bone like a floppy hand puppet.) The whole thing was like some out-of-body experience. So painful it was almost spiritual. This is probably my worst memory of the whole labour.

My waters refused to break. I threw the gas and air pipe down. I couldn't stand how horrible it made me feel.

Our baby's heartbeat, once again, dropped off the monitor.

Hugo looked absolutely traumatised.

'Baby didn't like that; I don't know how he'll take to contractions,'

Midwife Number Six said. 'And this is the first time I've *ever* failed to break waters.'

Then Midwife Number Six looked at me apologetically, 'I'm so sorry, I've scratched the baby's head.' *SORRY? YOU'VE DONE WHAT? HOW?* 'Seems your waters have already broken, the baby might be at risk of infection. We have to get him out as quickly as possible.'

Suddenly it became very real that there was something inside me that was mine to protect.

A drip induction was advised. Luckily, I had watched *One Born Every Minute* the night before: a woman had a drip induction and the midwives recommended an epidural at the same time, because the drip can rapidly bring on extreme and intense contractions, and the pain can shock the mother and baby.

An epidural. Intervention. Was this a 'get out' card? Would I be able to feel anything? I ran through the risk factors in my mind: with an epidural you have to trust the midwife who has to steer and navigate the exit of your baby with control as there's more chance of tearing when you can't feel anything, including pain, properly.

I demanded an epidural. Any ideas of my 'natural' birth had vanished and, for my vagina's sake, I started sucking up to Midwife Number Six – *hard*.

II

An anaesthetist introduced himself and his massive needle. He was obliged to run through the risk factors to the epidural: there was a small chance I might become paralysed from the waist down . . . *right* . . . then chattily said he was just recently qualified.

Oh, great. *Congratulations. Well done you.*

Luckily, by this point I was so bewildered that whatever dignity I had left had completely gone. I sat on the edge of the bed in a curled-up prawn position, my whole bum exposed. I was clocking out. I was handing myself over, and as soon as that injection went in, I lost all contact with myself. Goodbye, Laura.

I left myself behind in that labour room; my soul levitating out of the room like a scene from some terrible eighties movie.

Midwife Number Six now seemed very impressed with my bravery. As far as improving my relationship with her was concerned, clocking out was a brilliant strategy.

The epidural was like a bubble bath for the organs. I felt warm and cosy and relaxed. I couldn't feel a thing.

I've since asked Hugo about how I was in this moment and he said, 'You were so relaxed it was unsettling.'

When Midwife Number Six looked at the monitor and told me that a contraction was coming, I felt nothing more than a small tightening around the waist. We started chatting. She told me her boyfriend's name. The bonding was going extremely well; I could do this.

Then a bleeping panic alarm started going off. Hugo was panicking and Midwife Number Six was *not* happy. A doctor arrived and told us in a 'Bad News Voice' that our baby was going to be born 'small'. He said that my placenta had possibly failed and when Hugo asked what that meant, he replied, all matter of fact, 'That he'll be born *small*.'

With the drugs in full swing, I ran away with the idea that I was giving birth to an exceptionally tiny little being, a Tom Thumb-type. I began babbling away on this positive rant, reassuring Hugo that no matter how small our baby was, we were just *so* lucky to even be able to *have* a baby and of course we would love him regardless.

'Well, that goes without saying,' Hugo agreed, but he also knew that I was completely out of my box. I wasn't capable of taking anything in, never mind the fact that our son could have complications and what that might mean for us.

'Of course we will love him regardless but can you elaborate on what you mean by *small*? Nothing was picked up in the scan,' he asked the doctor.

The doctor proceeded to both baffle and terrify us with lots of confusing jargon and then simply said, 'It means he will be small. Potentially, chronic.'

Chronic?

Midwife Number Six obviously felt for us and, defrosting into an empathetic half smile, she explained, 'Laura, every time you are having a contraction, your baby is struggling. Every time your heart rate goes up on this machine, your baby's heart rate is going down. He's struggling to survive because he's so small.'

'What does that mean? That I'm *killing* the baby?' I said, a horrible panic overwhelming me. I was killing the very thing I was meant to be *growing*.

'I've seen this before. Most likely he will be fine but he'll just be very small. I think the best thing to do is to keep a close eye on things and see how the induction goes,' she replied.

Midwife Number Six was going on her break. I could sense that she didn't want to leave us, but at this point there was nothing that anybody could do.

Midwife Number Seven arrived. She was solid. She covered me with a blanket and apologised that they were so understaffed, 'It's because of—'

'Valentine's Day, I know.'

Midwife Number Seven was reassuring. She said that all a 'small baby' meant is that they are born *hungry*. She thought that it meant that my baby had been starving in the womb. Chances were that he could have been full weight at due date but since then he'd been losing reserves inside me.

I felt guilty. I thought he was going to be a prize pumpkin. I should have had an induction two weeks earlier. I should have had an elective Caesarean.

'Let's just see how these contractions go and see how he copes.'

Hugo and I started to cry. We didn't know this was going to be so hard. We thought we had done everything right.

Our little baby, swimming like the Nirvana *Nevermind* baby, lost, alone, hungry and distressed, trying to get to us.

Midwife Number Six returned. Things sped up, and got even *worse*. There was meconium on my bedding. My baby had pooed in the womb, which is dangerous: he could inhale it. I knew it wasn't good.

And then, I called it: 'I want a Caesarean. I feel like my body is killing him. I want to get him out.'

Midwife Number Six agreed. 'It's probably going to have to be a C-section. We think that's the safest route.'

I was frightened. Of what might happen next. Of giving birth to a dead baby.

I felt like I was pooing myself again. Was I? Was it sweat? Blood? Was it my waters finally breaking? Was the baby coming? *Make this all be over, please. I just want to see my baby in that plastic dish, alive.*

The theatre was particularly busy – I was in 'the queue'.

I grabbed my phone and texted my mum. I was terrified, needing reassurance. 'Will I be OK, Mum?'

It was dark outside. I wanted my sister. I wanted my mum. I realised that I hadn't done a wee for a really long time, then I saw a catheter, my dark yellow urine trickling into a little pouch beside me. I hadn't even noticed. I would say I was embarrassed but I was way, way beyond the point of all embarrassment.

Midwife Number Six dimmed the lights. She turned down the sound of our heartbeats on the monitor because it was making me feel scared. She watched my baby's heart beating on the screen instead. I watched her watching and she didn't miss a single beat.

Hugo and I held hands under the soft silver glow of the monitors.

There was a gentle knock on the door. Midwife Number Six jumped up like a security guard to open it.

It was my mum.

My mum smells of Mum. Of home. Of log fires. Of her perfume. Woody. Floral. Heavy. Deep. Musky. Of the dogs. *Please take me home.*

I began to cry. A lot.

12

Not long after my mum arrived, Midwife Number Six hinted that I was about to go into surgery. Mum had to leave.

We held on to each other and cried some more. In true Mum style she left us bags and bags full of crisps, sandwiches, potato salad and pots of hummus. An emergency picnic.

Hummus was the *last* thing I wanted.

It was the end of Midwife Number Six's shift. I didn't want her to leave. We'd become so close. I wanted to cling onto her scrubs and beg her to stay. 'Please don't leave me. You're by far not the warmest of midwives or who I ever imagined doing this with us, in fact, you're quite mean, but I've grown really fond of you. You're *my* mid-wife. Please don't leave me.'

Instead I simply said, 'Thank you for everything.'

She gripped my hand and added, 'I'm not going anywhere until you go in.'

Her icy heart had finally thawed. And I understood why she does her job.

Midwife Number Eight arrived. I started crying again.

'Nice to meet you too,' she joked. Midwife Number Eight was older and broad, and clearly had a good sense of humour.

A new doctor, a female doctor, came in and explained how the emergency Caesarean was going to proceed. They couldn't find my birthing notes. Hugo burst into tears and I started up again too. Neither of us could stop crying. Midwife Number Eight chuckled and stroked my hair. And then she began to sing. It was the most beautiful song I'd ever heard.

'It's from my church. It will give you strength.'

We cried even more.

Hugo changed into scrubs. All Ikea blue and a hairnet. He looked like he worked at a cheese counter. I took a photo. It was time to take me to theatre.

I had this horrible feeling that something really bad was going to happen to me. I clutched Midwife Number Eight's arm. 'His name is Jet,' I said. 'In case, if you need to talk to him, he's called Jet.'

As Midwife Number Eight pushed me towards the theatre, I listened to the sounds of the squeaky lino floor, soft rubber shoes and Midwife Number Eight singing her church songs.

The surgeons moved together like an orchestra, sparky and full of energy, unlike me.

A cloth was held up like a screen at my waist so I couldn't see anything. I was suddenly so glad that Hugo had shaved my fanny.

The surgeon pinched my thigh. 'Can you feel that?' she asked.

'Yep,' I lied. I couldn't feel a thing but I was scared that I would feel the knife. It's a real-life fear, isn't it? So I decided to keep lying until I was numb blind.

'OK, what about now?'

'Yep,' I lied again.

'What about now?'

'Yes! I can feel that.'

'I didn't touch you!' She winked. I'd been rumbled. 'I think we're ready.'

Damn.

I had to use all my strength to not freak out. A friend who had a C-section had told me that she was completely numb but could feel them rummaging around her stomach like it was a handbag. Another friend said it was like being punched in the stomach by a heavyweight. I looked straight above at the white lights. I focused on Hugo holding my hand. The surgeon said she was pregnant herself and was having an elective C-section. 'They're the best,' she said. 'This guy here is gonna do mine.' And the second surgeon waved at me with a grin as if to say, 'Guilty!'

'I can see a fountain of white horses and I can't wait for a can of Sprite,' I replied, and everybody laughed.

Could I actually see horses? Am I dying? Am I dead?

It felt like I hadn't even had a chance to blink and Hugo was squeezing my arm.

'Laura! Laura! Look! Look!'

And the whole world drowned out as my long skinny bloody screaming naked child was held high like that scene from *The Lion King* except instead of Simba, it was a scrunched-up angry, starving, distressed, tortured goblin.

Oh. God.

They took him away very briefly to do some checks and clean him up. Hugo was pacing backwards and forwards, running between the two of us: the scrambling tiny dinosaur and me, open and bloody, dissected like a real-life Frida Kahlo self-portrait.

Turns out that as well as my placenta failing, he was facing the wrong way and the umbilical cord was wrapped around his neck, twice. They reckon he had been pulling on it when I was contracting, essentially strangling himself.

A womb is supposed to be a sanctuary. A heaven of floating and feeding. A place of living and growing. Mine seemed like a dungeon of starvation and strangulation. A place to slowly die in the darkness, alone. *I'm so sorry.*

Hugo kept coming back to me with wide big blue eyes, 'Laura, he's amazing. He's so beautiful. He isn't small, just skinny. He's just really skinny.'

The whole thing was over in about fifteen minutes. I was lying there, turned inside out, thinking *what the fuck* was that?

It was ten o'clock at night. They stitched me up, and I said, 'Well done everybody!' As though we'd just wrapped on a film shoot.

I couldn't stand my annoying self.

13

It was not how I'd imagined giving birth to my baby. I had just been sliced open and then a wailing starving livid newborn was thrown onto my chest. Hugo was kissing my face, saying over and over, 'Laura, Laura, look, look at him.' And I was crying and shocked. And then the baby grabbed a hold of my nose and began to suck, like it was a nipple. Already latching on, already demanding milk.

'Small babies are hungry babies!' the surgeon said.

I kissed my baby on the head.

Bloody scratches from the breaking of the waters were etched into his soft scalp. It reminded me that this was just as traumatic for him as it was for me; we were in this together.

He is mine. He is safe. I'm alive. All is well.

'Hi, Jet,' I said. 'I'm your mummy and I love you.'

We were wheeled to a warm twilit ward. I was disorientated, drugged up, tired, emotional and so very thirsty. Midwife Number Eight was in her element. She drew the curtain around us, chatting and singing away, but she was also on a mission. What was the problem? The baby was OK, wasn't he? Couldn't we all relax so I could go to sleep?

Apparently not. I had a furious newborn to look after who was desperately trying to survive. Welcome to motherland. It doesn't matter what the circumstance is, you show up and you stick around. The midwife moved quickly and calmly around the bed, and plugged oxygen tubes up my nose. They were irritating and itchy and keep falling out. I didn't understand why I needed them. She ordered Hugo to hold them in my nostrils.

I was allowed the tiniest sip of water but I was so thirsty I kept begging her for more – for some reason I wasn't allowed to drink too much. Next she put a woolly red hat on Jet, to indicate that he needed special care and attention. They are called 'Red Hat babies'. I didn't like seeing him in this hat at all, but he had to keep it on at all times.

Then she handed him to me.

Jet.

I began to breastfeed him. I felt paralysed, my arms so loose from the medication that I didn't have the strength or energy to hold him to my chest. He was so skinny and scrawny and delicate, and he kept slipping from my hold.

My breasts were empty. Nothing was coming out.

'You have to work at it,' Midwife Number Eight instructed. 'Sometimes with a Caesarean the breast milk takes longer to come. Keep trying, it will come. You must. You have a hungry boy on your hands.'

Jet was sucking. How did he know what to do? But there was no milk. He started to cry. Raw empty gums. Lizard tongue. Screwed-up unsatisfied demanding face.

I kept falling asleep. Midwife Number Eight was shouting at me to wake up, she shoved my nipple into Jet's mouth and manually pumped my breast. The plastic tubes kept falling out of my nostrils. Holding them in, Hugo texted our family to let them know that everything is OK.

But everything was not OK.

'Get off your phone!' Midwife Number Eight ordered, suddenly very serious. 'You need to focus!' she snapped. She handed Jet to Hugo, guiding him to my left breast.

'Hold him,' she demanded, and then with a little plastic pump she extracted a thick yellowish cream from my right breast. Colostrum.

'Listen to me. Wake up!' She patted my cheek. 'This is gold dust. It's nectar. He needs this. It's very important: don't waste a single drop.'

It was as if I had been woken from a drug overdose.

'You,' Midwife Number Eight pointed at Hugo. 'Did you bring baby clothes in your hospital bag? I need you to get every item of clothing.'

Hugo jumped to attention. It felt like we were in an army camp.

She took Jet and placed him under a warm lamp, like a baby chick. Midwife Number Eight rubbed Jet's skin and muscles, like she was trying to start a fire.

'His blood sugar is very low,' she said, as she dressed him in layers, the clothes hanging off his tiny body.

Midwife Number Eight was working hard. I could see her back, elbows sawing in and out, blowing on his front, feeding him the magic colostrum with a syringe.

The room turned dark with a circle of glow, like a fairy fluttering away.

14

Early the next morning, we were wheeled round to a new ward, and into a shared room with perhaps seven other sets of parents and their babies. All with their own reasons to be held here in this maternal prison. It was boiling hot.

We must just be spending a couple of hours here, I thought.

While I had been sleeping, Midwife Number Eight had spent the whole night warming Jet with her hands. She had given Hugo a leaflet with a frightening bullet-pointed list of the dangers of 'low-sugar levels' in newborns – top of the list was permanent brain damage. Hugo told me that he'd held Jet at my breast to feed for three hours and then Midwife Number Eight had taken over the shift. Without her, Jet would have had to go into Intensive Care. When I look back at Midwife Number Eight I see her as an angel in a blue uniform. I will always be grateful to her.

I felt like a part of my brain had shut down. All the midwives and general staff, who served food and did the cleaning, were women. It was quite confusing and I struggled to remember who was who. Someone came round with a menu for the day and I was reluctant to even look at it because I was so sure I'd be going home soon.

'How long will I be here for?' I asked.

'Let me get a midwife,' the woman said, and told me I had to keep my curtain open. I didn't want to keep my curtain open. The room was full, there were other dads and men around, I was trying to teach myself to breastfeed and it was *really* not as easy as it looks. I was also mostly naked, had just been sliced and was urinating into a bag.

I sat up in my bed. Hugo helped me to cover myself and at last I got to see my Jet in the daylight.

For nine months he'd been a secret to me, a message in a bottle, a clay pot in a kiln, a proving loaf. And now here he was.

OK. Let's have a look at you, little one.

For a second, he was satisfied, quiet and still and then I could see his beautiful features, the deep sunken eyes, the perfect pink mouth and the milky ski-slope nose, but he looked nothing like the 'mini us' we had visualised. Everything was overshadowed by his severe skinniness, the empty feet of the babygrow hanging limp like dead rabbit-ears. I peeked underneath his layers of newborn clothes. His thin translucent skin was violet and blotchy, spiderweb maps of blue veins spiralling beneath, his tiny ribs bulging, chest rising and falling, and within moments his squirmy red face scrunched into a painful cry.

Contorting there in his little red hat, Jet was an evil goblin about to embark on an urgent mission, the objective being FEED ME, FEED ME like that monstrous blood-eating plant, Audrey, from *Little Shop of Horrors.*

I didn't know him at all. He was a total stranger and he frightened me. I stuck him back on the breast and he sucked away; feeding was the only time he was quiet.

I was wearing these hideous thick off-white surgical stockings, like something my grandma used to wear. I don't even remember having them put on me.

'Sexy!' I joked.

I didn't dare look under my own hospital gown, I just knew it was a big old mess. I imagined my pelvis the centrepiece of some hideous grossly indulgent feast from the past, a bloody basin with half-eaten seafood pouring out; tentacles and fins and scales, foetid and fleshy.

I asked Hugo to look at my scar. 'Is it bad?' I asked.

'There's dressing on it. I can't see,' he told me.

I'm the kind of person who will get talking to anybody, but here, regardless of the 'mothers meeting' stereotype, none of us mothers wanted to talk. We all just wanted to wrap the little curtain around ourselves, set up home there, please, let us make it ours.

Jet was constantly feeding, it was all he wanted to do. As the day went on the babies started to cry more and more. The other parents began to get annoyed with each other as crying babies took turns to wake sleeping babies up, which in turn woke up the napping mums. It was like some cruel fairground game. Nobody really knew what was going on, everybody was tired, hot, cramped, frustrated and emotional, and tensions were high.

Jet only cried if I tried to take him off my boob for a single second. So I didn't. I didn't want to annoy anybody else or wake up the other babies and he obviously needed to feed.

I attempted my grey hospital scrambled eggs with one hand and then Hugo tried a bit of 'skin to skin' with Jet so I could eat, but Jet just wailed and wanted to go back on my breast. His need was *exhausting*, relentless.

'Excuse me,' I said to one of the midwives, 'my baby won't stop feeding. Is that normal?'

'Because he's a *small* baby, he's hungry. He's working at it to get a flow,' she reassured me.

I'd just given birth to the world's hungriest baby and my milk had yet to come in. Jet was starving and the colostrum wasn't enough to satisfy him so he wouldn't be able to sleep. *Ever.* Which meant no sleep for me either. *Ever.* I couldn't just sleep while he fed because he was so small and if I didn't hold him tight he might roll off the bed. And anyway, even if I did get a second to sleep, I wouldn't have been able to because there was this one baby who would *not* stop crying.

Sometimes, my brain could zone it out for a minute or two, then it remembered that the dreadful sound was still there, and my head was back in the grinder. The father kept apologising to everybody, 'I'm sorry, I'm sorry, I don't know what to do. I don't know why she's crying like this.'

And then the itching started – a rare and unlucky side effect of an epidural. Naturally, I was gifted it.

I had never felt anything like it. It was venomous, underneath the skin, crawling, a million times worse than any mosquito bite. And what with the heat of the room and the irritation of all the babies crying – which had to be up there with one of the most disturbing sounds in the world (deliberate, I know, like an ambulance siren) – it was too much to stand. I couldn't *not* scratch. Once I scratched, it was bliss for a second, then was followed by a fiery burning pain that made me want to chop off my limbs. But I couldn't stop. With fragile Jet on my chest and connected to all these various wires, I found myself scratching incessantly with my toes. (Which I had manicured for the photo ops. Ha. Ha. Ha.)

I'm not joking when I say I itched and scratched so much that I had fresh blood underneath each toenail and raw scabs on my feet and ankles. *If I could just get up and take a cold shower. If I could just get outside into the cold winter air and feel it in my chest. If I could just . . .*

We were only permitted three visitors at a time. I told Hugo to invite his family and mine too, and he sweetly tidied up around our little home-corner and borrowed a chair from the corridor.

My sister, my mum and my stepdad arrived first. I can't remember their visit. I don't remember if I cried or smiled. It's a total blur. But I do remember them smelling of the wind. Of the snow. Of the rain. Of outside. Of the real world. My mum brought more bags of picnic-style food, celebratory beers for Hugo, and an actual real posh glass for me: some tonic and gin and even ice and lemon slices wrapped in foil. My reward – my gin and tonic. But the last thing I wanted was a gin and tonic. I had a sip anyway because it was so sweet and thoughtful of my mum. Maybe the alcohol would numb me for a minute? Help me escape from this place? The room was so hot that the ice instantly melted. The beers went lukewarm and the picnic food already seemed to be steaming.

They had brought me the bags of stuff that I'd apparently texted to ask for – tiny, tiny newborn clothes and extra-extra-small nappies made for premature babies. I didn't even remember sending them a text. (It's odd how the rational instinctive mother in you does those things subconsciously.) I don't remember saying goodbye.

Hugo's family arrived. His dad, his dad's partner and his brother. There were beer bottles and a half-drunk gin and tonic by my bed. It's embarrassing. I looked like a neglectful alcoholic mum, but I was too exhausted to move. I was hoping to close my eyes and get a second to rest while they held Jet, but I couldn't. I was a rabbit in the headlights, pale and ghoulish, covered in red itchy welts. I don't remember anything else from that day.

I'm in the photos but I couldn't be found.

Things that May Happen to You After You Give Birth that Nobody Tells You About

Y ou might cry like you've never cried before.

You might feel confused. Disconnected. Weird. *Like, what the hell was that?* Especially if you've had intervention.

You will probably bleed like all your periods have come at once. Even if you didn't give birth vaginally. It will look like there has been a mass murder in your knickers that no sanitary towels can mop up. You will need padded knickers.

You might forget that you like food.

You are so thirsty.

You might be constipated.

You don't sleep. At all. Ever. And even if you get the chance, you might not be able to sleep.

Your own baby's cry seems to speak to you and only you: it's like your name is remixed into the piercing melody of it.

You might be in a lot of pain.

Your milk doesn't come in straight away – colostrum first and then it's usually between day two and day five before the milk arrives.

You might struggle to breastfeed.

You might not feel proud of yourself.

You might feel weird about your partner.

Your wees and poos won't be the same.

Fitting into your jeans will probably be the *last* thing you think about.

You might feel the most trapped you've ever felt in your life. You might think to yourself, *Why did I ruin my life? What have I done?*

You might want to order a taxi and run away.

But even if you could, you might not be able to move.

You might not instantly love your baby.

15

It was Saturday morning. Jet was three days old. I woke up to a midwife injecting me in the thigh. She gave me pain relief and something called Labetalol for my ever-escalating blood pressure. She removed the catheter and helped me to get out of bed and stand up.

It felt amazing to straighten my legs but my scar felt taut, like it was ripping open. I sat back down. The bedding was covered in violent flashes of red.

Nobody warned me about the blood.

'Try and take a few steps throughout the day if you can. When you go to the bathroom, please urinate in this.' She handed me an upside-down cardboard bowler hat. 'And would you like something to help with constipation?'

So now I was constipated too?

'And try not to scratch,' she added.

My mum brought in a duvet for Hugo. He was so humble and said he didn't need it but I could tell he was grateful. My head kept lolling back into some strange lucid dream and then I'd wake up with a spasm, Jet nearly hanging off the bed but still there in his Red

Hat, his splayed little starfish hand on my breast, mouth sucking away. Clinging to me like a barnacle clings to a whale.

I asked to speak to one of the midwives. 'Please, can I give him some formula? I'm so tired. If he could just eat something then we could both sleep?'

'Honestly, you're doing so well,' she said encouragingly. 'It will come.'

I started to cry. 'I'm so tired. Please, if I could *just* sleep.'

My body was confused. He'd been starving inside me for two weeks. I immediately went into a spiral of negative thoughts: *I know what's happened here. There's no milk in my breasts because my body thinks my baby has died! It thinks I've had him ripped out of me.*

Why couldn't I just feed him some formula?

'We don't recommend it because he'll get too attached to the bottle and won't want to latch. Breast is best. He needs the antibodies.'

Maybe that's why I feel so low? Because I'm grieving. Because my body has decided that my baby has died?

Then again, Hugo didn't exactly seem jumping for joy. Nobody here did.

That was the mood! This was a wake. We were all grieving the birth we were 'promised', that we'd invented in our heads.

No . . .We were grieving for ourselves.

It was so depressing. Why would anybody want to work here? But just when I thought I couldn't do it any more, my milk came in!

I had enough milk for the whole ward! Now I was beaming. *Oh, that's why people work here. For wonderful moments like this!*

'Hugo, Hugo, wake up, look, I've got milk, I'm making milk!' I squeezed my boobs and milk squirted out, white and brilliant. I'd done it. I was a mother. I was legit!

The midwives were pleased. They told me I'd done really well, my milk had come in sooner than they expected. Jet was satisfied; happy, gulping, swallowing, pressing his face into me, and making sort of greedy guinea pig noises, snuffling away. I had this boost of adrenalin and euphoria and instantly felt capable and maternal. I was happy I hadn't given up and used formula. If we had been in the wild he would not have starved because of my boobs!

Everything was going to be OK.

16

I can't remember when the fear about my stitches splitting began: a potent festering worry that I couldn't get out of my head.

'I think my stomach is splitting open, the stitches,' I told a midwife. 'I think they are coming apart?'

The midwife looked doubtful but checked my stomach anyway. 'No, that looks normal. See? These bandages are really good – that's just dried blood.'

I plucked up the courage to look down and it wasn't as bad as I thought. There was a translucent gel-like plaster over my wound. The blood underneath was dark and dry.

'Look, if I just draw a line here . . .' She marked the dressing with a biro. 'If the bleeding goes over that mark then let me know.'

With my milk in full flow, I was looking forward to Jet having a long sleep with a full tummy, even for just an hour. He was drifting in and out but it didn't seem to be happening.

'I don't know what's wrong,' I told the midwife. 'I'm feeding non-stop but he doesn't seem to be full, has my milk dried up?'

The midwife scooped up a pillow.

'Try the the rugby-ball position ...' She latched Jet to my boob. '... and he should ...' She stopped. 'Aha, he's tongue-tied.'

'Tongue-tied?'

'Yes. He might have trouble latching.'

'OK, how do we fix the tongue-tie?'

Hugo sat up with a 'What now?' expression on his face.

'Just a small operation, they cut it. It's very common,' the midwife reassured us.

No. No. No. So we'd been given the hungriest baby in the world and he couldn't feed? The irony.

I couldn't help think about the Hungry Ghosts in Chinese Buddhism, folklore in which humans who do bad deeds are reincarnated as beasts with long necks and small mouths so they are constantly starving. Never satisfied.

Was this bad karma? Was this my fault?

I'm sorry, Jet.

'Ah, look, if you do it this way, he can latch,' the midwife said as she arranged him on to my breast.

Jet began to drink. And swallow. I breathed again.

'Isn't *my* tongue tied?' I asked Hugo, opening my mouth for him to get a good look.

'Looks like it.'

'And I have *no* problems eating.'

There was no way I was giving Jet an operation unless he really needed it. He'd been through enough. So I sat up, held Jet in the rugby-ball position and he fed.

He fed and fed and fed.

17

Families around us began to be discharged and I resented their happy faces when they strapped their newborn into their immaculate car seat and left the sweaty purgatory. Nobody seemed to be there as long as us. I felt guilty, like I'd put Hugo into an irreversible position. Like I'd trapped him by having a baby. Like it was my fault.

The midwives were reluctant to discharge us. Both Jet and I were patients in our own right and they couldn't let us go home until we were both given the all-clear.

Because we'd been there for a while and were still opposite the crying baby that never stopped crying, the midwives kindly moved us to a room with a better . . . wait for it . . . view.

The view *was* nicer. The Houses of Parliament reminded me of how small I was. But the mood on this ward was sombre and low-beat, a complete contrast to the heated chaos of before.

All of a sudden, I went all super-practical. I was going to make the best of the situation. I told Hugo to go home and get some supplies: clean clothes, underwear, our pillows. The sheep thing that glows red and makes 'noises of the womb'. I told him to shower and eat something. Nap, if he wanted. I asked him to get me some fruit. Some lemonade? The second Hugo left I called my mum. I'd been pretending to be OK the whole time, ever since I was overdue, thinking any hour could be *the* hour, living in this false-start adrenalin-ignition limbo, only to then power down over and over and again. Now I collapsed.

'Mum. Mum. Please. It's so bad. It's so bad.'

'I know, I'm so sorry, sweetie, I'm so sorry. You'll be home really soon, I promise.'

Why did I feel like I had to hold it together? Like I couldn't cry in front of Hugo?

I didn't want him to know how hard I was finding it; I didn't want him to worry or think I was having regrets; I didn't want him to think I couldn't cope and that I'm not a good mum; I didn't want him to doubt me.

I could hear the couple in the bed opposite crying and the odd sounds of a baby, whimpering. I peeped out from my curtain and saw that their curtains were completely drawn shut.

When Hugo came back, I tried to hide that I'd been crying. He smelt of toothpaste, of the air, of our home. Of our life.

The ward fell silent with only the soft shuffle of quiet steps and the sucking of babies feeding. We turned off the lights. We made the bed all cosy and squishy with blankets and pillows, Hugo got in with me and we cuddled. The room was lit like a reptile tank. It was so quiet and still and peaceful and finally, Jet fell asleep.

I gently put him into the plastic basin and I got a full hour's sleep. It was rich and deep and wonderful: the best sleep of my life.

I woke up on Hugo's chest with Jet ready to feed again.

I felt recharged. 'I feel *so* much better,' I kept telling Hugo. 'Honestly, I feel like I can focus now. That hour was all I needed.'

There was some commotion as a new family arrived. We had neighbours. The new mum didn't say a word, but I could sense her exhaustion and fear as if she was communicating to me in some strange new maternal telepathy: I heard her whale song, so did the woman opposite. We could all feel this different undeniable energy around us.

And then all was calm. Hugo snoring softly beside me, Jet feeding, relentlessly, and me, slipping in and out of sleep.

18

Hugo and I woke to furious shouting from the bed next to us. It was a midwife. My neighbours had fallen asleep without feeding their underweight newborn.

When we opened our curtains we were faced with the devastation of the family opposite now too. The ones who were crying. From what we could make out, the mother was expecting twins and one of her babies had not made it.

Ever since she was shouted at, the young mother next to us had been feeding and her husband had been replaced by the girl's aunty, a huge, cool-headed woman with a beautiful face and full make-up. She arrived laden with bags of food in Tupperware: home-cooked chicken and rice, soup, salad and cake. She even brought a tablecloth, salt and pepper in silver pots and hot sauce. The whole ward filled with the smell of savoury cooking and spice. She was kissing her teeth, speaking in simple bite-size orders, bossing her niece to 'wake up' and 'eat'. The communal sink doubled as her makeshift kitchen. The midwives turned a blind eye.

The aunty took charge and sang the baby girl to sleep with lullabies so that her niece could rest. Aunty's yellow-gold bangles clanged, the baby lost in her fabrics and curves. She'd done this before.

Aunty seemed to do the trick and it wasn't long before mum and baby were discharged. I wished that I had an aunty like that to come to the rescue.

A woman a few years older than me was the next occupant of the bed. She also had an emergency C-section and her son's head was also covered in those horrible scratches. She was fuming. Pacing the ward in her fluffy pink dressing gown, insisting that she talk to the midwives. She said she'd had two children before and this had never happened. She didn't want a Caesarean, she wanted to know why her son's head was scratched, and demanded to see her birthing notes.

Why was I such a pushover? Why wasn't *I* demanding to speak to the midwives? Why was I such a passenger in the biggest moment of my life?

Out of my depth, not wanting to cause a fuss, I stayed quiet, and continued to feed Jet. It was all I did. He'd come up for air for a second and then would cry his eyes out. Every few hours, I was tempted to give up and let him cry it out but I couldn't. I followed his lead. *He must need it.* At one point I caught sight of my notes and saw that I had fed him for eighteen hours straight with a ten-minute break and then for another five.

One night, the boss of all the midwives suggested giving him a bottle of formula to help him sleep. She said, 'I'll just leave this here.' And I considered it, watching the bottle like an addict needing a fix. I kept saying, 'If he doesn't fall asleep in the next hour, I'll use the formula. Hugo can feed him and I'll sleep.' And before I knew it I had fed him all night again.

One day I fed him for twenty-four hours straight. I'm not telling you this so you can call me a hero, I'm telling you so you can see how sleep deprivation can help send you to madness, because sleep I did not. My stomach ached and it hurt to laugh and move and cough.

I became pretty primal in there. By now everybody had seen my boobs. Seen my blood. Heard me cry. The laxatives had kicked in and I was shuffling backwards and forwards to the shared bathroom so they'd all smelt my poo too. I was mostly naked, sweating, scratching, bleeding, unable to wash, feeding myself just to feed Jet, feral, sobbing, and I felt so dirty.

I started to lose my inhibitions, wondering if we'd *ever* go home. I couldn't be bothered with the fussy plastic cup any more and was drinking water straight from the jug because I could drink litres. I no longer had the patience for pleasantries. I went from dreading the sight of a needle to literally just rolling over on my side to let a nurse inject my thigh every morning without even a 'Hello'. My legs were covered in purple-and-black bruises and scabs, I was fed tablets three times a day, had my blood pressure taken, had to wear the weird horrible stockings, and my head was spinning, it was *so hot*. I had to take iron, which made me constipated, so then I had to take more laxatives to make me poo. I am a vegetarian but I was literally eating anything they gave me – I tore a chicken carcass apart with my nails and teeth like a crazed Viking. I asked everybody about my scar like an impatient child repeats 'are we there yet?' in the backseat of a long drive. No answer could pacify me long enough. *Are you sure the stitches aren't splitting? Can I see the doctor? It feels like they are coming apart. Is the blood over the biro line?*

Every hour a different midwife would thrash the curtain wide open and ask why the baby wasn't swaddled, only for another midwife to then tell me that swaddling is not recommended. Too hot. Too cold. The same happened with breastfeeding; the angle, the latch. Next it was the position he should sleep in. On his side, on his back. Then he would fall asleep for a second only to poo and need changing, all the nappies were too big for him.

One night in the ward I just lost it.

'WILL IT EVER GET BETTER?' I cried to a midwife.

'Yes,' she reassured me. 'It will one hundred per cent get better. I promise.'

Well, let me tell you, that chick was a liar.

Midwife Number Five (the one with the tattoos and piercings) came to see me. She'd looked me up and saw that I had an emergency Caesarean. 'I'm so sorry, what a shame,' she said, as though it was a sad ending to a story. 'It will be all good from here.'

It was sweet of her to come and say hello, but I was left with a bitter feeling like I'd failed at a test. I showed her my scar.

'Do my stitches look like they're splitting to you?' I asked.

'No, they look good; you look like you're gonna have a small scar! That's good for your bikini!' She was very reassuring, Hugo nodded in agreement (because he'd also reassured me himself 5,000 times by now that they weren't) but it didn't satisfy me.

Bikinis were the least of my worries.

'Are you sure you can't see it splitting? Has the blood gone over the pen line?' I insisted.

'Nope. You're all good.'

I felt like Midwife Number Five would tell me the truth.

We then had a visit from *our* midwife, Midwife Number Six. And she cried when she saw us and we cried too. We hugged and she held Jet and she said how proud of us she was.

'Before you go, can you look at my stitches?' I anxiously asked her. 'Do they look like they're splitting?'

19

Finally, I was discharged. I don't know how because I was sobbing non-stop. There should be warning signs around the ward saying, IT IS NOT NORMAL TO BE CRYING FOR TWENTY-FOUR HOURS STRAIGHT. Then again, it's not normal to be awake for almost a week.

Jet had not yet been discharged; we had to see the doctor first.

I paced up and down the L-shaped corridor like a caged tiger, pushing Jet in his clear basin on wheels. I should have been taking it slow but I was overtaking all the other traffic of trapped, worried parents pushing their babies; eyes locked, deranged, clueless.

When the angry woman next to us in the fluffy pink dressing gown was discharged, I decided enough was enough. The doctor had to see Jet. We had to go home.

Eventually, the doctor checked Jet. His hearing, his eyesight, his reflexes. I winced at every test, dreading another setback. The doctor weighed Jet. The doctor was still worried about Jet's low reserves and wanted us to stay on the ward. This was the setback I'd been afraid of: apparently, babies *lose* weight after they come out of the womb.

I got a call from the midwife we'd been seeing during the pregnancy, and, like some sort of secret assassin, she stalked onto the ward and convinced the doctor to discharge us: we would be under her care.

We were free to go at last.

Jet's 'going home babygrow', the grey one with the white stars that Mum got him, hung off his bony little body. People stared at us in the lift, murmuring that he was 'so tiny' and 'so cute and small'.

They obviously thought he was premature.

It was a clear sunny blue day. We stepped out into the fresh air, ice cold and pure spring. After the ripe vacuum-packed jungle we had just escaped, it felt glorious to simply breathe, filling my lungs. The car park warden halved our bill in sympathy at our long stay. We started to think that everything was going to be OK.

We loaded ourselves into the car, Jet in the back for the first time, and began the short drive home, Hugo, hugging the wheel, driving extra safely.

Jet screamed the entire way.

We laughed. 'Maybe the sun is in his eyes? Maybe he's scared of the car? He'll get used to it,' I said, but I was thinking, *Oh God. I thought it would all be OK now but maybe it's not? Why is he screaming like this?*

Who even is this tiny stranger that is coming home with us?

I told myself that it would be fine once we got home.

I had planned on bringing Jet into our house and introducing him to all the rooms, telling him, 'This is the kitchen . . . help yourself to anything you want in the fridge.' But I didn't. I couldn't. It was like a deserted holiday home, igloo cold.

I said to Hugo, 'Let's all get in bed.'

I'd dreamt of this moment. I had these visions of us all being together, naked and hippy and rolling around in a heap of blankets, falling in love and in and out of sleep, and ordering Deliveroo.

It *should* have felt so wonderful and it didn't. Hugo fell asleep instantly, Jet burst into inconsolable tears. I had this lurking feeling deep in the pit of my stomach. It had nothing to do with Jet crying, it was something worse. It was the feeling of terror. Of dread.

I put Jet on the boob and he quietened. My head was racing.

I've made a demanding screaming alien and I don't know how I did it. My body doesn't feel like mine any more. Why did I even have a baby in the first place? How can I even be thinking that? Maybe the baby has ruined everything? Maybe the baby has robbed me of my life? I've made a mistake. OH GOD! Having these thoughts makes me a bad mum. Great, I'm a bad mum and I've not even started. Give me a chance — no, actually, I don't want a chance. I'm a failure. I can't even put my finger on why . . . but I'm so scared. I don't want to be a mum. I can't do it.

'This doesn't feel right,' I whispered to Hugo.

''Course it does,' he answered, his eyes still closed.

'No. Something is wrong,' I whispered back.

'Nothing is wrong, you're OK and Jet's OK. We just had a scare, we just got off to a bad start. That's all. Try and get some sleep.'

'I'm not sure why, I know this is *meant* to feel right, everything is here, everything is as it should be, but I can't put my finger on it. It's not all right,' I shook my head. 'I'm not all right.'

Stuff that Scared Me Before I Had a Baby

Ghosts.

Home intrusion.

Anything you could knock your teeth out with – including rollerblades, roller-skates, skateboards.

Slopes.

Hills.

Mountains.

The roads that wrap around mountains.

The dark.

Sleeping on my own.

Streatham.

Touching chalk with my nails or teeth.

Witches.

Forests.

Halloween.

Zombies.

Cannibals.

Ghost trains.

Anything to do with the devil like that film *The Exorcist*.

Cults.

Clans.

Stalkers.

People not liking me for no reason.

Being left out.

Climbing over fences.

Letters from the bank, tax, bills etc.

The news.

Dying.

My family dying.

Drugs.

20

Fear came into my mind a lot during my recovery. What am I scared of? Did my imagination *do* this to me? Did I scare myself into this? Did I subconsciously *ask* for this? Was my fear so powerful that it overrode the 'happiest' time of my life? Had my brain seen something as a child and it needed to entertain it – play it out? And why now? Why did my life *have* to choose now, of all moments, to break me? I thought I was so solid. To think I thought I knew myself. I can't help but go back . . . maybe I would find an answer hidden in my past?

When I was twelve we moved from our cosy, squishy, busy Brixton flat that I called home to a big, old rundown house further out. It had beautiful high ceilings, working fireplaces and original wooden floorboards but it felt hollow and cold. We felt like intruders, borrowing somebody else's space; ghosts of odd socks behind the radiator; eyelashes on the windowsill; dust on the mantles. There was something about the place that wasn't right. Something that made my brother, sister and I share a bed every night.

Mum told us that the house was haunted. She would spindle up these far-fetched stories of the house's legacy. That she could hear marbles rolling over the floorboards. That there was a wooden chair that would drag itself across the room. That if we listened closely we would be able to hear little children singing in between the walls. That the second stair on the staircase would make you slip if you weren't careful.

One night my brother said 'a ghost' lifted him up and smashed his face into his headboard and tried to break his nose (although he did sleepwalk). My sister Daisy said that once her bedroom door swung open in the night and a man wrapped in bandages stood staring at her, mouth agape, a gust of wind behind him bellowing like a sandstorm. And once my stepdad's mum thanked Daisy and me for bringing in a glass of water to her in the night. She said the little girls were wearing bonnets.

We never brought her a glass of water or owned a bonnet.

My mum thrived on the idea that some 'presence' shared our home with us. She said we should see the spirits as our friends. Sometimes, to spook us, she pretended to talk to them. She even commissioned someone to make her a big wooden Ouija board with gothic-style letters in a rainbow arc of doom.

She filled the house with taxidermy, jarred jellyfish, pinned insects, accessorising with religious paraphernalia, thick Roman candles and dubious ornaments. She would go on holiday and bring back obscure artwork, relics and antiques – weird masks, dead stingrays, old browning bones, bits of rubble, and ancient musical instruments. The house began to look like a junk shop. A haunted museum.

I grew up trying to normalise the clutter. To rationalise every chipped clay face, every string of a violin, every page of an unwanted book, every sweep of paint on a canvas, every beetle's back, every crocodile tooth, hoping it wouldn't come to life like in *Jumanji* and exile me to the jungle for forty years. *It's just stuff. It's just stuff.*

And it *was* just a house, but as a child, when the growling fire was burning and the yellow flames danced off the blood-red walls, it was a house of horrors.

My imagination is both my superpower and my kryptonite – it keeps me happy but it can also turn on me and play nasty tricks. I do not underestimate it. No outside danger could terrify me as much as the workings of my own brain – it can scare me better than anybody.

And one day, when I was at home alone revising for my exams, it happened. I heard the rolling marbles and the dragging chair. *Oh God, it was my turn. I was about to be attacked by a poltergeist.* I launched up, running outside the front of the house with an iron in one hand and the cordless phone in the other shouting, 'I CAN'T help you! I don't want to see you. Leave me alone.'

Most people are meant to be more scared of the streets than their home. Not us.

This was the house where my parents broke up. The house soaked up all that sinister emotion. My fear of ghosts and intruders was real but not as real as my fear of my family splitting in two, of things falling apart. Of people you love, leaving.

Stuff that Scared Me After I Had Jet

Anything bad happening to Jet.

Anything bad happening to Hugo.

Being a bad mum.

Jet not wanting to come to my house for dinner when he's an adult.

Being trapped inside my own head.

Losing my mind.

Having Jet taken away from me.

Not being able to care for Jet.

Not trusting myself.

Doing something stupid/ dangerous in my sleep.

Being sectioned.

Becoming an insomniac, not being able to take it, losing my mind
    and then being sectioned.

Living in a different reality to everybody else.

Living in a different reality to everybody else and not knowing it.

Living in a different reality to everybody else and knowing it.

Thinking I'm unable to cope.

Committing suicide.

My family finding me dead after I've committed suicide.
Lullabies.
Hallucinating.
Hearing voices.
The songs that come out of baby toys.
The sound of white noise.
Nursery rhymes.
Play groups.
My blood pressure.
Interventions.
My imagination.
Not having an imagination.
Shock therapy.
Not being able to access myself.
Not being able to be creative.
Addiction.
Racing thoughts.
Being scared.
Paranoia.
Phantom pregnancy.
Knives.
Prison.
Isolation.
Dying alone.
Becoming pregnant again.
Meeting my unwell self.

21

The expectation that I'd fall head over heels in love with my baby was overwhelming. I'd see those photos all over social media, the kind with the smiling-crying happy mum and the naked baby on their chest. *Skin to skin.* Their big reunion. Both breathless and bound. I'd seen it in movies since I was a kid. A woman in labour screaming in roars of pain, the baby being born, and the mother suddenly laughing and crying tears of agony and joy and relief at the same time. Isn't the mother beautiful like this? She's never been more beautiful. Sweaty and teary and glowing after she's just done what she was 'born to do', she's performed her 'woman's work'. And she looks down at her newborn: *Isn't she beautiful? She looks like you.*

That feeling never came in those early weeks. Not for me. For me, Jet was like the ultimate pet that I couldn't give back. When would I start to feel anything like love?

During the day, we grew like bacteria, spreading out in the living room. I'd sit in the corner of the couch wearing padded knickers and a maternity bra, feeding, with a giant pregnancy pillow stained with tea and blood and baby vomit behind me. I had a side table with my necessities: nipple cream, tea, water, paracetamol, phone, tissues, biscuits, the remote, muslin cloth after muslin cloth that I'd use to clean sick, spilt milk, wipe up spilt tea and tears. Sometimes we played music but everything sounded too loud. I didn't want to listen to the songs I loved before because I didn't want to associate them with feeling like this.

I couldn't read or watch TV. I couldn't laugh.

I didn't want to go out. I didn't want to see anybody. But then I had this awful guilt, like I *should* be showing Jet the world – *my* world – introducing him to the people and places I loved.

Jet's skin began to shred and peel off (it happens with overdue babies and is completely harmless) and I found it unbearable. Such a small thing was somehow too much for me to take, and bizarre thoughts went racing. *Is he an alien? Is he peeling to death? Is he skinning himself alive? Is he sick?*

My stomach was flipping, my head was mazing and my heart was pounding. I knew I was at home but it felt like a parallel universe. Everything was the same, but different.

It was *me* that had changed. I'd never been so unhappy.

'*Oh, it's tough work but it's SO rewarding,*' the midwives had said.

No. It. Is. Not. Where was the reward? Maybe everybody feels like this? Hugo didn't. He couldn't have been more besotted with Jet, his little mini-me. Yes, just to add insult to injury a baby looks exactly identical to the *dad*! A midwife in the hospital had explained that it's evolution's way of bonding the father with his baby. Like nature's paternity test.

Are you friggin' joking me? Why? For Dad's ego? So he doesn't think his girlfriend has cheated? Because it's so comforting to watch a mini version of themselves sucking on their girlfriend's boobs?

Hugo hadn't even held a newborn before Jet, in fact he asked me just moments before he was born, 'Is he going to be born with teeth?'

I felt this added pressure that I *had* to be besotted with the baby and also to know what to do. That *I* had to steer the ship. Maybe it was my naivety but I trusted that instinct would take over. But nothing felt natural or instinctive.

Hugo is the man who once upon a time made me a 'salt and cheese' sandwich for lunch. Now he came into the bedroom every morning with a green smoothie and a cup of tea. Gave me my medicine and injected me in the thigh. He had to take care of us while I took care of Jet.

And he was *in love*. He was exactly the same as he always was. In fact, no, he was *happier*. He was complete. How was he managing to be the exact same guy he always was before this tornado? How did he have this immediate bond with the baby and I didn't? How could he think that Jet was *cute* and laugh at everything he did? How could he already be talking about having *more*? *Stop taking photos! I hate cameras. This can't be real. I've been tricked into having a baby! The world has lied to me. I can't believe I fell for it. I am LIVID.*

I watched Hugo capturing Jet's gargles on his phone. Kissing him, scooping him up, already dressing him up like a mini-Hugo and playing him the guitar and singing. Why wasn't I being the same? I wasn't the fun playful mum I knew I could be. I wasn't like this with other people's babies. Why was I like this with my own? Why was I so bad with my baby?

I wanted to say, 'Listen here, baby, I was cool once too, you know.

I had a life before you too. I am funny too, just like your dad. No, in fact, in all honesty, *I'm* actually the funny one. Ask anyone. I have stuff going on. I have friends. A past. I have an imagination. A personality. I was even a bit sexy for a minute before I was a bedraggled braless mule carrying baby crap around. I have dreams! I just can't seem to find them right now. But I do. I promise. I am someone. I am . . . I really am.'

22

The days would drag. I knew I should be napping when Jet napped. But I couldn't. *You really should be sleeping, Laura.* STOP TELLING ME TO SLEEP! I **KNOW** THAT! DON'T YOU THINK I WANT TO SLEEP? The pressure just pushed sleep further and further away from me, and all the while, Hugo would be blissfully snoring away.

So I just sat there in my diseased corner, zoned out in front of the TV screen, light flickering across my vacant dilated pupils. I look at photos of myself from this time and I am *dead*. Glassy-eyed like a waxwork model.

I thought back to how we used to spend our Sundays: hungover, falling in and out of sleep, looped in each other's arms watching films and eating takeaway. Why couldn't it be like that now but with a baby? That sounded like an impossible dream.

Time became abstract and didn't make much sense. I would crawl through the day, desperate for it to come to an end so that it could strike midnight and be a new day again, and maybe tomorrow would be different.

But the nights were the worst. It was February and the days were short and lonely, leaving the night to swell and suffocate in its drowning numbing silence.

The doom would build.

The plan was that Hugo would sleep during the night so that he could care for us in the day. I was 'meant' to sleep for forty-five minutes at a time, be woken by Jet crying in his cot, feed for an hour or so, which wasn't easy with the complication of Jet's tongue-tie, sleep for another forty-five minutes and do it all again.

If the plan worked I guessed I'd sleep a few hours in total, but it didn't quite work out like that.

I remembered someone, a man, once saying, 'It's so easy with a newborn: you just go to sleep, wake up, feed the baby and go back to sleep. Simple.'

Yeah, right. Some cunning primal sixth sense makes the new mother alert to every noise, every unusual smell, like a watchdog. As if the umbilical cord was never cut. He communicated with me through the dust particles in the air, waves of sound, the beating of our hearts.

The clock very quickly became a bully, prodding me in the back. Counting down the minutes.

I was on panic mode the entire time, and it was so draining. I was beyond exhausted, but I couldn't relax. And this was soundtracked by white noise, which Jet had to listen to all night from a broken iPhone, a muffled scratchy sinister siren song scoring the seconds.

There was the added pressure of knowing that he was born so underweight and that he had to catch up, so we couldn't afford to miss a feed. Feeding was my job: if I didn't, he'd starve.

I fed Jet, and made a note on my phone of how long he had fed and either L or R breast so I knew which side to start the next feed on. It sounds so simple, but I found it all so overwhelming and confusing.

Paracetamol
Start right breast 23.05 – 15 mins
Change nappy – poo and wee
L – 23.29–23.35
Change nappy – poo and wee
R – 01.19–01.34

L – 2.30–3.30
R – 3.30–3.45
Change nappy – wee and poo
L – 3.55–4.01
R – 4.53–5.13
Change nappy – poo and wee

I couldn't grasp it. It was blowing my mind. All the numbers made no sense. And I was getting *no* sleep.

Jet would often fall asleep on the breast and I'd have to keep him awake to feed, tickling his toes or stroking his hair, to ensure he drank and then *he* could sleep and so then *I* could sleep.

A bit of me was certain he was going to die anyway. I thought, *well, why should I bother feeding him? Am I just delaying the inevitable?*

Would I feel relief if he did?

I hated myself for thinking like that.

Even if he did sleep a bit longer than anticipated, I would have to set an alarm to wake me up for his next feed. My phone was full of alarms at all kind of obscene times in the night. My basic maths went out the window.

I also couldn't just do a 'dream feed' because he wasn't encouraged to fall asleep on the boob because he was so underweight so I'd have to wake him to eat. It felt so wrong, shoving a nipple in his resting mouth.

Never wake a sleeping baby, they say. Well, I did – over and over again.

Boob in. Lights dim. I would fight sleep. I had a fear of dropping him, that he'd slip and shatter when he hit the floor. I'd visualise the midwives from the ward thrashing my curtain open instructing me to place him in his little plastic bed. Not like that, like *this*. So I'd sit, in my bedroom, in the twilight, zoning in and out of consciousness.

This is impossible. How is everybody doing this? WHY would anybody do this? How do we exist as a population? How have we not DIED out as a species? Please get easier.

The second I'd put Jet down and raced back to close my eyes, he would scream, rigid with agony, want more milk, or have a wet nappy and cry and I'd have to get up to change him, moving like a bumbling thief in the dark next to the glow of the little night light, only for him to need more milk to settle him back down. Or sometimes I'd think he was drinking but he was just using the nipple for comfort, and I'd have to feed him again. And I was doing it all on no energy.

'Just put him in the bed with you,' my friends said.

But what if we crushed him? What if he fell out of the bed and died?

And anyway, according to the midwives on the ward, co-sleeping was out of the question and made to feel illegal. So I paced, back and forth, up and down. Rock, rock, rock until he was settled, which could sometimes take several attempts, placing him so gently in the cot, chest to chest, until I was basically face down in the cot myself, and holding my breath like a real-life game of Jenga. I'd finally tiptoe back to bed, back to a sleeping Hugo, and know I would only have a tiny forty-five-minute window to sleep. Sometimes I'd only have fifteen minutes, because I had to start the feed at the beginning of the last one, not the end, and the longer it took to fall asleep the less point in sleeping there was, because he'd only just wake up needing another feed. It was absurd. No, it was torture.

The pressure to sleep became enormous. If I didn't sleep I wouldn't be able to cope and function the next day. Yet I felt oddly wired. I became terrified of caffeine. I didn't want tea or coffee or fizzy drinks or chocolate during the day. Basically, the stuff most parents rely on as fuel to get them through.

Hugo would wake every morning and ask how I slept and I'd say, 'I didn't.'

I'd feel so resentful of the sleep in the corner of his eyes, the evidence of blissful rest that was so out of my reach, and then even more disappointed at myself for being angry at him for that.

He offered to stay up with me, but what was the point in us both being worn out? I knew the deal. I knew I was the feeder. I knew I wasn't meant to sleep.

But I didn't feel *tired*.

And that was the problem. I was pumped with adrenalin.

'Just go to sleep, Laura.'

YES THANK YOU, I KNOW HOW TO SLEEP, I'VE BEEN SLEEPING FOR THIRTY-ONE YEARS BEFORE THIS.

I'd just lie there, heart beating, head spinning, blood pouring out of me, running through worst-case scenarios and hurtling down this ugly track in my brain.

How do I know how much milk he's getting? What about the tongue-tie? Was he actually swallowing? Was he just sucking for comfort? What if he dies? What if I think he's sleeping but he's actually dying right now? Maybe I shouldn't love him too much in case he DOES die? I am too tired to take care of him. What if I never sleep again? What if I have a heart attack? What if Hugo leaves me because I'm a bad mum? I'll end up alone. Mad and alone. What if I can't do it? What will people say? Why don't I feel normal? I'm never going to feel normal on no sleep – BUT I CAN'T SLEEP! I'm trapped.

And what if my stitches split open? What if they get infected? What if I run out of blood? What if I had to go BACK to hospital?

I'd heard of infected Caesareans – it happened to one of my friends. That was going to happen, I *knew* it would.

I should wake Hugo up. This could be an excuse to wake him up so I'm not alone. Hugo, sorry to wake you . . . Are you SURE my stitches aren't splitting open? Is there blood over the biro line? Hugo, wake up.

What if I'm so exhausted and delirious that I drop Jet by accident?

Wait, what if I kill Jet by accident? I should tell somebody about this . . . Is this normal?

What is wrong with me?

23

Something wasn't right. I'd never felt like this before and it frightened me.

I needed help but I didn't want to admit I was struggling. I was terrified that the health visitor would become concerned and take Jet away. I couldn't speak to my friends because I was scared that they'd judge me. I couldn't even look after my own child. It wasn't the practical stuff, the pooey nappies and rocking him to sleep. It was something else.

I didn't feel human. I wasn't warm, or friendly or loveable. Not maternal. Not womanly. Not like a 'mum' is meant to be. I couldn't do it. I was overwhelmed. I needed real-life serious help.

I'm grieving for myself. I miss myself and never got a chance to say goodbye to me.

I was jealous of my friends. There was so much I haven't done, and now it was too late.

I'm traumatised. I'm in pain. Please help me.

People say that depression can be caused by sleep deprivation, which is true, it can be a contributing factor. But sleeplessness is a *symptom* of the illness. I didn't get ill because I couldn't sleep. I couldn't sleep *because* I was ill.

I'd talk myself down, get up every morning with a new improved sense of enthusiasm and positivity.

It's OK. Today I'm going to nail the routine and get back on track.

My parents told me we never had a routine when we were small. We would be rocked to Kylie Minogue and sleep on our parents until one in the morning. If we were out, we would run around until we dropped and then sleep on pub tables with leather jackets thrown over us, and here I was wrestling with the blackout blinds and plug-in room thermometers.

Throughout my chaotic labour and time on the ward, I had had to relinquish all control. Now I was in my own home, I was *determined* to get things back on track. I decided that Hugo should keep a record of what Jet was doing at all minutes of the day. Mostly it was the same thing: *Sleeping. Pooing. Feeding.* I made him draw up in a routine book all these little columns (with a ruler! Can you imagine?), which he then had to fill every hour with feeding data (left breast or right breast and duration of feed) and napping (duration) and changing (time and what was in the nappy).

I became obsessed with analysing the times, the gaps between, imagining a pattern and tricking myself into thinking that a routine was emerging, trying to convince myself that Jet was running like clockwork.

He was a newborn; he was behaving like a newborn baby.

I had disapproved of following any baby guru's routine and yet here I was, creating my own bizarre set of rules. God bless Hugo for going along with it. I've since thrown that book away because it made me shudder.

I sent a long-winded text message about the labour and Jet's low weight to pretty much everybody in my phone book. I felt the need to explain what had happened to us and why we'd been so quiet. I read it to Hugo afterwards and I remember him being a bit confused as to why I sent it out. 'I don't think people will be expecting to hear from us,' he said. 'We've just had a baby.'

He was right. It was weird and I knew it.

I got a few concerned sympathetic replies, which only made me feel weirder.

A few days in and we had our first midwife visit. At the time, I thought I'd *smashed* it. God, it was really *not* OK.

When you have a newborn, it is a given that you'll be unwashed, in pyjamas, the sink piled up high with dirty dishes, the washing basket full and mugs of tea everywhere. My flat however, was immaculate, and I am *not* a tidy person. You could have eaten off the floor. My house was also silent, and I am *not* a quiet person. You could have heard a pin drop.

When the midwife arrived, I was like a 1940s wife trying to hold it all together with perfectly curled hair and immaculate red lipstick. I had Jet perfectly dressed in his fresh baby whites, sleeping peacefully in his Sleepyhead, and was checking my emails in an almost, 'Oh! I wasn't expecting you,' sort of way. Creeeeeeepppy.

I had plugged in a diffuser blowing out scents of lavender and camomile and, I'm embarrassed to say, had even put some classical music on the stereo. What the actual FUCK!??

And then, there was my *pièce de résistance*: I had the horror-story 'routine book' wide open, on display, ready for the midwife to survey my strange scrawls and impressively rigorous time-keeping and applaud me with a gobsmacked, 'Well done, you! I've never seen anything so incredible. You've totally *nailed* this motherhood thing.'

Except she didn't. She looked concerned. '*Hmmmm . . .*' she murmured, looking me intently in the eye.

I wanted her to tell me how well I looked, but she didn't.

'You've got make-up on?' she said, in the tone you might use to accuse somebody of lying.

I showed her the routine book again. Did she not see how fantastic it was? *Sorry, are we looking at the same thing here?* Maybe it was too complicated and profound for her to understand? She looked confused, and worryingly, more to Hugo than me, said, 'It's good to have a rough idea of feeding times and nappies but you don't need to go overboard.'

Overboard? I was livid.

She weighed Jet. The sight of his scrawny naked body wriggling on the scales made me shiver. I was nervous, but he'd put on weight! It was such great news. She told me I'd done really well and I felt proud. That was all that mattered. 'Keep doing what you're doing,' she said. It had all paid off.

I told her I was worried about my stitches splitting open (they were fine), but she told me to keep taking the iron because I had lost some blood during the Caesarean. It was normal. Apparently. I hadn't even thought about that before she mentioned it. She told us to 'enjoy this precious time' because 'it goes past so quickly'.

Does it? It felt like I was doing the breaststroke through concrete.

She smiled and I smiled back.

Crrrraaaaccck.

Hold it together, hold it together . . .

I closed the door behind her and when I heard her heels clapping on the street outside, the performance was over. The lavender mist was switched off. The classical music was silenced. I washed off the make-up and my smile slid away.

I was privately panicking about my blood loss. I was convinced I had a severe iron deficiency. I was still bleeding heavily on my pad too. *I might lose all my blood? How do I make more blood . . . and QUICK?*

I didn't want Hugo to go out so I asked him to ask his best friend to bring steak and liquid iron and spinach immediately, as if we were in hiding and in need of supplies. Hugo fried me a bloody steak and I wolfed it down like a beastly carnivore, washing it down with a green spinach smoothie while I breastfed Jet.

Something bad is going to happen. I know it is.

I started looking at myself in the mirror. *I'm falling apart. I'm getting paler. I can see it. I've got vitamin-D deficiency. I'm low in iron. I've got no immune system. My teeth are going to fall out. I'm going to start losing my hair. I'm so weak. I'm so frail. I haven't got enough milk to feed my baby. I need to sleep if I'm going to make milk. He can't lose weight. He will die. We're* both *dying.*

I told Hugo to put away all of the congratulations cards. They kept coming every day, along with flowers, cookies, cakes, babygrows, mobiles, rattles, toys, teddy bears, bunnies, baby books. YUCK. All ugly and hideous and mounting up on the table. I said, 'There's nothing to celebrate about. Why are we celebrating *this?*'

We'd just had a beautiful baby boy but I felt like somebody had died. Hugo looked hurt. To him, it was a celebration, but he did as I asked, and threw everything away. Afterwards the flat looked sad and deflated. I felt even more guilty.

We moved about like Quentin Blake illustrations, grey, washed out. I pretty much refused all visitors. I felt sick most of the time.

Jet's poo looked a weird colour. I sent photos to the midwife who said it was fine. I felt like she was lying to me. I wanted to ask her to reassure me by taking photographs of every nappy I saw, but I stopped myself.

One morning, Jet's umbilical cord snapped off in his nappy and this put a spring in my step. I woke Hugo up with the little clip and cord on his chest and we smiled. I had some faint hope that it would get better, that this was a mark that time was passing.

A different midwife visited the next time. *They probably sent a new one for a second opinion on me. Maybe she'll appreciate my routine notebook*? No. She really didn't like it. And why would she? It was like the secret diaries of a stalker. She said, 'You need to see the day as twenty-four hours – there's no such thing as day and night for a newborn. You can't impose a routine on a baby under six weeks. Just get naked and be together.'

That's exactly what I wanted to do but I couldn't. I told her that I didn't feel normal, that I had this horrible pressing on my chest. A burning sensation. I told her that I didn't feel well, I couldn't breathe.

She said that the pressing on the chest could be the feeling of the milk coming down, it wasn't unheard of. I knew it wasn't that. This was not a physiological thing. It was a psychological.

I became paranoid that people were taking about me. It started as a little seed, but once planted in my mind the suspicion began to flourish very quickly. I began to unpick and overanalyse messages from my friends, picking up on signals from my family and Hugo.

My behaviour was getting more and more bizarre. I started ignoring my friends so people couldn't talk about me. I didn't trust what

I was saying so I stayed quiet so I couldn't overanalyse it. I started to take less and less care of myself. I was crying quite a lot. Mostly in secret. Tears splashed on to Jet's sleeping face.

'What's wrong?' Hugo asked.

I said I was having flashbacks from the birth, but it wasn't that.

I became erratic. Next, I started reaching out to friends of friends, vague acquaintances, anyone I knew with kids. 'I feel really weird and bad, is this normal?', 'Did you love your baby straight away?' I wrote, and all of them replied that they had felt exactly the same as me. They all told me it gets 'so much better'. That one day I'd 'just push the pram outdoors and be like, OK I've got this!'

Friends told me to switch to formula. 'It's no big deal,' they said. But it felt like the only thing I knew how to do, and because I felt our bond was so absent I worried that without the breastfeeding we would come apart at the seams. Then Jet wouldn't be mine at all.

I'd just got the 'Baby Blues'. Apparently. 'Everybody gets them.' 'It's very common. It's hormones and acclimatising.' 'How do you expect to feel after a birth like that? Course you're not going to feel normal.'

'It passes. Don't worry, it passes.'

We took Jet for a walk. It was arctic cold. He looked tiny in his pram. Hugo and I trembled our way around the park, jumping at every noise, like everyone was looking at us. In Tesco, some young guys admired Jet sleeping, they said, ' Awww he's so tiny.' And I felt like screaming, 'How *dare* you?' I had to go and sit down. The world was spinning.

I wanted to go home. But I didn't want to go home either. I had a horrible feeling I was going to die there.

24

The *only* thing I knew how to do was breastfeed. *What if I couldn't?* I bought £50 worth of nipple cream as a preventative measure and asked my sister Daisy to come over to help me cut clingfilm into tiny squares to cover my nipples so they didn't dry out or become sore. If I wasn't breastfeeding, I was covering my nipples in cream and clingfilm. I set up little breastfeeding stations all over the flat, with tubes of cream and stacks of clingfilm in piles.

Before long, Jet started spluttering when I was feeding him. He had almost choked on a square of clingfilm, which I'd forgotten to remove.

Later, with the window open, the wind blew a pile of clingfilm squares into the cot. I visualised it suffocating Jet while he was sleeping and immediately went frantically rummaging around the entire house getting rid of every single square that Daisy had only just cut up.

Jet was steadily, incredibly, gaining weight, but as the numbers on the scale were recorded in his little red book, and he notched up the centile chart, I felt myself sliding away. I couldn't care less any more. About him. Or myself. I was disappearing.

It was snowing outside, London was at complete peace. I was on the sofa, convinced I was having a heart attack.

I called the midwife and asked if that was a possibility.

I finally had the guts to tell Hugo that I had to see the doctor. I couldn't do this.

My mum told me I had postnatal depression, but I ignored her. I didn't feel depressed. I could still appreciate the soft twinkling secret magic of snow, the way it silenced the world and sank the streets to sleep. But what did I know? What did depression feel like?

I booked an appointment with my doctor. Mum watched Jet, and Hugo and I set off for the GP surgery visit Number One. The black streets were dotted with patches of snow like a cow hide in reverse. I felt paranoid and scared of everybody. My steps didn't seem to be hitting the ground. I held Hugo's hand, but couldn't get a proper grip.

'It's so cold,' Hugo said, but my body was numb. I didn't feel a thing.

The GP stared at me with her big kind blue eyes. She calmly asked me if I was haunted by images from the birth.

I said yes. But it wasn't the entire truth. I felt terror, doom and a storm brewing. And then this other feeling, like a cat that has its hairs brushed up the wrong way, like I'd been struck by lightning. I was static. Charged.

The GP suggested that I was suffering from post-traumatic stress disorder. I nodded, but I knew it wasn't just that. She could prescribe me some antidepressants but perhaps I should wait to see how I was when my hormones had settled down and I'd slept?

She told me to express milk if I could, and let Hugo do the night feeds and to come back the next day after a good night's sleep. She promised that it would get better. She looked so beautiful and healthy. And normal. And problem-free. She could go about her day and eat a sandwich for lunch and go home to kids that she loved like a regular healthy person. I *wished* I was her.

We stopped at a cafe on the walk home and I was not OK. Hugo ordered a coffee and a croissant and I looked at him like he was eating dog poo. The colour faded from my vision. I was trapped inside my own head and didn't know how I got there or how to get out.

What did I used to think about before all my brain thought about was what I was thinking about?

I'm too inside myself. I have no distance. No space.

I won't be able to live like this for much longer – I won't be able to watch a film. Listen to somebody talk. Read a book. Walk two steps without my internal thoughts clanging around my caged-in head.

We got back and the baby was *still* there, my mum hugging him, watching TV and laughing. Being the same as she always was made me feel even more inadequate and wrong.

The GP rang and spoke to Hugo. It was so nice of her to call, to go out of her way like that. She had spoken to her colleagues who suggested that I could just be struggling with severe adjustment disorder, and prescribed me with a week's prescription for a low dose of a drug called quetiapine as a sleeping aid. She added one more thing: quetiapine was prescribed to medicate schizophrenia, but I wasn't to worry. I could breastfeed with it and it would help me to sleep.

Hugo tried to reassure me, but it was too late. Even the word 'schizophrenia' scared me. A seed of fear had been planted.

My mum and Daisy stayed over so Hugo and I could get some

sleep. She said that back in the day when she had me, the midwives used to let the mother sleep for a full week straight. They would just bring the baby in for feeds. She said you need the rest to recover after labour, and that's what TuTus (that's what she calls herself because 'Grandma' makes her feel old) are for.

I didn't want to take the pills, but I didn't want to let anybody down either. So I did as I was told. I had a bath. I fed Jet. I took the quetiapine, and waited for it to work. Hugo held me and read to me in bed.

The drug hit me instantly, like I was falling through a bottomless elevator. My muscles jerked and then I slept. A full eight hours – my first full night's sleep in about two weeks.

When I woke, my boobs were full with milk, swollen and massive like balloons. Ready to bust open. I couldn't believe how energised and refreshed I felt. My mum and sister laughed at my porn-star boobs. I expressed and felt the relief.

'Good morning, baby,' I said to Jet and I could have sworn he smiled at me.

The GP was right. I was just adjusting to motherhood, the shock of the labour. I returned to the surgery and told her I had slept for eight whole hours. 'That's better than most people!' she said. 'Especially a new mum!'

It would get better she said, but warned me that there could be good days and bad days, and I thought, 'Yeah, yeah, whatever, stop raining on my parade.'

Then she said I should to stick to the quetiapine for the full week.

WHAT? Couldn't she see that I was back to normal and everybody could stop worrying? What was her problem? It's like she wanted me to fail, to get me hooked onto the quetiapine. I didn't trust her. You couldn't trust doctors.

'I'm better,' I told her but I didn't mention the fact I had now decided that I had schizophrenia. That was my secret.

Paranoia took over. I told Hugo I didn't like the GP. Mum and Daisy came back to watch Jet again while I slept. I forced down a bowl of pasta, fed Jet, and climbed into bed . . . but this time, the sleeping tablets didn't work.

I woke Hugo up. 'Hugo, I can't sleep, please wake up, please don't go to sleep, don't leave me.'

He grumbled, held me and kissed my head, then he rolled over and went back to sleep. Of course, he was just as battered as me.

Panicked, I ran in to my mum and Daisy who were sleeping on the sofas in the living room and I cried to them that I couldn't sleep in a whisper so as not to wake Jet. Daisy looked worried. I didn't like to see her worried so I curled up next to her on the sofa and pretended to be asleep. But my mind was whirling.

My baby slept softly in between them. When he was sleeping I could almost pretend he didn't exist.

I didn't sleep the next night or the one after that. I started to build a web in my head, that this was the REAL me. I was a secret schizophrenic, trawling for evidence of my illness. *Oh God. Oh God. Oh God.* These beliefs became more sinister: I've been lying about who I am, living as somebody else for my whole life. I started to persecute myself for stuff I had done when was I was seven, nine, fourteen, beating myself up for not taking care of my pets or of plants when I was younger. The signs were there. All the things I should have done for people, all the times I'd let people down. *I'm selfish. I'm unreliable, untrustworthy, disloyal.* Any generosity or kindness I'd ever shown had a cruel intention behind it. *I'm a fake. I'm a liar.* I was a joke. A freeloader. An imposter. Pretending to write for children when I clearly hated children. On and on and on, I tortured myself.

I began to care more about my own freewheeling downfall and less and less about Jet. I was a time bomb waiting to go off. I was racing against my own insanity. OH GOD.

25

Hugo sent a video of Jet sneezing to our friends and family and everybody was obsessed with how *cute* it was. To me, it was scary. The idea of him getting a cold frightened the life out of me. I ordered a giant bottle of antibacterial hand gel as precaution.

My mum and sister had to go to work. I didn't want them to leave me but I rocked Jet. I was doing all the 'Mum' things. Nobody could see what was going on in my head.

At some point, I thought about giving Jet formula to alleviate some of the pressure but my mum disagreed, she said, 'Stick with it, Laura. Honestly, it will strengthen the bond between you and Jet, and once this passes you will love breastfeeding. Besides if you give up feeding now there will be more hormones and you'll feel very emotional.'

She stroked my hair encouragingly, 'Plus, you're very good at it.'

I didn't feel very good at it, but Mum was right. It was the one thing that let me know I was being a good mum; the one thing I could do that nobody else could.

*

One day Hugo's family came over, and I locked myself in the bedroom with Jet and just lay down in the dark. I wished I had a trap door out of my own life.

Friends told me to just 'relax and watch Netflix'. To 'enjoy this time'. To 'take a sleeping pill while your mum has him'. To 'let Hugo do the feeding'. To 'swap to formula.' To 'be kind to myself'.

Kind to myself? How?

I hated myself. Not in an angsty teenage diary way . . . no . . . I really, really actually hated myself.

We went back to the GP surgery, this time with Jet.

It was a different doctor who was friendly and warm but again, I decided I didn't really trust him. Jet cried and I pretended I knew how to soothe him in front of the doctor. I didn't want them to take him away and give him up for adoption. The doctor watched me.

They are all in cahoots these lot. I know their game.

He suggested that I take a stronger dose of the quetiapine to help me sleep. *Of course he does, he wants me hooked.*

My head had already decided that the stronger dose wouldn't work.

My family were now staying every night. My living room was like Glastonbury, full of blankets and clothes and bags of food. Everybody camped out. Each night the pressure rose and tension mounted. Everything revolved around my sleeping. Each morning, everybody was on tenterhooks for a report, like I was some storybook princess that the whole village was willing to slumber. Everybody was giving me tips and remedies. Stretching, yoga, lavender, camomile, cherry juice, eating, reading, bath, meditating. They kept sending me off to bed but I just lay there thinking of all the things I should be doing. All the things I couldn't do.

I never thought for a second that I was robbing Hugo of his time with Jet too by handing the baby around the family.

When he told me he was feeling claustrophobic and trapped, that he could look after me and Jet by himself, a new fear began its steady drip feed. It was Hugo who was the real threat. *He* was incompetent and unable to care for our baby . . . *Hugo was the ill one.*

I kept expressing but my milk was dwindling. I would sit with the pump and frantically squeeze away. The picture on the front of the box showed a professional woman in a power suit, silky blonde hair and a full face of make-up, on the phone in deep discussion, cutting some fat business negotiations while her copious breast milk flows as she effortlessly pumps.

For me, it was like getting blood out of a stone.

Drrrrriiippp.

My milk was poor. Dribbly. It could feed *nobody*. But it wasn't because I was not eating or resting . . . I knew really, deep down, it was because I'd been feeding Jet less and less. It was simply a case of supply and demand. I was too in my own head to do long feeding stints. I couldn't sit still, I needed to be pacing around. Looking out for danger.

The less I fed Jet, the less milk I produced, and Jet just cried, face scrunched up, hungry and neglected. He didn't understand. It wasn't *his* fault I didn't know how to love him.

Hugo talked to Jet like he was a person. I found it awkward. I couldn't think of anything to say.

Hugo told me he noticed him developing every day. I just saw a baby. And it could have been anyone's.

But, at the same time, Jet was also like my heart that had been ripped from my chest. I wanted to put him back where he belonged.

My mum gently told Hugo to buy some formula, JUST IN CASE. It felt like I was being disarmed of the one thing I could do.

After doubling up on the quetiapine I got out of the bed in the morning from yet *another* night of not sleeping. In the living room Mum told me she had fed Jet with the formula in the night. She had no choice. I saw the empty bottles and my sleeping baby. Content. He had got what he needed. I felt myself collapse inside.

I wasn't even capable of feeding my own baby. To think I had just been lying there awake the whole night while my baby was starving. I felt utterly useless, like I wasn't his mum.

Oh God.

I couldn't even blame my not sleeping on having to feed all night. This really was just *my* problem now.

My mum and Daisy were exhausted; as well as waking up all night to feed and rock Jet they still had to go to work. This couldn't go on for much longer.

Mum told me to go for a run.

'Go for a run?' I snapped. 'Are you mad? I haven't slept for two weeks! I can't just GO for a run!'

'Burn off some of that . . . *adrenalin*.'

'What adrenalin?' I asked, sparking with electricity like I could ignite. 'I've just had an operation! I'm meant to be taking it easy for six weeks!'

Yet there I was, pacing around the flat. I stalked by the window and watched the frosty road outside. I flinched at the grumble of every passing car. I thought it was an ambulance coming to take me away. And that's when I suggested to Hugo that we get a Maternity Nurse.

26

Hugo really didn't want a maternity nurse. This private, precious time would no longer be ours, but I was so disconnected by this point. Every time I looked around Jet was having more of that formula stuff. This was not how I wanted it to be.

A very practical and rational part of my brain took over here and I became strident and pragmatic and pushed ahead. Even now, looking back, I know I was unwell but I still prioritised Jet and Hugo with every action I took. Even if those actions seemed bizarre or bold, it was *always* for them. I had visions of a Mary Poppins flying in to save the day. Pulling an umbrella and a lamp out of her little floral carpet clutch bag. She would get me breastfeeding again.

I had never employed anybody in my life – I didn't know what or who I was looking for! I just went with the first CV I read. (I say 'read' but all the words looked like hieroglyphics to me.) I didn't know how much she cost or how it would even work. But I did see she had experience with working with postnatal depression.

I don't want anybody coming in who's going to hog, or 'mother', or fall in love with my son. Who's going to judge or to patronise me.

Was this a terrible idea? But instead of worrying about my tiny family I was simply paranoid about what other people would think. *A Caesarean and now a maternity nurse? ARE YOU FOR REAL?* They'd say I couldn't face the nappies and the sleepless nights. Would people think a maternity nurse was the same as a wet nurse? Would people think that somebody was coming to breastfeed my baby?

I panicked. A maternity nurse seemed so outrageously lavish, snobby, spoilt, posh, ridiculous: a luxury. I was shrouded by shame. Shame of my failed labour, shame of my Caesarean, shame of this postnatal depression talk, shame of my schizophrenia, shame of not being able to feed or take care of my baby, shame of not loving him, shame of my maternity nurse. Shame of actual shame.

I was meant to be his mum, but I knew I was in trouble. I couldn't do it.

The Maternity Nurse sounded upbeat and friendly, and told me straight away that she was 'happily' married – I guessed this was important for some women to know in case they are concerned that their husband might run off with them? I saw it on a documentary once, but at this point I did not even have the capacity to think about affairs.

She managed to tell me that she had two children of her own but after that I didn't really give her a chance to speak. I talked at her at a frantic pace about routines and feeding, and basically WHEN CAN SHE START?

(Now that time has passed Hugo tells me that this was a horrible disturbing phone call to watch because I was so frantic and neurotic.)

I said I'd call her back to confirm.

In the meantime Hugo and I battled it out: he just wanted our home to feel like a home again, and didn't mind taking over. He pointed out that we hadn't even met this woman and now she was moving in to take care of Jet. Could we not at least meet more maternity nurses? I ignored him.

Secretly, my rationale was this: I didn't want Hugo to be on his own with the baby when the ambulance came to take me to the asylum. I couldn't cope, and that's why somebody was coming to take care of our baby. And that, at the time, was probably the best decision I made as a mum.

I called the Maternity Nurse back and said, YES, YES, YES.

But because I was so not with it, I didn't think the logistics through properly. We didn't have anywhere for her to sleep. Before we knew it, we had bought a single fold-out bed on the internet, sheets and towels. Then we got a detailed shopping list for food for her stay – food we don't eat. The list was so specific, I became obsessed with getting everything like an assistant shopping for a popstar diva's dressing room.

27

The midwife came to remove the dressing on my Caesarean scar.

I found the courage to look down and saw the neat fresh red line along my pubic bone. Hugo said it looked cool and I managed to laugh.

It wasn't infected and was healing well. The midwife named it my 'Jet Scar'.

I told her that the baby was sleeping but I wasn't. 'That can't be right? That's the wrong way round? Isn't it?' I asked, and what about the hot pressing on my chest and the confusion? She bit her lip, 'Anxiety?'

I hadn't had anxiety before. I didn't know what it felt like. Maybe that was what it was! Ah, so I had anxiety, I was worrying about stuff. Not schizophrenia?

'Or . . . could I have postnatal depression?' I asked.

'It's a bit too soon to diagnose you.' She held my hand, empathetically, trying to understand, then asked, 'Have you had any . . . *dark* thoughts?'

'What do you mean?' I asked her.

'*Extravagant* thoughts?'

'Like what?'

'Like, I don't know . . . thinking that you're God? Like you . . . think you could fly or anything like that?' she replied.

'What? Fly? NO! And God? No!' I thought I was the opposite of God (which I suppose also counts as an extravagant thought).

I'm not mad! What is she on about?

There was an elephant in the room and then she just came out with it, 'Do you blame me?'

'Blame you how?' I asked.

'For not spotting that Jet was small?' she said.

And I started to cry. I really did like her. I called Hugo in from the kitchen. We had an awkward and sad and upsetting conversation. I felt like my organs had been scooped out.

'Did you feel like this when you had your baby?' I asked her.

'I was so young I just . . . kind of . . . got on with it,' she replied.

Why couldn't I *get on with it?*

She weighed Jet. His weight had gone down.

'They lose weight, remember,' she reassured me.

But I knew that he was hungry, and I wasn't feeding him. I was so preoccupied with what was wrong with me, I hadn't the capacity to care that Jet needed me. I needed somebody to tell me what was going on.

The buzzer rang and Hugo came back from the door with a ginormous, and when I say ginormous, I mean gigantic, man-sized teddy bear for Jet from one of Mum's work friends. It was so sweet and thoughtful and funny, but I gulped with horror. I didn't know what I needed in my life at that point, but I knew it was NOT a 6ft teddy bear in my house. Hugo read my thoughts and said it was terrifying.

'No, no,' I said. 'It's brilliant!' If I showed I was afraid of it, that would make me seem 'mad'. The old me would have loved a massive hideous bear in the house.

It's just a bear! It's just a stuffed bear.

I phoned my mum. 'Mum, I need to get another opinion. I'm truly not well.'

A private midwife arrived in 'emergency hours', dressed in a two-piece business suit. She had glasses and thick dark hair. Round cheeks and twinkly eyes. She asked for a decaffeinated tea. She smiled at me. Assessing me.

She asked me to fill out a questionnaire, answering the questions as honestly as I could. It was the Edinburgh Postnatal Depression Scale (by the end of this experience, I would know it pretty well). The answers were a multiple choice of 'hardly at all' 'mostly' 'most of the time' 'all of the time' etc . . .

1. I have been able to laugh and see the funny side of things . . .
2. I have looked forward with enjoyment to things . . .
3. I have blamed myself unnecessarily when things went wrong . . .
4. I have been worried or anxious for no good reason . . .
5. I have felt scared or panicky for no very good reason . . .
6. Things have been getting on top of me . . .
7. I have been so unhappy that I have had difficulty sleeping . . .
8. I have felt sad or miserable . . .

9. I have been so unhappy that I have been crying . . .

10. The thought of harming myself has occurred to me . . .

It was probably the only test in my life where I scored almost 100 per cent.

'You have postnatal depression,' she told me, confident and certain. 'I could tell as soon as I saw you.'

I burst into tears. I fell into my mum's arms and sobbed. It felt so amazing to have a name for what was happening to me. The private midwife hugged me and said it was treatable with medication. She was confident because she'd had postnatal depression herself: she had taken antidepressants and then was a completely different person.

I couldn't stop crying, and kept telling Hugo how sorry I was. The private midwife said she would take care of me, she would nurse me back to health. She was like a superhero.

'We will get you better in no time, don't you worry,' she told me as she left.

Mum and Daisy ran me a bath and I got in with Jet. I could see a hole of sunlight in this sky of iron that had been above me. I kissed Jet, saw how beautiful he was. Properly. I even managed to eat a meal. Now I knew what I had, I could deal with it. I could get better. But I never saw this midwife again.

Almost as quickly as I felt relieved and diagnosed, I decided that she was a fraud and I didn't trust her. She was too kind to be genuine. The questionnaire was a flimsy homemade sheet that she'd invented in her spare room. She just wanted me hooked on medication like the rest of them. I felt I could trust nobody at all.

My thoughts had arrested me. This midwife was actually the first person to officially diagnose me and understood my illness better than anybody else. She really was kind and warm and genuine – like all the other health professionals and my family, but in my ignorance, my miseducation about depression, I decided I didn't 'look' like a depressed person. I wasn't acting how I thought a depressed person should act. I felt overactive and busy and erratic, so in my naivety I dismissed my diagnosis. They were wrong. I didn't have postnatal depression.

I wouldn't take the antidepressants. I would push through. I could do it alone, with the help of the love around me, with the help of my little baby.

But by the next day the giant 6ft teddy bear was watching me. He had surveillance cameras in his eyes and was reporting me. To whom, I didn't know, but he was monitoring my every move.

I tried to shake off this thought, but I couldn't. I'd turn away from his big plastic shiny eyes but his stare seemed to follow me, his horrible smile. I could feel his eyes drilling in the back of my head, waiting for him to say something.

I moved the bear away into the other room but he just spied on me from there, scaring me. It was almost as though I could hear him sneering. *Ha ha ha. You think that by moving me into a new room I'll leave you alone?* I tried to tell myself it was all in my head, repeating to myself over and over, 'It's just a toy. It's just a toy. It's just material and fluff. It's not real.'

That night I had to do everything in my power to stop myself from tearing that smug bear to shreds, gutting him open with a knife to find that damn hidden camera and smash it to pieces.

28

Jet's nursery was no longer my little boy's bedroom but a makeshift emergency campout for the Maternity Nurse.

I started panicking and told Hugo that I didn't want her to come any more. I'd changed my mind. Hugo, understandably, put his foot down. We were sticking to a decision, even if it was just for a week.

She arrived. We were like opposites: she was a warm sweet sponge cake drenched in custard and I was a blade of glass. I told her my birthing story; about the postnatal depression 'theory'; about not sleeping. She told me that she had suffered from postnatal depression herself after her emergency Caesarean. I showed her my weird frantic notes about Jet's routine and she laughed affectionately and put it to one side.

The Maternity Nurse kept trying to get me to breastfeed. It was like she was trying to corner me, pin me down so I kept feeding Jet, and I kept finding excuses to get up. She liked daytime television, chat shows, reality TV and the news. She made so many jokes about the people on TV, filling me in on their life stories and celebrity scandal and I sat as numb as a zombie. My head was banging. She was trying to relax me but it was doing my head in. I couldn't be my normal self with her.

She made me lots of tea and gave me bits to eat. If I was well, I would have ADORED her, but I was just there, stewing in obscure thoughts of paranoia and delusion. Odd observations started running though my head and festered there. *She thinks I'm weird. She thinks I think I'm better than her. She thinks I'm a bad mum.*

The Maternity Nurse and Hugo got on well, cooing at Jet and laughing at the TV and I began to hate them both. I resented them for feeling OK. When she said how 'amazing' Hugo was with Jet, I knew what she really meant was that I *wasn't.*

At bedtime she would come to my bedroom to take Jet to put him to sleep. I didn't want to let him go, holding on, my arms wrapped tightly around him.

I didn't want to take my sleeping pill either.

She's going to steal Jet.

I know she is.

Laura, don't trust her.

Don't sleep, Laura, you won't be able to hear the latch on the front door when she steals the baby.

But no, of course, she didn't steal the baby. She fed him formula in the night and then came whistling in, first thing in the morning, for me to feed Jet. I felt almost repulsed at myself for being 'handed' my baby by a nurse.

Who did I think I was? Some queen?

She'd tell me all the 'cute' things he did in the night and I'd just stare at her blankly. Already I felt like Jet might think that the Maternity Nurse was his mum.

When she asked me if I'd slept I'd have to tell her 'no'. But I'd be thinking to myself, 'Oh, you just want me to sleep so you can be with Jet all by yourself.' It was so sad, because deep down I knew that she was patient and kind and gentle and funny. She was always only trying to encourage me, not to sabotage me.

The days were really hard.

The Maternity Nurse could soothe him, nap him, feed him, play with him, change him, oil him, bath him, all the while cracking up at the TV, telling stories, eating and playing Candy Crush. And I just ran around behind her, tripping up over myself, picking stuff up and putting it down again, thinking I was helping but not doing ANYTHING at all. Just getting in the way. I reminded myself of a really bad basketball player that had been told to mark a professional, stumbling by her feet, trying to keep up. She tried to explain the times of her new implemented (practical and logical) routine but I couldn't get my head around it. It sounded like the hardest algebra in the world.

Then every night she waved goodnight to us again and slept with my little baby next to her in his Sleepyhead. He would look to *her* in the darkness when he needed milk or comfort. And once again, the cot in our room was empty.

The Maternity Nurse told me I had to eat. But I didn't want to. I had decided that was scheming to fatten me up. *She wants to make me fat and ugly. She thinks I'm boring and plain. Stupid and uninteresting. She thinks Hugo's too good for me. She thinks I don't deserve to be a mum. She's punishing me. This is all part of a larger plan to break me.*

Hugo and the Maternity Nurse had started sharing food and eating together. I hated them both. They ate and I starved. I watched Hugo eating one of her microwave sausages and I couldn't believe it. A MICROWAVE sausage?

I'd invited the enemy into my house.

She started avoiding me, telling only Hugo what to do with Jet, telling only Hugo about the feeds. I was like Piggy in the Middle screaming I'M HERE YOU KNOW, but she talked over me. She stopped bothering to make eye contact with me. She'd sit laughing at the TV with Jet asleep on her chest. He was so cosy, smooshed into her lovely *proper* boobs and I'd just hover about, not knowing what to do with myself. I'd flit between despising her and idolising her.

She started asking us why we didn't have certain stuff – a rattle, a teething toy, a play mat, a beaker, Napisan, a bucket for his dirty clothes, *these* kinds of bottles, *those* kind of teats, Bonjela for his gums, gripe water, Infacol, vitamin D drops . . . and why wasn't I taking stuff for my milk supply. *Why wasn't I expressing? Why wasn't I feeding more?*

It was all a trick.

I didn't know how the steriliser worked. I didn't know how to make up the bottles. Why was she *boiling* extra water? I couldn't take the information in about how to make the formula. I didn't understand the 'scoops' or how much water to put in. I didn't understand what a 'top up' meant. And Hugo was her A-grade student, smashing it.

At one point, I'm not joking, I had to ask her how to take off the plastic lid of a bottle. It was like I had amnesia.

She would ask me what I would like Jet to wear each day and I was so confused. All the clothes looked the same to me. Tiny and white. So she'd ask Hugo and he'd dress him up all cute in all these wonderful clothes that I didn't even know we owned – leopard-print leggings, rocket shirts – and I'd feel annoyed, like – *I could have done that.*

Sometimes, Hugo would try to include me but I just thought he was patronising me or setting me up for a fall or it was a test, and so I'd refuse to play.

Then, next thing I knew, Jet had a dummy. In his mouth. Sucking away like it was no biggie. I looked at the Maternity Nurse as if to say, '*Oh you snide bi—.*' How DARE she? I didn't want him to have a dummy. And he loved it. Suck. Suck. Suck. Great. I turned my back for one second and he was a dummy addict.

I felt like I'd died and was seeing into a portal of what Jet and Hugo's life would be like without me.

I'd cut myself out of my life.

29

I was still ignoring all my friends. Once one of them caught me off
guard and I answered the phone. 'I'm really sick,' I blustered and
hung up.

Hugo was doing ALL the research he could to work out how to
fix me. He stocked me up on vitamin D. One evening, he got a
reflexologist to come to give me a session. Hugo had warned her
that I was potentially suffering from postnatal depression. I felt *so
much* from her. That she was wise. Kind. Strong. That she'd lived
a life. It was the first time I felt *touched* with a gentle hand in a
really long time.

The second she saw me she looked worried. She rubbed my feet
and it was the closest I felt to a release from my coma of self-hatred
and illness, but when she finished the massage I sprang up like somebody was burgling the house.

'I thought you'd be asleep by now,' she said, but I was like a Tas-
manian devil on turbo power.

'Sorry, no,' I replied. I felt like I'd let her down.

Then she looked me right in the eyes and said, 'If you don't mind me saying so . . . you need help. I've had what you're experiencing. Please believe me, it can spiral, it can get out of hand, it can tear your whole life apart if you're not careful. I lost everything to it and I'm still rebuilding my life now.'

I nodded. 'I know it's bad. I will. I know I have to.'

30

The arrival of the Health Visitor stirred up in me much of the same emotions as that of a visit from the tax man. A churn. But, on this occasion, my fate wasn't measured in VAT and expenses. It was a test of love and I was worried that I'd fail.

How much do you love your baby, Laura?

How *do* you *show* somebody that you love your baby? I was so scared of this baby bailiff. In a cold sweat I kept thinking, *They are going to take my baby away. Oh God. Oh God. Oh God.*

'Cooey, it's me, the Health Visitor.'

And I was the opposite of *health*.

Jet's weight was improving the Health Visitor said and she was very happy about that. The tongue-tie didn't seem to be getting in his way. I said that I wasn't doing so great. I was honest but played it down too because I worried that she would put Jet into care if I told the complete truth. It was a fine balancing act. But when she read my birthing notes she sounded genuinely upset. 'I'm so sorry,' she said. 'This should never have happened.'

'It's not your fault,' I said. 'And I love the NHS so . . .'

'Yes, but we are here to provide a service,' she said.

She started to write in Jet's little red record book.

Was she making a mock adoption advertisement for my little son?

She asked me if I was breastfeeding. I said yes but with formula top up.

~~NOT REALLY. TRUTH BE TOLD, I'M SCARED OF MY OWN BABY.~~

She wrote it down in that little book. She asked me if I felt like myself. I said no, not really.

~~WHERE HAVE I GONE?~~

She wrote it down in that little book.

Hold it together. Smile.

She asked me if I was coping. I said, no but I had the Maternity Nurse and Hugo to support me.

~~AND I WISH ONE OF THEM WOULD DO ME A FAVOUR AND MURDER ME.~~

She wrote it down in the book.

Was I eating properly? No, not really.

~~I HATE FOOD. IN FACT, I'M ON A SECRET HUNGER STRIKE STARVATION MISSION. IT'S SERIOUSLY MESSED UP.~~

Again, she was writing away in the book.

Then she asked if I felt like I could put my make-up on in the mornings? I snapped back, 'Do *any* new mums feel like putting their make-up on in the mornings?'

She stopped writing.

'Could I have . . . postnatal depression?' I asked.

She looked at me from over her glasses and replied, 'It's still very early days. We wouldn't like to diagnose you with postnatal depression *just* yet. It would be normal to feel a little unsettled after your experience. See how you go.'

I nodded.

Have I passed the test? Do I get to keep my baby?

'Lovely,' she said. 'Now, you must talk to your baby all the time. Even if you can't think of anything to say, then simply say, "I can't think of anything to say." It doesn't have to make any sense; he just wants to hear his mum's voice. Some people say don't shower your baby with love, but in my opinion you can't show your baby too much!'

He just wants to hear his mum's voice. I looked at Jet whimpering on his back in the mat, like a helpless beetle. Blue eyes staring at me like I was his idol or something.

The Health Visitor squeezed my shoulder as she left, getting her silver-ball identity tag in a tangle with her wet mac and spattering umbrella. 'I think you've done really well,' she said.

We'd passed, I thought. For now. I'd dodged the bullet, but had I? I really didn't want my baby to be taken away from me but I also didn't want to be a mum.

The Mum I Want for You

Your mum has a skin-care routine. She drinks a glass of fresh orange juice every morning and takes her vitamins. She keeps a pack of tissues in case you need them when your hands get sticky from a doughnut on the bus after school. She wears long dresses and big floppy beach hats. She wears clear mascara. She gets you a puppy for your fifth birthday. She understands politics. She can have *just* one glass of wine. When she sleeps her hair is all spread over the pillow. She enjoys sitting alone outside a cafe with a coffee and a newspaper. She buys crafts from independent shops. She can have a sandwich in her bag and not scoff it down immediately. She reads instruction manuals for appliances. She knows where everything is in the house. She has a stack of novels by her bed that she actually reads. She has photos of you all over the fridge. She lets you skip a cheeky day off school to go bowling and eat cheeseburgers and buy new trainers. She makes sure there are always fresh apples in the bowl on the table. She actually *likes* the taste of grapefruit. She's photogenic. Your school uniforms will never be too big or too small.

Sometimes she has to stop walking and physically hold on to your arm because she's laughing *that* hard.

She will say to you, 'I love you.' Because she does.

She loves you. She's your mum.

31

My dad and his partner came to look after Jet so Hugo and I could go out for lunch. I was going along with it because I felt like I should, because it was 'normal' to want a bit of time away from your kid. Dad texted me on his way to see if we needed anything.

I wanted to say, 'Yes. A time machine. To take my baby back to the shop. A one-way ticket to Mars. Pain-free poison that would kill me successfully. A gun. Something to put me in a coma for a few years. *Help*. I need help.'

Instead I asked him to get paracetamol, milk and sunflower oil.

I dressed up like myself. Blue velvet, sparkly boots and bright pink lipstick. I felt like an alien that had gobbled up 'Laura' and was pretending to be her.

My dad couldn't be prouder of us, our little family. He was beaming and I wanted to run into his arms and say, 'Dad, I know I look OK but I'm not. I'm really struggling, I'm really not happy. Please make it all go away.'

But I didn't.

As we were leaving, my dad's wife said, 'You've taken to mother-hood like a duck to water,' and I swallowed down the sick that was building in my throat and sort-of-ish kissed my son goodbye on his little head. And we left.

Walking down the road with wobbly Bambi knees towards the restaurant at the end of the street, I felt nauseous and nervous. In the restaurant the menu overwhelmed me. I didn't care about any of the stupid fiddly fussy tapas. *What would Laura order?*

Why I didn't tell Hugo how I was feeling I'll never know. I guess it was a part of the illness. The shame. The fear. It corners you, it bribes you, like a kidnapper: 'if you tell anybody, I'll kill you.'

I tried to eat but the panic and anxiety made it hard for me to swallow. Hugo ordered champagne, and the celebratory bubbles tasted bitter and disgusting and made me feel more on edge. I was clinging onto my chair with my nails. *Everybody knows that I'm the town weirdo. Everybody knows I'm the woman who doesn't love her baby.* If I had walked past a cat it would have hissed at me. Hugo knew I wasn't normal. And I knew he knew it too. It was a horrid silent game.

Can we quit now? Can we acknowledge that I'm definitely not OK? Put me out of my misery. I feel like a killer on the loose. I need to turn myself in. Please, Hugo, read the signs, you know me . . . please . . .

We took a photo and I posted it on Instagram, already dreading the 'likes'.

'Congratulations!'

No. I'm drowning. Someone. Help me.

My new novel, *Big Bones*, was being published that week. It was about body positivity, self-esteem and the love of life and meanwhile its author was an absolute mess who hated herself. I had a radio interview scheduled and I couldn't do it. I couldn't pretend to 'love myself' when I'd unlocked the 'forbidden' door of my brain's castle and ended up imprisoned in a torture tower.

I didn't know the girl who had written that book. And if I ever got glimmers of her, I seethed with jealousy, I was livid at her joy. I pitied her naivety, snubbed her ignorance. She was gone.

Big Bones was being published to coincide with International Women's Day – but I felt like the worst example of a woman on the planet! I was set to be an ambassador for a big charity group supporting young people and mental health and here I was wishing I'd been flattened by a steam roller. It was all so ironic.

It was also my sister's birthday which just made me feel even worse.

I had another piece of publicity to do, a phone interview for a magazine article, but my publisher managed to swerve it so they emailed me the questions. My brain just wouldn't work. Typing in the answers on the laptop was like trying to eat a bowl of soup with a sewing needle.

My editor called me up with the plan of asking me the questions and me answering them on the phone. She had kindly offered to type them up. But I couldn't speak. I slurred, 'I'm sorry, I can't do this.'

Cancel everything.

We went back to the doctor's again, pleading with them to help me.

'We've all spoken here,' the GP said. 'Initially, we thought you were suffering from severe adjustment disorder, but we believe you do have postnatal depression.'

'Do I *have* to take the medication?' I asked.

'No, you don't *have* to do anything,' she said, 'but it can escalate very quickly if it's not treated correctly. It can go two ways. There's postnatal depression, which we think you have. And we can give you a short course of antidepressants and that should treat it until your hormones settle. These antidepressants are completely safe to take while breastfeeding.'

'And what's the other way?' I asked.

'In the unlikely case, but it's very rare, it can escalate into something called postpartum psychosis,' she told me.

Psychosis.

That was to do with serial killers, wasn't it? Crazy exes. Stalkers. Cannibals. Monsters. Why did I suddenly have all these illnesses that I could barely spell? All I did was have a baby. I felt sick. My hairs went on end.

'You haven't . . . *seen* anything that's not real? That nobody else can see, have you?' she asked.

'What? Hallucinated? No! Of course not,' I said.

I'm not MAD, you know!

'Have you . . . sort of . . . I don't know . . . *heard* a voice, maybe somebody calling out your name and turned around only to find nobody there?' the doctor acted out the action of turning around.

Oh God. She was actually asking me if I was HEARING voices.

'NO!' I almost scolded her. 'I've not heard any voices!'

'Well, that's very good news, but you must tell us if you experience anything . . . *scary,*' she replied.

I didn't mention that I thought a giant teddy bear was filming me, but instead I asked her how long I might feel like this. The doctor explained that it could take up to six weeks for the antidepressants to start working.

SIX WEEKS? I hadn't GOT six weeks. By then I would be

seeing things and hearing things. I knew I would. I might even be dead.

'And we think it's anxiety-led so . . .' she continued.

There was that anxiety word again. She opened her hands out to me as if to say, 'It's up to you really, how long do you want to drag this thing out for?'

'Now what do you want to do? Do you want to have a think about the antidepressants or see if you can battle through?' she asked.

'*Can* I *battle* through?' I said.

'Some women can, but in your case . . .' she trailed off.

'It's all my fault. I feel so guilty,' I cried but no tears would come. Not real ones. I was so numb. *Why couldn't I feel?* I couldn't normally get past the first five minutes of the episode of *The Simpsons* where Homer eats the poisonous Blowfish without sobbing. Now, I was a sociopath.

She prescribed me the antidepressants. As I left her room, she said, 'Don't worry about the guilt. The guilt never goes. I've got a daughter at home and I'm guilty all the time. Guilty for working, guilty for not working. It's a part of a mum's life. You'll get used to that.'

We walked away from the surgery.

My beloved South London suddenly looked so ugly.

What was the point? Why should I even try to get better?

I could just leave.

I could just go.

I could just make it all stop.

I didn't want to go back home to my mum and Jet with the Maternity Nurse there to do everything, and I'd be on the couch, useless, turning to stone.

I texted my best friend, 'I have postnatal depression.'

She said something along the lines of, 'Yeah, I thought so. Don't worry. It will be OK because it HAS to be. I promise. I'll help you through it. I love you. X'

We had to go into the chemist again. I hated it in here. The woman behind the counter stood like Dracula's wife, with her blood-sucking smirk.

Back again, I see?

This time for antidepressants. Oh, she was gonna *love* that.

'Where's *baby*?' she asked me, as if I'd left *baby* on a park bench to rot somewhere.

'At home with my mum.' I bit back and handed her my prescription.

'You have postnatal depression?' she asked me, *smiling*.

'Yes,' I tell her.

'It can happen. This your first?'

I couldn't even bring myself to look at the baby dummies and bottles. The nappies with the squishy pleased-with-themselves toddlers on the packaging. *Oh God.* I was going to have to face baby paraphernalia for the rest of my life, reminding me of the baby I couldn't take care of. No matter where I ran away to, there would always be babies everywhere. And no matter how far away I ran, I would always, *always* be tied to Jet.

I was going to have to run away. But the guilt. I couldn't live with that. But I couldn't live like *this*. I was going to have to die.

Suddenly London felt really small. I felt like I was THAT woman, everyone was talking about me. Laughing at me. *Whisper whisper . . .*

She's the one who . . .

That's the one that . . .

Ooo . . . isn't that the mother of . . .

This was how it happened. I saw it now. I knew the directions to madness and I was on my way. I had to get out of that chemist to get some air.

I called my dad.

'I've got postnatal depression, Dad,' I erupted, 'I don't know what's wrong with me.'

'OK, Lolly. It's OK. It's OK. It will be all right. Tell me where you are.'

'I'm just waiting at the chemist. Hugo's just getting my . . . they want me to go on antidepressants.'

'OK, OK, Lolly. I'm at the pub. The one where you had your birthday.'

I found myself running. It was early in the day and there were just a couple of locals and my dad, leather jacket, silk scarf, scooter helmet under his arm. I fell into his arms, but I still couldn't cry.

'I don't want to take the medication,' I said.

He was trying to stay calm but I could see the concern all over his face.

'Well, maybe you can find other ways? Other things to do? You haven't exhausted all other routes yet?'

TRUE! I could do an art class? Yoga? Life drawing? Meditation? Golf? *Find myself* through trampolining?

'Mum's at the house. I need to feed Jet, will you come back and talk to Mum?'

'To your mum?' He hesitated. His face dropped. But he came.

My mum nearly jumped out of her skin (and the window) when she saw Dad. They had not been this close up and personal for about fifteen years.

I felt drugged. My jaw was locked. I was buzzing like an electric fence. I was trying to be normal, but every move felt like a performance. Something as simple as folding my hair behind my ear felt orchestrated and disingenuous. Everything felt really slow but then sped up. I couldn't make eye contact. I didn't want them to see my big black air-balloon eyes.

When Hugo arrived back from the chemist with my prescription, I was ranting, saying I didn't want to take the antidepressants.

'Laura, you have to listen to us. Take them. Take the medicine,' my mum instructed.

'Listen to your mum!' Dad shouted.

They *never* agree. This must be bad. They couldn't both be conspiring against me, could they?

My mum popped the chalky white pill from its silver foil packaging and held it out to me.

'Laura. Take it. Now. You are seriously *not* well. Take it.' Her voice was stern.

'Laura, darling, take it,' my dad added, in deflated desperation.

I grabbed the pill and swallowed it down.

32

In my teens, I used to actually think depression was sort of *cool and interesting.*

I had never experienced it. I felt short changed, jealous of the girls in my school who dyed their hair black and wore kohl around their eyes, and who scribbled angsty poems in biology. They used to engrave 'I want to die' on their desks with a compass. They were *suffering.*

I used to think I just wasn't cut out for depression. I didn't have that level of intelligence. Of emotion. Of sensitivity. I wasn't gifted to understand the depth of what life was really about. I had no excuse to say my life was difficult.

I remember a girl at school once said to me, 'You're fake. Nobody can be THAT happy all the time.'

And I remember feeling gutted about that. What was I supposed to do, apologise for my resilience? For my ability to take life in my stride? To be open and upbeat and positive?

I would sometimes *try* to be 'depressed', but I would have forgotten that I was in misery by break time and be laughing my head off munching down on a chocolate chip cookie. I could never *go there* and say I hated myself. Because, well, I didn't.

I always felt I wasn't legit as a writer because I wasn't a 'tortured' artist with mental health issues. I thought that mental illness went side by side with creativity, sensitivity, wisdom. That geniuses *had* to suffer for their art. I didn't have any actual experience to write about because nothing of note had actually happened to me. My parents had split up. *Great. Whose didn't?*

I wanted to be *that* artist. I wanted to write great novels on my bed sheets only to tear them up. To have a trillion lovers. To not get out of bed and scream and rage and be in a tumultuous relationship. I wanted to be an enigma. To be heartbroken. To be intense. To be extreme. To have lost. To have 'experienced'. To live in a warehouse. I wanted sleepless nights up creating, slurping black coffee and not eating.

To be taken *seriously*. I wanted my work to come from somewhere real.

Happy, secure artists weren't 'genuine'. Happy meant boring.

TOTAL RUBBISH. 'The depressed creative' is one of the biggest flawed stereotypes in our culture. It's glamorised. Sensationalised. You do not have to be kissed by the lips of mental suffering to be creative or create brilliant work.

I would choose to feel any physical pain over the pain of depression or poor mental health. Scrap that – poor mental health *is* physical pain. It cuts deep. It's not a joke.

Depression is not 'because you make art'. You don't need *it* to make art.

It's not a trend. It's not a fashion. It's not aspirational. It's not 'because you're creative'. It's not sadness. It's not 'grumpy'. It's not 'snap-out-of-it'-able. It's not 'your fault'. It's not a choice.

And it definitely is NOT cool.

33

People have in mind a stereotypical insidious 'tabloid' version of what postnatal depression looks like. Horror stories from what they've seen in the movies.

Laura . . . They think you're a baby killer. That you are running around the streets in a flowery blood-stained nightdress with an empty pram. That you will walk into the roaring waves of the sea with stones in your pockets. That you will smother the baby. Shake the baby. Strangle the baby. Bite and scratch the baby. You're the threat. You're the danger. People will lock you up and you'll pace the corridors muttering nursery rhymes to yourself.

If a new mother *does* have negative feelings towards harming the baby in her illness, it is because she is ill. She might find the world a greater threat or danger to her baby. She might think she is protecting her baby. She might be having delusions about herself or her baby or the rest of the world. It is not her fault. Yes, she may be scary but *she is scared*.

When I was unwell, nobody was more scared of me than ME. I would have given anything to not feel this way.

I became so afraid of hearing voices or hallucinating. I was scared of what nasty surprises my own mind had in store for me. It was all I could think about.

Maybe, I thought, it was like when you are so scared you can smell gas in your house that you actually *start* to smell gas. It's a bug in your brain. And it won't go away.

If I tell you not to think of a pink elephant . . .

What are you seeing now?

I was changing Jet's nappy one early afternoon when it happened. I heard a voice. In my head. But also not in my head. It was mine, but not mine. It sounded just like me but it wasn't me. I had no control over it at all. The tone of the Voice was so dark, like it had been waiting for this moment, with a sneer on its face.

You're a really bad mum. You've really messed this one up, haven't you? You are really, really sick. It's coming. Something is coming. Something really, really bad.

I froze.

I am hearing voices. Am I? Does this count as hearing voices?

In the same way that wishing a train would hit me probably counted as a suicidal thought, *what more proof did I need?* I was hearing a voice and it was goading me. It pitied me. It was sarcastic and mean.

I asked Hugo to finish changing Jet. I didn't tell him what I was hearing. I walked to the bathroom, my stomach flipping, the Voice following me down the hallway.

Where are you going? Are you trying to run away? You can't hide. I'll just come with you.

'Go away, go away.'

I looked in the mirror. My eyes were mine but they were *not mine.*
Tee. Hee. Hee. Hiya.

Oh God, oh God, oh God. It's happened, I thought. *I've gone mad.*

I didn't tell anybody about the Voice. I just tried to control it the best I could. I hid it. I didn't want to engage with it, so I just let the thoughts thump about, internally boxing my brains in. My veins, nerves, hormones, chemicals, shooting signals and messages and were getting all tangled in a constant trespass of racing thoughts.

My brain was burning down. I knew I was ill. And I knew *it* had got me. ('It' being the Voice, I guess?) That this would be how I would die.

I tried to listen to the radio to distract myself but the thoughts became rapid. I found it difficult to concentrate on anything. I tried to focus on Jet, but my mind would flit and panic, drown, come up for air, take a breath only to get dragged back down again.

I panic-downloaded a meditation app, and signed up for a full year, praying that it would save me. The words were like pouring petrol on to a fire; the man's voice scared me. I decided he was hypnotising me. Making me sicker.

I would sit on the sofa next to the Maternity Nurse.

Don't try and suck up to her. She knows what a dirty piece of work you are.

I'd get up and walk to the bathroom.

Oh, running away are we?

Every time I saw anybody, spoke to anybody, said hello or goodbye to anybody, so much as looked at anybody:

What are you doing? Stupid girl. Don't tell them about us. If you tell ANYONE I'll fucking kill you. Hold it together. That's it. Play along. Keep it together.

143

As soon as I was alone again or turned my back or shut the door the Voice would snarl:

Ha, so you managed to fool them then? Nice work. But they'll see you soon, the real you. Don't you worry. You won't be able to hide yourself away forever.

YOU'RE NOT REAL. YOU'RE NOT REAL.

Something really bad is about to happen. Something really, really fucking bad and you won't be able to face it. You won't be able to take it.

I'd always wanted an imaginary friend. Trust me, I didn't any more.

I'd always 'talked' to myself, 'Come on, Laura, get on with it', snapping myself out of the gaze of a daydream window. But *this* wasn't that voice. Somebody I didn't recognise had crashed the cocktail party . . . and I guess it was *me*?

. . . but also not me.

OH GOD. Please. NO. What kind of witchcraft IS this?

I wanted to run away from the Voice but where could I go? I couldn't escape from myself. I wanted to punch my head but that only aggravated the Voice – and made me feel more mad. I didn't want to upset the Voice. I was scared it would get angry.

Wait. Who will get angry?

The Voice!

But the Voice is ME! It's MY voice.

OK, so in that case I've been hijacked. By the devil. By an evil twin. Somebody is using my body as a host. I'm possessed. By a spirit. Or a ghost.

Telling myself, 'It's just in my head' didn't help, because yes, that's correct, it *was* in my head.

I could no longer steer my brain to sanity. I could no longer distract myself. I no longer had any control. I was no longer Laura. I had been holding on to any scraps of myself that I could, anything that was me, a sense of self, shreds of thoughts, anything at all, but if I opened my grasp I would find that my hands were empty all along.

I was holding on to nothing at all.

It was a horrible feeling to know that I was quietly going mad and that everybody knew but nobody was saying anything.

It won't be long
And I'll be
In a white hospital nightie.
Crawling.
Bloody knees.
Screaming, 'Where is my baby?'
Oh God.

Also, the whole time this was unfolding, I was bleeding so much. I started taking photographs of my bloodied sanitary towels on my phone and texting them to the midwife. It was a lot of blood.

Oh God. I'm going to bleed to death, I thought.

Yes, and you're not eating, are you? And you're exhausted. And you're feeding. Look at you, you're not sleeping and you lost blood in the Cae-sarean too. Boo hoo hoo. You're a right old mess, aren't you?

My ears were compressed like I was on an aeroplane and I decided that my hearing was going.

I was prescribed some diazepam for my nerves to take alongside the quetiapine and antidepressants, oh, and some mild hay fever tablets too – but *ha. Yeah. OK.*

You're too robust for these drugs, you stupid girl. They won't even touch the sides!

In the chemist, I was in a really bad way. I couldn't stand seeing normal people getting on with life. The world was carrying on the same as usual, but for me, it wasn't. I no longer fitted in.

Can everyone just stop being normal?

My family joked that they were jealous of my prescriptions! Apparently, diazepam was 'amazing' for jet lag. Well, that's what I had. Literal. Actual. JET. LAG.

Hugo was scurrying around trying to do anything to make me well. At some point he passed the phone to me and it was an emergency helpline. I was slumped on the couch with my sister and Mum across from me, holding snoozing Jet, while a young woman asked me questions. I remember answering in drunken slurs, not wanting to go into detail in front of my worried family. I turned the volume right down on my phone. I didn't want them to hear the questions because I didn't want them to know my answers.

'Have you had dark or negative thoughts?'

'Yes.'

'Have you thought about harming yourself?'

'Yes.'

'Are you fearing your baby's safety?'

'Yes.'

It was a bit like one of those quizzes you get in teenage magazines to find out what celebrity you will end up marrying. Or to find out which member of a girl band you're most like. I answered the questions with a *Yes* or *No* and followed the arrow as it slid me to the next question until I got to the result.

And all options seemed to lead to suicide.

I thought about all the tablets mounting up by my bedside table. *I could just take them? I wanted to love you, Jet. I've been looking*

146

forward to you for my whole life. This is the worst thing that's ever happened. I'm so sorry.

Wait. His little hands. His baby feet. His belly – his gentle breathing, up and down. His little nose. On his sleeping face I saw another little baby face staring back, holding on to me. You *do* look like me.

I saw myself as a little girl, running with long hair, singing with Daisy. Strawberry Minnie Mouse ice cream; panning for fool's gold at Legoland; watching *Jaws*, eating tangerines with Mum; driving to Chichester; jumping off the top of the wardrobe with Daisy and Hector. Watching *Gladiators*. Pretending to be in the Victorian days; my bunk bed; my Old Bear that if you squeeze three times you can whisper a wish into his ear; my rainbow leggings; my doll's house; my purple lava lamp; the Beatles; my first desk that Dad built when he was drunk – the stationery wrapped in yellow tissue paper; Hector and I listening to audiobooks before bed. Trying on my next-door neighbour's high heels; dressing up as a boxer for a fancy-dress party; wearing a bin bag to my birthday party. Being made to go to chess club where it smelt like smoky bacon; getting my ears pierced; Dad throwing us in the bath in our pyjamas; Siobhan and I making poison in a plastic cup for a burglar to drink; sitting in the van waiting for Dad; tomato soup with melted cheese at the bottom with Graham; tuna pasta, baked beans; my dream house in Krissy Ward's garden; getting stung by a wasp; my crush on Jaz with the gold tooth that worked at the newsagent's. Mr Gordon teaching me guitar; decorating the Christmas tree; Holland and the man with the ginger biscuits; when I burnt my shoes on the bonfire. My mood ring; Polly Pocket; Happy Meals; sparkly Tinkerbell talcum powder. When I played the Innkeeper's Wife in the school nativity; jumping over the toadstool at Brownies. The American clowns that came to school.

My first red Apple bike. Ribena. Having a braid plaited in my hair; sour-apple sweets; Greek mythology; Zoe my beloved Barbie doll; *Mr Bean*. Notting Hill Carnival; the stick insects at school; learning how to draw a tree; *Charlotte's Web*. My cats; my dad telling me I had a nice silhouette. Coco Pops; driving through London at night. When my mum popped my dad's blisters with a pin. Sunny Delight; Dad's packed lunches – he would write messages on the banana skin; the adventure playground at Battersea Park; the elderflower tree. *The Snowman. The Land Before Time.* Jacqueline Wilson. The butterfly house.

My mum dancing.

It can't all go. It can't.

I woke Hugo up in the night and told him to move the tablets away from me. He was half asleep and chucked the tablets across the room.

I didn't tell him that I had an urge to run to the park and take an overdose in the night: I had to do it out of the flat, away from everybody, so that Hugo and Jet could still live there without the memories of what I did. Hugo wouldn't have to *clean up* the mess. I hated that I had to see it practically like this. I couldn't even plan a train journey without running the route through with Hugo – how on earth was I going to do this effectively without his advice? But you can't ask anybody how to kill yourself because they'll talk you out of it.

Your only way out of loneliness couldn't be more alone.

Don't do it, Laura, hold on.

34

Hugo booked an appointment with his therapist for both of us. She had treated him for grief after his mum died and he swears by psychotherapy.

I had high hopes and was feeling positive. I got dressed in one of my actual dresses rather than the bobbly leggings I'd been living in.

We decided to drive and take Jet with us. The Maternity Nurse asked if I was sure. (She was being nice and sweet and obviously wanted me to focus in the room.)

Oh, I know your game. You just want to steal him.

Jet cried the whole way. I sat with him in the backseat but I had no idea how to pacify him.

The therapist was gentle and humble. I felt like she took one look at me and was terrified: unless she was an exorcist she wasn't going to be able to heal me or my massive planet eyeballs. My temperament. My panic. I believed that she could sense my disturbing 'spirit', my unnerving energy. Her hands were clamped on the arms of her chair like she needed to hold on in case the demon in me started thrashing about just because of *even* being in her treatment room. She was bracing herself. She told me to sit down.

I was suspicious, defensive, frantic, aggressive.

She folded her arms. I thought, *She's trying to show me she wants me to leave with her body language. She doesn't like me. She's worried for Hugo. She thinks I'm a nasty piece of work.*

She considered me and said, 'I think you need to get some sleep.'

And I said, 'I know. But I can't!'

Jet began to cry. I got him out of his car seat and became irritated. I frantically began to rock him and then in a harsh and mean tone I said, 'I feel like I've been raped.'

I think I was trying to say that my body felt assaulted, abused, exploited, physically and now mentally too.

The session was meant to be fifty minutes, but the therapist let us talk for well over an hour – well, Hugo didn't get a chance to talk – he just listened to me, ranting.

Back in the car behind Hugo in the seat next to Jet, I was suddenly embarrassed. I felt like I'd contaminated that sacred space for him and Hugo regretted taking me there.

The Voice was waiting for me.

Ah ha ha ha, idiot. What was that back there, eh? Pulling the sob story, were you? Raped? Please! That's a bit of an exaggeration. You stupid girl, what do you know about rape?

Leave me alone, I snapped back in my head. *I don't have to listen to you. You're not real.*

Ha ha! Don't you get it? This *is real. Everything you knew before this was fake.* You *were fake. And now you've been exposed. You go on and on like you're some feminist Wonder Woman and when it gets tough, you can't take it.*

I caught Hugo looking at me in the rear-view mirror. I smiled but I couldn't hold it together. He smiled back politely, but his eyes flickered. He knew he had a monster in the car and he was thinking, *Who did I have a baby with?*

35

You're in a theatre and the second the lights go down you suddenly have the urge to scream every swearword you know. Or on an aeroplane, to shout out, 'I've got a bomb!' To push somebody onto the tracks at a station; squeeze a stranger's spot; to jump out of a window; throw your phone into the sea; kick someone's dog. The more you know that it's a terrible idea, the more you feel you want to. The more to lose, the more at stake, the worse the urge.

I'd experienced intrusive thoughts before, but had never really thought anything of it. I just thought it was one of those weird brain things that happen – like *déjà vu*.

When I was doing a primary school tour for my children's books, I got so exhausted I'd start believing that I was going to strip naked and call them all 'little sh**s'. It got so overwhelming for me that on the way there I *almost* had to get off trains and tell my publicist to cancel all visits because I didn't trust myself. As if I would ever do that? Was it Tourette's syndrome?

Later, when I was on the psychiatric ward, a therapist explained how intrusive thoughts occur. Imagine you're having a row with your partner and you're chopping carrots for dinner with a sharp kitchen knife. Your partner is annoying you so much that you think to yourself, *I'm so angry and I hate you so much, I'm actually going to stab you.* You know, however, that you wouldn't so you just carry on chopping the carrots and arguing and that fleeting murderous thought passes; you calm down and you eat dinner. But when you are highly anxious and in the throes of terror and you have a thought like that, you might suddenly throw the knife down in fear because you believe that you *will* murder your partner. You don't trust yourself. You fixate on the thought and convince yourself that you are not in control of yourself and are capable of using the knife. That's what makes intrusive thoughts so disturbing.

I became *obsessed* with setting up mini 'dares' for myself, a constant flood of 'imagine if I . . . ', 'what if I . . .' I didn't trust myself. I wanted to handcuff myself to the bed because I was so afraid of what I *might* do.

My mind became like a spider's web and everything was sticking to it. Every thought seemed like an 'idea', which would develop into a 'need'. I started looking for clues around the house about what I should do, reading messages from my friends incorrectly, linking them up, looking for signs. Thinking that the TV was talking to me: every contestant on every game show and every drama villain seemed to be called Laura.

The joke is on you. Your worst nightmare has come true. Play the game, Laura, play the game . . . it's been building to this your whole life, can't you see it? Kill yourself. Kill yourself. Kill yourself.

OH GOD.

I started to believe that the fig tree outside our house was trying to tell me something. Its branches were black and naked (it was winter after all). In my head, I connected the fig tree with a play I had seen when I was pregnant, which also used a tree for symbolism, and in which the protagonist, who is losing her mind, becomes more and more disturbed, isolating herself and, eventually, stabs herself in the stomach. With the logic of a Greek tragedy I now believed that this play was trying to give me a sign. To warn me. And I missed it. I had been given a chance to escape and I was too sloppy in my naive Hollywood pregnancy to see it.

But now I saw it all and it was too late.

Hugo and I were meant to meet when we were kids. We were meant to fall in love. We were meant to have a baby. And then I was meant to kill myself . . .

The end.

36

Lying in bed one morning after another sleepless night I began to feel every vein in my head fastened to my brain. My skull was shrinking. The inside of my brain was itching.

I saw stars.

I touched the empty cot where Jet should be with his soft baby white rabbit, the one thing I bought when I was pregnant.

I gasped. My breathing was low and crackly, like my lungs were filled with old leaves. I was so convinced I was dying.

I heard the sound of the Maternity Nurse's suitcase wheeling down the hallway. Of course – it was Thursday, she was going home for the weekend. She had her own kids to get back to. And Jet was crying.

I would do it in the next couple of days. I just had to get the courage. And then I wouldn't be in pain any more.

What if I got it wrong? What if I *survived*?

I'd thought I'd be a wild old granny, collecting art and wearing chunky magnificent jewellery. I imagined Hugo and me growing old together. Swimming in the freezing cold sea. Having white wine and lobster. Holding hands while we slept. I wanted to see Hugo become an old man. I wanted to see Jet grow up. Oh *God*! I couldn't die like that.

The pressure was mounting for me. I was lying in bed ignoring all the publicity about my book. Ignoring all the phone calls and messages. Not publicising my campaigns or retweeting my adverts. Not only this but it was Hugo's birthday the next day and I hadn't got him anything or organised any celebration.

I was trying to remain calm; to avoid eye contact with the giant bear. Trying to keep my head straight. Trying not to think of the fig tree. Or schizophrenia. Or the play I saw and of stabbing myself. Or insomnia. Or the hints and messages from the TV, or the song lyrics.

I sent a weird text to Hugo's brothers and his best friends organising some last-minute half-attempt at a birthday lunch for the next day. I tried to make him a miserable birthday card out of normal A4 printing paper. I drew a wonky heart with the words TRUE LOVE written on the front and it took me so long because I couldn't seem to keep my hand steady. Hugo was sitting on the other side of the room watching me make it. I threw it at him from across the room.

He said, 'It's not my birthday until tomorrow.'

'Yeah. Sorry,' I replied.

A year earlier, Hugo's birthday had been one of my favourite days ever. I had got him an over-the-top bespoke three-layered sky-blue cake made by my friend with marshmallow fondant clouds, and fruit and gold leaf stacked on top. His family came over for breakfast. Afterwards we went to a spa and drank champagne. The next night we went to see one of our favourite bands and drank beer from plastic cups and the night after that we threw a party.

This year, it was very different. Daisy and her boyfriend, Ramsay, had stayed over on the sofas again. Ramsay was on my 'night watch' and got up when he heard me moving about in the early hours.

'I need to go,' I whispered to him. 'Daisy needs to let me go. I have to do it but I need her permission.'

'Permission for what?'

Ramsay suggested we went out for a walk. It was the crack of dawn; I wore my sunglasses to hide my horrible eyes. We must have looked like we were staggering back from a big night out. The roads were end-of-the-world dead. It must have been freezing cold because I could see my breath smoke in the air.

'I'm going to take all of the tablets,' I said. He didn't react. Which I was grateful for; we turned around and headed home.

On the way back to my flat we bumped into one of my neighbours, walking her dog. I'm really good friends with her daughter. I looked at her and took off my sunglasses, our eyes met. 'I'm really bad. I'm really ill,' I told her.

When we got back into the flat, Ramsay held my shoulders. He wasn't scared of me like everybody else. He *knew* me. He was trying to save my life. He said, firmly, 'Laura, you can do this.'

'I can't,' I said.

'You can. If this was me I would be fighting with everything I had to get through it and make it OK. You don't give up. It's not even an option. You *don't* give up.'

And I nodded. But I knew what I was going to do.

The day got worse. My moods switched within the hour like bi-polar disorder sped up. I was experiencing racing thoughts, anxiety, severe delusions. I felt frantic. Insecure. Wired. Full of energy, like I was some sort of bionic woman. Nothing could slow me down. I started following whoever was holding Jet around the flat, shadowing their moves. If they asked me to 'help' (I was *never* unsupervised when it came to Jet), I crumbled and shied away. I didn't want to hold him. I didn't want to look at him.

I kept cornering members of my family, one at a time, except for Hugo, asking them what I've done wrong, anxiously whispering to them, like it was a secret, *'I'm a bad person, aren't I?'*

They weren't listening to me properly. They were (understandably) just trying to get on with taking care of Jet and calling my doctors to get me help. But I didn't know this. I was just pacing around thinking that nobody understood the severity of what I'd 'done'.

As the day crept on I began, physically, to feel my moods change. I could feel myself morphing – my voice, my posture, my gait all changing in quick succession – with every shift in my mental state.

The neighbour from earlier texted me saying she had experienced postnatal depression herself and that it got pretty dark for her. She said she understood, that it would get better and to take my meds.

This text was a hand in the darkness. It brought me comfort. But not enough to change my mind.

To give him a rest, Hugo went to meet his brothers and friends for lunch. With him gone, I could tell my family the 'truth'.

I said that I was a dark, deceitful person, but we couldn't tell Hugo. I gave my sister my bank details.

'What are you saying all of this for?' she asked.

I said it was for when she was taking care of Jet.

'Why? Why can't you just take care of him? Where will you be?' She began to cry.

'Just please, Daisy, just concentrate, OK? It's very important, just give me permission, just let me do it,' I told her.

'Do what?' she asked me, panicking, 'Do what? Stop it now. Stop talking like that, stop saying that stuff. You'll be here, *you'll* be right here. I don't need to know your bank details, Laura, you'll be here.' She swallowed. 'Won't you?'

37

S uicide. The S-word.

Since this illness, I think I understand so much more about faith. I understand why people have a God. It's a comfort to trust that everything happens for a reason. It's nice to think that some-body/ something is listening. That something has *got* you and that your prayers *can* be answered. That paradise exists (in whatever form) and there will always be a place where you will be forgiven, loved and accepted, regardless. That there is an open door for you – especially in times of hell.

I understand addiction, the want to wash yourself away. And now I understand suicide too. Well, my own version of it.

I was one of those naive, ignorant (perfectly kind and well-intentioned) people who thought that people killed themselves because life was too hard, because they were unhappy, in pain, heart-broken or bereft, in too deep with debt, or in other trouble. I probably thought that it was 'selfish' or 'cowardly'.

Now, I understand a suicidal thought as a heart attack to the brain. If you are at *that* place it *is* an emergency.

I didn't know or understand that you could kill yourself because suicide was a *symptom of your illness*. That when you decided to kill yourself, it wasn't *you*. *You* weren't there. That it's like jumping out of a window in the middle of a night terror.

Nobody who is of healthy mind *wants* to kill themselves. But, in the grips of this illness, you could kill yourself in a state of mania or by accident. You could also be suicidal because you're afraid of *yourself*, because you're trapped. The ill *you* can't see a way out. Because your head is a prison of the worst, beyond imaginable, suffering, you believe that you don't have a choice. And believe me, at the time, no matter how many people tell you that you do have choices, you feel like you don't. And there is no lonelier place. You are saving yourself from what you believe to be a bigger threat: the place you have to be in to do that is horrific. (People jumped off the *Titanic* once they found out the boat was sinking.) It takes guts.

Your illness tells you that you are a burden, that everybody would be better off if you didn't exist. And your illness is so powerful and all-encompassing that you believe this. You believe that you are doing it FOR other people, not for yourself. And yes, it will hurt your loved ones, but your illness makes you believe that you're saving them from worse suffering and stress in the long term. You also feel like you need permission from your loved ones to do it. It's self*less* because you think you are a burden, not worth your spot on the earth and you don't tell anybody because they will try to stop you.

But it's ALL lies. There is no world where anyone or anything would be better off without you. You *have* to tell somebody.

We are human beings, built for survival. For that very reason, the act of killing yourself deliberately is difficult. We want oxygen. We want our hearts beating! We are resilient. And stronger than we think. We are robust. Having been there myself, I know now that it is not *easy* to kill yourself and there is absolutely nothing *selfish* or *cowardly* about wanting to take your own life. It is terrifying.

I became suicidal during what could be considered the 'happiest' time of my life. I had everything I wanted. There was no reason for me to be 'sad'. It was the postnatal depression, the pain, the shame, the guilt, what I had *seen*, the *ill* me, that wanted me to take my own life.

I didn't want to get sicker. I didn't want to do something stupid. I wanted people to remember me well, healthy, happy, fondly. I remember saying, 'I want to go out with a bang. That's how I want to be remembered.'

I would spend hours on end thinking, *How am I going to do this? Why is it so hard? Why do my family have to love me so much? Why can't they just let go? I'm suffering. I'm in pain. Why don't I have a choice? Let me have some control over my destiny.*

Later, in a meeting with my psychiatrist, I remember he put his pen down and said, 'You would have done *it*, wouldn't you? You were *there*, weren't you?'

And I said, 'Yes.'

38

Jet was just under a month old, and I was manic, running around the flat. My boobs were out for most of the day. I was going to the toilet, forgetting to wipe – I was still bleeding so this wasn't pleasant for anybody. I would forget to wash my hands. I would forget to flush. (CRINGE.) Then I would remember I hadn't flushed and run to the bathroom to check the toilet bowl over and over again.

My best friend FaceTimed me and I told her I'd gone mad. The line cut out and I tried her again but it didn't ring. I decided she hated me and didn't want to be my friend any more. (In my crazed state I was calling an expired number which was out of date by about ten years.)

Then I forgot all about that and was manic and frantic some more, running back and forth checking the toilet again and again.

Daisy high-kicked the door in.

'What are you doing?' she yelled.

'Changing my pad,' I said. I showed her the blood.

'Oh. OK. Sorry. It's just I heard rustling.'

'You thought I was taking tablets, didn't you?' I asked accusingly, even though it wasn't unlikely that that's what I would be doing.

When the Maternity Nurse wasn't there, the house was in chaos. Fast-forward panic. The heating was on full blast, the washing was mounting, Jet was crying and Hugo, who had had nothing to eat, was feeling increasingly trapped and suffocated. He asked me to go and give Jet his bath with him.

Then I had an idea. I should suggest to Hugo that we should both die. That he could kill us both and my family could take care of Jet? Then we wouldn't need to live with this terrible decision we made. (I know. I was seriously ill.)

Luckily this idea jumped out of my head as quickly as it swam in. It wouldn't work because Jet would have two dead parents instead of just one.

I started watching Hugo with Jet and got it into my head that he didn't have a clue what he was doing. *He's doing it ALL wrong. He isn't capable of taking care of a baby!*

The delusional thoughts took hold at this point. I thought that Hugo was the fourteen-year-old boy I fell in love with. We were underage kids that had got ourselves into a mess. I kept whispering to my mum and Daisy, 'Hugo can't be trusted with Jet, he doesn't know what he's doing. Please take Jet off of him.'

It reached breaking-point when Jet was sick in Hugo's arms (as babies are!). I saw the sick as projectile alien vomit, like he was dying and snatched Jet from him, ripping him out of his arms like a territorial chimp, and ran down the hallway to hand him to my mum.

Jet was screaming. I was screaming, 'Mum! Mum! Mum!'

They all just stared at me. And I realised I was the problem.

39

My family were on suicide watch.

The irrational part of my brain wanted everybody to leave me alone so I could get the 'job' done but then the rational side of my brain could not stand the idea of being by myself.

I asked Daisy to sleep with me. I felt like I would have more chance of sleeping if she was in the bed with me, and we could pretend that we were little again and none of this mess had happened, but as the night approached I could see she didn't want to. She made a million excuses but the truth was, she was scared of me. I knew her inside out.

I didn't push her – I didn't want to put her in the position where she had to say that she was frightened of me out loud.

Mum climbed in bed with me. I took my medication and tried to close my eyes. She was watching a thing about cavemen on her iPhone and I kept saying to her, 'I'm not asleep yet,' until I fell asleep . . . for about forty-five minutes.

When I woke up, Mum was texting Hugo who was in the living room. I watched over her shoulder.

They're plotting to get rid of me . . . no, they are arranging for me to be sectioned. They are going to lock me up and give Hugo sole custody of Jet. My mum is helping Hugo to organise it so she can still be in Jet's life as his grandma.

For a whole night, for nine hours straight, I had a panic attack. I'd never experienced anything like it. I had it *all* worked out. I'd put some serious thought into it. I seemed to get to a solution and then remember why I had to commit suicide and then go through it all again. It was like having amnesia. It was absolute torture. I was on repeat, trying to get up but Mum was holding me down in the bed. I threw myself around. Thrashing about in the bed, I said, 'Oh God, oh God, oh God, oh God, it's bad, it's bad, it's bad, Mum, please let me go, Mum, please let me go.'

I said, 'Don't make me suffer, Mum, please help me, please make it stop, Mum, please. You can help me. Mum, it's so bad. It's so bad. What have I done?'

And then, in my delusion, I 'heard' her say back, in the darkness, in a whisper like she was angry, 'I can't tell you because you won't be able to take it.'

And I whispered back, 'I've fucked up, haven't I? I've really, really fucked up.'

And again her whispering back through gritted teeth, 'Yes, yes, you really have.'

(I later asked Mum about this 'conversation' and she said it didn't happen. It's strange, I remember it so vividly.)

I said, 'Mum, please. Please take me to hospital.'

And she said, 'Please go to sleep, Laura, or just try and rest. In the morning, if you still feel bad, we can go to A&E.'

Please, please, please, Mum, let me go. Round and round and round. *They are going to take Jet. I've been exposed, I have to kill myself.*

Mum held me tight, falling in and out of sleep, her legs wrapped around me in case I dared sneak out and hurt myself. Imagine physically holding your child in bed so she doesn't kill herself.

I can't imagine doing that with Jet. I can't think of anything worse.

I don't know how my mum dealt with that. Talking to my mum since, about that night, she has said, 'I felt like I couldn't love Jet until you were better. At that moment, *you* were, the baby, not Jet.' She got teary and said, 'you were *my* baby'.

It was the longest night of my life. I watched the sky go from black to white. It was unforgiving and mean.

The next morning, Mum got up to get tea. Daisy came in with Jet, buttered toast and water. I couldn't touch the baby. I didn't want to see him.

She said, 'But Laura, you can just say good morning to him.'

And I said, 'I don't want to. Please don't make me.'

I couldn't keep the act up any longer; I didn't want him. Daisy looked absolutely gutted and, tears in her eyes, she took Jet away. His little gargles left the bedroom.

I was in a catatonic state, a trance. I could barely move or function. I was slow and delirious. Daisy ran me a bath and I sat in the water. My sister washed me and began to cry. I looked up at her and said, 'Why are you crying?' As if I was disgusted by her. Like she was just as bad as me for loving me.

Pathetic.

40

It was Saturday. Jet was booked in to have his BCG that morning at an open clinic. We'd been warned that it can be really difficult for the parents to see their baby have an injection.

My mum asked if Hugo and I would be OK and I accused her of Munchausen's syndrome by proxy and that she was making me ill just so she could take care of me. It was all her fault, her postnatal depression and her adoption had caused all this and she'd known that this would happen to me. She'd had a daughter *deliberately* to pass this cruel illness on to me.

I also accused of her of being overly weird with her sausage dog. (No, I don't know what all that was about.) Daisy laughed a bit at that; maybe she thought, *That's more like the Laura we know.*

I had hurt my mum. She never cries but she did then. She tried to hide her tears; it only annoyed me.

She's only crying because I've exposed her.

At the surgery, I sat slumped in a stupor. I couldn't speak. Blinking felt like an effort. I'd completely shut down.

Coincidentally, our midwife was on duty. She was passing through the waiting area when she saw me. She looked genuinely shocked. She took off her glasses and got on to her knees and held my hands.

'Oh, Laura,' she gasped. 'Oh, lovely Laura.'

I gazed at her, blankly.

The midwife said, 'After the jabs, I think you should get down to A&E.'

We were called in to see the nurse for Jet's injections. 'Is the mother present?' she asked.

I looked around as if to say, 'Oh, you're talking to *me?*' and raised my hand like I'd been snapped out of a daydream by a teacher in class. My face was frozen in a 'mother's grin' but inside I was screaming, ' **COME ON, LAURA! WAKE THE HELL UP.** *Act normal or they'll take your baby away. Act like you care.*'

And the needle went in. And my baby cried, my fixed smile plastered on my face, like I was a mannequin.

LAURA

LAURA

LAURA

Your baby is having an injection. You are IN there! Laura, come on. You are THERE. You are THERE. Come on. Come on. Come on.

We left the surgery and went to Hugo's dad's partner's house and from here onwards everything of that day is a dimly remembered blur of my bizarre behaviour. They made me tea and toast. I couldn't stomach anything. I was too lost in the filing cabinet of my head. But I didn't feel afraid now, I had surrendered to the feeling.

I should just say here that this was all from the viewpoint of me at my most unwell. The below is the version of events how I 'remember' them.

Hugo's dad talked to me at the kitchen table. He was actually trying to rouse me out of my catatonic state, but *I believed* he was attempting to hypnotise me. In my delusion we were having some kid of 'face off' – it was like a psychological interrogation in a scene from a Kubrick film.

The world drowned out. It was just him and me. I heard classical music: maybe a loud and overpowering opera. I thought Hugo's dad was using this as a technique to draw me out of my walking coma. And for about half an hour, I did come back to life, and I could think and see clearly, like I'd sobered up. It felt as though I had confessed to something but I didn't know what. With this 'weight' lifted, I was enlightened, relieved. *I've been healed! I've been fixed!* I thought, and hugged Hugo's dad. I almost felt a kind of euphoria – but not quite because the rational part of my mind still knew that I was in a heap of trouble.

Hugo's dad suggested that we go for a walk in the park to get some air. *I can do this. I can get better.* If I could un-spiral myself out of this for even a few minutes, I thought, I could practise and then maybe do an hour, then two hours, then half a day, then a day, then a week – until I was better.

But then I turned around, like in a super slow-motion glance, and 'saw' Hugo for what he really was: a lonely, isolated little child with a very low level of intelligence. I remember thinking that his IQ was really low and that *he* was the vulnerable one in the family.

He was a perfect subject for my dark advances and intentions. I plucked him out as a child when we were kids. I targeted him. And he fell for my trap. And it all went wrong. And everybody knew. Except for Hugo.

Oh no, that's not true: I didn't know either. The good side of my brain didn't know, but the schizophrenic, anxiety side of my brain, did. She knew. One half of my brain was keeping a secret from the other half and now the secret was out.

We walked around the common. In a few hours, I'd be dead. Children looked at me in disgust. Women with buggies stared at me and whispered. Stupid, gullible Hugo was swinging my hand, happy to have me back, and I was swinging my hand in his, pretending to be 'back', acting like 'the happy couple'.

I don't love you. I don't even KNOW you. You're not who I thought you were. You only love me because I've manipulated you. I've tricked you. And you're too stupid to see it. This isn't real love. I'm not capable of that. You've had a baby with a 'master of the dark arts'. I'm Lady Macbeth. It's been me all along. I'm the terrible one. I'm not the victim. I'm the perpetrator. My labour exposed me.

I don't remember how we got back to our flat but it was there where it all went horribly wrong. I snuck away to use the bathroom and I FaceTimed my best friend. I said, 'It's happened. It's all out about me. Everybody knows the truth. The game is up. Everybody knows what I've done.'

'What do you think you've done?' she asked. She looked worried.

'Everything. It's bad. I'm a master of the dark arts. I'm a liar. I'm a fraud. I'm a fake. I'm a manipulator. I'm an actress,' I said. I told her that Hugo's dad had hypnotised me. 'They have me here, at home, trapped. There's no more running or hiding. It's time to confess.'

I walked back into the living room, half-naked and shaking. I couldn't touch Jet. He was crying but I couldn't pick him up. I said to Hugo's dad, 'I can't. Please take him.'

I know they made me food. Chinese-style rice and vegetables. Hugo's dad was telling me to eat and I was crying saying I couldn't. I believed I had a mission to starve myself. That my brain had conjured up the worst possible scenario – the most messed up one of all that would hurt the most amount of people, to repeat history – it wanted me to die by starvation or by stabbing myself, then Jet's mum would die, just like how Hugo's mum did, and Hugo would have to raise Jet alone. The chain had to continue. That is what had to happen.

'I'm killing myself, aren't I?' I asked, and they nodded.

I'm so sorry. I'm so sorry. I'm so sorry. I can't handle it. I can't handle it. It's so dark. It's so sick. It's so fucked up. I'm so fucked up. I can't take it. Please make it stop.

They told me to try and sleep. I didn't want to go into my bedroom because I was scared of it, so they set me up on the sofa in the living room. I took my medication and closed my eyes.

'She's sleeping,' I heard them whisper, but I wasn't. I could have run a marathon. I don't know how much time passed, but as I lay there, my eyes crinkled shut pretending to be asleep, a new train of thought started to form . . . *I've been obsessed with Hugo since I was a child. I want to kill him and myself like some weird twisted love story. I love him so much I want to kill him!*

I heard them making plans; someone said something about 'holding on until Monday'.

And then Hugo's dad's partner said, 'Laura, we're going to go to hospital, OK? We think you have something more acute.'

'OK,' I said, and got up. To be honest, I was relieved. I was going to hospital. At last.

I didn't have to pretend any more.

Jet wasn't even a month old.

41

Hugo's dad and partner would watch Jet for the night. We all went back to our flat and Hugo packed a bag for me, which I then unpacked. I put in some leggings and jumpers but nothing else I actually needed. I forgot underwear, pads for the bleeding, socks. I forgot to put in a toothbrush.

It was 1 a.m. We were waiting for Daisy.

Jet was asleep in his bedroom. I couldn't go in there. I kept telling Hugo that I loved him. I had to keep telling him because I'd tricked him so much that if I didn't tell him I loved him, then *he* might kill himself.

Daisy arrived and we met her outside. I got into the car. I felt like the whole street was watching, like I'd been arrested. We drove through central London in the night.

My best friend FaceTimed me and I was screaming, I was a 'master of the dark arts', my cover had been blown.

We pulled up at an odd building I didn't recognise at all. I was completely disorientated.

Inside, the foyer was bright and light. A front desk. Blue carpets. A water cooler. Sofas. It didn't look like a 'hospital' or an asylum. We sat and waited in the waiting area, like we were asked to. Were we waiting for the police?

I held onto my case and Hugo and Daisy sat either side of me, hands on top of mine.

A doctor came. She was pretty, and my sister whispered, 'She looks like J.Lo.'

J.Lo smiled at me, 'Hello, Laura.'

She led us into a small room. This would be my bedroom for the next couple of weeks.

A nurse joined us. Doctor J.Lo sat on the end of the bed and began to ask me questions. Did I want to talk to them in private? Was I comfortable answering in front of Daisy and Hugo? I said that they could stay.

I don't remember all of the questions but I do remember the questioning seemed to last for ages. They asked me if I'd had a history of mental illness or had ever suffered from depression. I said no. They asked me if I was prone to taking drugs or alcohol when stressed? I said no. They asked me if I'd heard any voices. I said yes. Daisy and Hugo looked saddened by this.

They asked me if it was a woman's voice or a man's voice. I felt sick. I remember looking to the right-hand corner of the ceiling as though I was trying to *find* this man's voice. The idea of 'hearing' a man's voice in my head started to really terrify me so I couldn't concentrate on the other questions. I really didn't want to hear a man's voice . . .

Laura . . . Laura . . . Laura . . .

Had I thought of hurting others? No. Had I thought of hurting my baby? No. Had I thought of self-harm? No. Had I thought of hurting myself? Yes. Did I have suicidal thoughts? I said yes.

They asked me if I had a 'plan'.

'A plan?' I was confused.

'A *plan* . . .'

'Ohhhhhh! On how to kill myself?'

I asked if Hugo and Daisy could leave the room then. They hugged me and went to find the communal kitchen where they could make themselves tea.

Once the door was closed, I told Doctor J.Lo and her assistant as much as I could; everything that had gone on before this point since Jet was born. The doctor took notes while I talked. It was a shock to hear myself describe my plans to stab myself in the stomach out loud and mean it.

'I just want to sleep,' I said.

Hugo and Daisy came back in. The doctor told me I would see a psychiatrist in the week and I'd attend group therapy. My doctor would see me on Monday morning.

'Tomorrow, it's Sunday, so just chill out in here. See it as a day to get to know the place. There's a TV here, and if you need anything there's an alarm. The nurses' station is just there and a nurse is on call twenty-four seven.'

Chill out? And why would I need an alarm? I noticed a massive stain on the carpet. I imagined it once to have been sick. Or blood. Was I in rehab? What *would* happen to me in this room?

The doctor asked if I wanted somebody to sit in the room with me. I can't remember my answer. I don't remember taking the medication. I just remember Hugo and Daisy, in the darkness, lying over me, stroking my hair. Kissing my face. My pounding heart, slowing down. My muscles, taut with tension, gently powering down. My rigid bones, softening.

Shhhh . . . shhhh . . . shhh . . . it's over now. Shhhhh . . .

42

I've tried to recall everything I did and felt during my psychosis in as raw and truthful a way as I can, but I realise I haven't been completely and entirely honest. It's not to protect myself or my dignity – I really don't have much of that left any more – but some parts of this experience have been harder to confront than others.

I have to go back a bit.

When I wrote about the conversation in the kitchen when Hugo's dad 'hypnotised' me, I played that down. I have tried to understand why until now that particular moment was so difficult to write about wholly honestly, and it is because I didn't want to upset anybody.

After what has happened over the past year, some family members just want to move on and pretend this never happened. I can understand that. I want to be sensitive to that. But at the same time, it's not something I can just forget.

After Jet was born, I had quietly become convinced that Hugo's dad was judging me. That he didn't like me. The negative delusions and paranoia about him came on thick and fast and took a very long time to lift.

I decided, in my delusion, that on that night before I was admitted to the psychiatric hospital, he had deliberately played this intense classical music to put me under a spell. I believed – in my psychosis – that he was performing some kind of self-taught shock-treatment hypnosis therapy, a sort of home-baked lie detector/interrogation/torture process. In my mind, he had taken off his glasses and stared me straight in the eye. His eyes were like a microscope lens. He was dissecting me.

Tears falling down his cheeks, he said he was 'vulnerable' about Hugo. Then, he was angry, furious, red faced, and he said to me sternly, 'You *know* what you've done, don't you?' and I remember jolting out of the catatonic state that I'd been locked into and coming to, nodding like I *did* know what I'd done.

Stammering, I had 'confessed' to him. I'd led Hugo on. I was the devil. I was sinister. I was dark. And I felt shame.

Thereafter, I became terrified of Hugo's dad. I became absolutely fixated with my fear of him – obsessed that he was out to get me, to expose and embarrass me. Ultimately, I reached the conclusion that Hugo's dad was the mastermind behind project 'Getting Rid of Laura', and I told the hospital I didn't want him to visit me.

It's horrible and sad and embarrassing to even put this into words. Most people get embarrassed about their partners' dads seeing them in a towel – not losing their minds in front of them.

All of the delusions and symptoms of my illness, I know and understand as symptoms of the illness. But I couldn't shake this 'moment' with Hugo's dad. I'd known him since I was a kid and somehow always felt like we would be family. I'd always looked up to him and respected him. We lent books to each other. We had the same taste in films. He even cut my hair. And no, he is not a hairdresser!

For the past year, I thought all that had been threatened, beyond repair perhaps, because of my illness. The trauma leaves you with so many unanswered questions and lingering feelings, elephants in the room and awkwardness. Shame. You feel like you got really drunk at a wedding, got naked, told everybody what you truly thought of them and ruined the day for everybody. But at the same time you are annoyed too that you should even feel 'apologetic' because you didn't do this to yourself! It's not your fault – but at the same time it *is*. It's like murdering somebody in your sleep! But you did nothing wrong except have a baby.

I'd never had a chance to *talk* to him about it. I was too scared of the truth, the answers, what this 'confession' was that I told him. I was scared for it to be real but scared to have invented it too. Both were frightening scenarios.

But today, Hugo's dad and his partner came over to visit Jet. We were having tea; Jet was showing them his train set. Suddenly I felt this sickness in my tummy, a churn, and I knew I was going to say it. Because I so badly wanted everything to be OK. To be better and repaired.

'That day, when we spoke in the kitchen, were you playing classical music?' I asked him.

He looked up at me, over his glasses, 'When?'

'*That* day. Did you play the music on purpose?'

'There might have been music on in the background, from the radio, but no.'

Confident with his answer I went further, 'And did I *confess* something to you?'

He laughed and shook his head. 'No,' he said.

OK. Wow. I'd been sitting on this for a year, Hugo and I had talked and talked and talked about it. I couldn't remember what this 'confession' even was. I would cry to Hugo saying, 'I said something to your dad and I can't remember what it is, and I'll never be able to live it down and tell him that it wasn't true,' only to now find out that I'd said nothing to him.

I fiddled with the wheels on one of Jet's toy cars. 'Did you say to me, "You know what you've done"?'

'What? No! Not in my memory.' He laughed. 'It was a very short conversation. But it was clear you were unwell. I don't remember it all but you were manic.'

'So you didn't hypnotise me then?'

He laughed again. 'Oh, Hugo said this. No, I didn't hypnotise you.'

I looked at Hugo. He looked to me as if to say, *I told you. It's OK.* Hugo smiled. And I just felt so relieved.

'I thought you hated me,' I said.

'The opposite!' Hugo's dad's partner said.

It's a textbook symptom. To turn on the partner's family in this way. I've heard cases where women think they've been poisoned by their in-laws. Or run away from them because they feel like the baby will be kidnapped by them.

I don't even know if I've managed to convey just what an epiphany this was for me – but I think it should go in here. Because recovery is not linear. I've spent a year in debt to Hugo's family, secretly begging for forgiveness for something I couldn't even put my finger on, for something that's not my fault, and I so badly wanted to breathe in clear air.

43

The next morning, I woke up in the hospital, alone and con-fused in a bed that wasn't mine.

It was my first Mother's Day. Hugo came to visit me with Jet, a sleeping bug in his fluffy snowsuit. Hugo handed me a card. It said 'Happy Mother's Day' and had a print of Jet's foot in green paint.

But I couldn't touch Jet. I felt like all the staff judged me. They all told me how beautiful he was, but to me this was code for, 'Why can't you just stop pretending to be ill and be a good mum?'

I know that someone showed Hugo and me around the hospital. My hair was over my face. I felt really shy and embarrassed, all my confidence gone – it was like starting a new school late into the term and everybody was settled and I wasn't. The new kid. And I believed I deserved to feel it all. I'd been caught out.

You're not unwell, you're just a bitch.

I had a simple clean bedroom on the ground floor so I couldn't jump out from any windows. I had a bathroom. The water didn't get at all hot so I couldn't scald myself. There was a bath but no shower so I couldn't hang myself – not that I'd have the slightest idea how to do that. I couldn't even manage the monkey bars at the park.

There were maybe ten or twelve rooms, with a communal living room at the end with a few sofas opposite a nurse's station. With nurses at computers. Paperwork. Flowers to 'cheer' us up. The desk was covered with thank-you cards for the staff.

You will never be saying 'thank you'. Because you'll never recover.

Downstairs there was a basic canteen. A salad buffet bar; grated carrot and diced beetroot. A hot food section. Chairs and tables and that school dining-hall smell of salty mashed potato and soup. Roast chicken and the savoury smack of melted cheese. A very small court-yard with a fountain with a water feature in the centre; a silver sphere with ripples pouring off it – *something peaceful, to calm the mind.* Cigarette butts littered the ground. Smoking was permitted there and *boy* did the patients take advantage. I saw a girl my age with an Afro, she was on the phone, crying.

We were shown the gym (a running machine in a cupboard) and there was framed work from art therapy class along the walls. Lots of dark scratches, flowers, sunny beaches, broken hearts.

The walk back to my room was totally confusing and I decided the building was deliberately designed to bewilder us, like a maze. *It's all a trick. It's a test.*

Then I suddenly decided I'd figured it out. *I had brain damage.* From all of the nights of not sleeping and not eating.

Hugo explained that this hospital was the best place for us: there were no strict visiting hours so Jet and my family could come to visit me whenever. And I could get better.

I wanted to shout, 'Please don't leave me here, please don't leave me here, please let me go home with you and Jet.'

With a bit of sleep and whatever meds they had given me, the frantic mania of the night before had receded, leaving me with a heavy feeling of displacement and turmoil.

Hugo told me that he had spoken to the psychiatrist the night before. He had described my symptoms to him over the phone, and he'd advised that I be hospitalised immediately. When Hugo said it was the middle of the night, the psychiatrist had replied, 'Put it this way, if it was my wife or daughter, I wouldn't wait.'

'What's wrong with me?' I asked Hugo.

'Do you want to read it?'

'Yes, OK.'

He showed me the NHS website page on his phone. Postpartum psychosis affects roughly one in one-thousand women. Its symptoms include hallucinations, delusions, paranoia, suspiciousness, insomnia, confusion, mania, mood disorder, euphoria (I didn't get *any* of that), suicidal thoughts, thoughts of harming yourself or the baby, strange feelings towards family members, severe anxiety with a lovely side order of psychosis!

I was nodding at all of the symptoms. I couldn't believe what I was reading. It was me. I hadn't invented it.

Postpartum psychosis is *not* postnatal depression although it is suggested that it can be built *upon* postnatal depression. In truth, there is still little understanding of the illness, which is why it is so difficult to diagnose.

It was my best friend who worked it out; after our FaceTime call she began googling 'going mad after having a baby'. She called Hugo after and said, 'Sorry, tell me to shut up if you want to but do you think Laura *might* have this?'

Psychosis. Halloween visions of *Psycho.* Of *Texas Chain Saw Massacre.*

Girl Interrupted. Outlandish documentaries that you watch with your mouth gawping open at. And now, me.

In what seemed to be an organised handover, Hugo kissed me goodbye and my family arrived. My whole family: my mum, dad, sister Daisy and my brother Hector.

The five of us had not sat like this in a room together since maybe the year 2000, and now we were all squished in this tiny space round my bed. Strange circumstances. It was awkward. Humiliating. Every time I said anything I felt like they were trying to catch one another's eyes.

They brought stuff from home for me: my multi-coloured woollen bed throw, my glowing pineapple lamp, clothes, a toothbrush. Toothpaste. A notebook. Hector gave me his oversized black Nike hoodie – I *must* be sick because he never lets me borrow his clothes. Mum gave me a card and Dad brought me a yellow teacup and saucer with strawberries on it.

How long would I be in here for? Why are they moving me in like this?

I started to panic. *They wouldn't pay me this much attention for ever. Yes OK, they are here now but this would only last a few weeks, surely? And then life would go on. Eventually they would stop coming. Maybe Mum would move me home to her house and I'd live in the top bedroom with the wooden bars on the window (so Hector couldn't throw himself out by accident when he was a little boy.) That would become MY room. Jet would come for visits once a week. He'd tell people at school that his mummy lived with his grandma in a little room at the top of the house with bars on the window because she was sick. Oh God. Let me just die now.*

Dad and my brother sat on chairs, their symmetrical mannerisms mimicking each other awkwardly, Mum and Daisy on the bed. I felt they had become a tight little unit since I've been ill, but not in a good way. It had always been the three of us. And now, I was the rotten egg that had let the team down.

A roast dinner arrived for me. My mum and dad made enthusiastic comments about the food, 'Oooh, delicious! Looks lovely.' It was like how they spoke to my great-grandma when she was in the old people's home. Plastic knife and fork.

'Happy Mother's Day to me,' I joked.

My dad looked sad.

'I can't believe it,' I said, 'I've never experienced anything like this. Where did this come from?'

Dad laughed and said he'd taken antidepressants. Mum said that she had severe postnatal depression with Hector; Daisy said that she'd been suffering from anxiety off and on for years; and Hector said his anxiety had been 'through the roof'.

We couldn't help but laugh a bit. We were the Addams Family.

Every fifteen minutes, there was a knock on the door and one of the nurses would pop her head in.

'Just doing checks.'

The incessant 'checking' would continue during my entire hospital stay.

Another knock, but this time it was an older woman, a happy high-pitched almost musical voice, big round eye-googling glasses. She was to do my 'vital signs'.

My blood pressure was still 'looking pretty high. Maybe it's because your family are here?'

Time for another form. I answered the questions one by one as she ticked the boxes, yes or no.

Hygiene – did I feel able to brush my teeth? Bathe? Change my clothes? Tick, tick, tick.

Thoughts of harming myself?

'No,' I answered truthfully. I was proud of that, I got one right at least.

'Thoughts of suicide?'

I could have lied, instead I said, 'Erm. Yes.' She didn't react. It was so normal here, no doubt.

How had I jumped over self-harm straight to suicide?

'Thoughts of absconding?'

'Oh no, no, I want to be here,' I answered, truthfully.

The others left but my dad stayed behind. He lay on the bed opposite me. Face to face like we used to when I was little. For the first time in a while, a tear fell out of my eye.

'I'm sorry, Dad.'

'Don't say sorry, Lollypop.'

'What if I don't get better?'

'You will. You've got to. For your boy. For Jet. He needs you. He's your boy.'

That night, a male nurse sat on the end of my bed and gave me my medication in a little paper cup not much bigger than a thimble. You get them in McDonald's to put your ketchup in. I could have another sleeping tablet if I needed one. *Great.* My Velcro brain had already decided that I definitely did need another one.

And then he left me in the darkness where the room was ripe with shadows and ideas. It was just me and the jury of monsters that nobody else could see, weighing the room down like some hideous fog.

I really don't want to see something. I really don't want to hear something. Please don't make me. I don't know who I'm even talking to but please, have mercy. I'm scared of being scared. I'm scared of being alone.

I thought about the stain on the carpet.

I don't know how long I was alone for, but suddenly I was pressing the panic button. A screechy siren went off. A red light flashed. The same male nurse and another female nurse rushed in, relieved to see me not in the middle of doing something stupid.

'I can't sleep. I can't sleep. I can't sleep. I can't sleep,' I said. 'I'm scared.'

They gave me another tablet. And I was out, like a wild elephant felled by a tranquilliser dart.

44

At 6 a.m. the next morning the nurse woke me to let me know that the psychiatrist would be there to see me in half an hour. The room felt too bright. My head was imploding with horrible ideas. The medicine made me feel like I'd been hit by a truck. I dragged myself out of bed and ran myself a lukewarm – verging on freezing – bath. I had no soap.

With my hands, I squeezed my full breasts and my milk ran into the water, clouding it white, like cigarette smoke. It was surreal, sad and satisfying all at the same time. *How did I get so sick?*

'Hello, Laura? Can I come in?' It was the psychiatrist and I was still in the bath. I hadn't moved.

I scrambled around to get ready. This meeting was really important.

Come on, Laura. Come on!

My room was a mess. Stuff everywhere. I tried to clear up but all I was doing was picking stuff up and putting it back down again somewhere else. And in he came.

Dr P. was the most eccentric-looking doctor I'd ever seen, which didn't help to assuage any of the delusions I'd been experiencing. He was small, middle-aged, with a heavy coat that was so long it swept along the ground, and his hands were tiny. He was a storybook doctor. It would be wrong to say he looked 'cute' but he kind of did, in a caramel-coloured guinea pig sort of way.

His voice was striking. I had never heard a voice like it: northern and posh and nasal and rusty. It was croaky and husky and hoarse, yet high-pitched at the same time.

He is the leader of this place. He has some kind of power. Is he God? No . . . the DEVIL. Is this HIS hospital? Am I even in London? Am I in fact the guinea pig here for an experiment and he is the doctor? Will he brand a number on my head and refer to me as his subject?

He walked right in and plucked a pair of my bloody, oversized maternity knickers up off the chair. 'Knickers!' he said, matter of fact, and holding them at arm's length with his fingers like a pair of tongs, placed them on the floor.

'Sorry,' I said.

'No, don't be sorry. How are you doing?'

'Awful. It's just awful.'

'What's so awful?'

'Everything.'

'The mornings are always the worst.'

I used to love the morning. It was my favourite time of day.

He seemed to already know me somehow. Like I'd been his experiment for a while.

'The truth about me is out,' I said.

'What truth?'

'That I'm such a bad person.'

'You're depressed,' he answered, matter of fact.

'Depressed?'

'Yes, you have a severe case, not the worst I've seen, but a severe case of postnatal depression.'

'Why do I feel like everybody hates me?'

'Because you're depressed.'

'So this is all just depression?'

'You had a psychotic episode and now you're depressed, yes. And you're going to get better.' He smiled.

'I don't think I will.'

'You will.'

I shook my head.

He continued, 'And it's not going to take years, it's not going to take months, it's going to take weeks. And then you're going to be completely back to normal.'

'Back to normal?'

'Back to normal. And you'll be Jet's mum and you'll go back to writing your poetry and children's books.'

'I won't. I can't. I feel so bad.'

'You're depressed.'

Yes. So I'd heard. 'How will I get better?'

'Because you're here. We've upped your dose of antidepressants.'

'I don't want to take antidepressants.'

'Why not? They are going to help you. It's medicine. You would take antibiotics if you needed them. And it's the same with the brain. You can't do this on your own. You need them.'

It was either suicide or going along with whatever experiment this doctor had in store for me.

'And we've given you an antipsychotic.'

Again, that word: psychotic. More disturbing images flashed

in my head: blood on walls, weird writing, screaming faces, a rattling eye, a naked woman with her ribs popping out, flashes of crucifixes, fire, of a cave, of monsters, of a man scratching his skin in a foetal position on a stained mattress, of a cold damp prison cell, of a child wearing a mask, an electric chair. Buckles. Straps. A straightjacket.

'Olanzapine. Now you might notice some weight gain with this one as it increases your appetite but we'll try to get you off it as quickly as possible. But so far you've responded to the drug really well. And that's very good news.'

'Can I breastfeed with that one?'

'Why do you want to breastfeed? All of my children were bottle-fed and they all went to university. Forget about that.'

'But I'm letting my baby down.'

'No, you're getting better. And you've got a very supportive family around you.'

I nodded. I wanted the ground to swallow me whole. He stood to leave.

'Why do I feel like this?'

'Because you're depressed. That's all there is to it. You're a text-book case.'

Depressed. Was this what depression actually felt like? Like you're made of metal? That you're a glitch in the computer game, fuzzy and fading?

'Now. Do you need somebody sitting outside your door tonight or do you think you'll be all right?'

'Errrrmmm. I think I'll be all right,' I lied.

Don't leave me!

'Good. OK?' He put out his tiny hand. 'Now if you need anything you can go to the nurses' desk and ask for me and they'll give me a call. I'm available to you twenty-four seven. Otherwise I'll see you on Thursday between seven thirty and eight.'

And that was it. It didn't feel like a doctor's appointment. It felt like a meeting with the ringmaster of the circus.

45

No eggs were bought to my room that morning and I had to go to the dining room. Alone.

I didn't know what to expect.

I changed my bloody pad, which was sodden and hit the bin with a thump, and then got dressed the best I could. I didn't really remember how, or even who I was. I knew my name, which I couldn't stand to hear, but I had no sense of identity. I put on some leggings and Hector's Nike hoodie. Socks and sliders. Like I was hungover and was popping to the shops to get milk.

I walked past the nurses' station.

'Good morning, Laura.'

I kept my head down.

'Laura, can I give you your meds?'

I pretended I didn't hear.

'Laura?'

I need to hide the meds under my tongue and not swallow. I shouldn't take them. They are making me sicker. I can't trust the evil doctor.

'What is it?' I asked suspiciously.

It was a young Italian girl. She smiled. 'Antidepressants.'

Stop it, Laura. You're being ridiculous.

I swallowed them down with water.

You haven't got the guts to be a rebel.

'Are you going to group today?' she asked.

'Group?'

'Ahh, maybe you've not been assigned yet.'

I heard a woman shouting from behind me, her bedroom door wide open. She was a bit older than me. Blonde. Slight. She looked up, her eyes were wired. UFO circles. Her room was immaculate, not like my bomb site. She screamed down the phone, 'I need to speak to my lawyer, if he thinks he can take the kids because of my mental health then he can—'

'Enjoy your breakfast,' the nurse said.

The living-room door was open. A young woman with short hair sat in a tracksuit staring into space.

Oh God. What do they do to you here?

The dining room was packed. Everybody looked 'normal'. Nobody was wearing 'gowns' or smashing their heads in like I had imagined. It was busy but it was all disturbingly quiet. We were all drugged up to our eyeballs; sedated, we moved in slow motion.

The hot food under the lightbulbs at the breakfast bar flipped my belly over. Sweaty sausages. Pink greasy bacon. Watery scrambled eggs. Baked beans with a wrinkled orange skin on top. *How was anybody eating?*

I couldn't think what I liked to eat so I took a box of Alpen – at least I recognised that brand – and a strawberry yoghurt. I went to the far end of the room where it was quieter and sat down at the end of a long table. I looked around my fellow diners, but couldn't spot a unifying factor. We were, in every way, all different.

So why us?

About seven young girls, two boys and a nurse sat opposite on another long table, politely making small talk. There were large plastic containers of cereal, cornflakes, Rice Krispies, on the table in front of them. They looked like a group of students away together on a school trip.

A purple-faced man maybe in his late thirties appeared beside me, interrupting my thoughts. His face was unshaven and swollen. In a very well-spoken voice, he asked if he might join me.

Oh God.

I nodded and he sat down. He was eating the full cooked breakfast.

'What are you in here for then?'

'Ermmm . . .' Oh God. Straight to it. I hadn't thought that we'd have to *converse*.

Still ashamed of the 'psychosis' bit of my illness, I said, 'postnatal depression', because I thought it was more palatable.

'Ah.' He tutted, sighing on my behalf.

'You?'

'Alcohol. My wife, she wants to have kids. She's been putting a lot of stress on me. And it just . . . escalated. I'm meant to be discharged on Friday. We'll see. I've done some stupid stuff so . . . yeah . . . we'll see.' He gazed out to the distance. The red veins in his eyes were pronounced.

I could see he had been *there* too. He had shaken hands with whatever monster I had.

Across from us, a dishevelled man in a dressing gown was sitting at another table alone, pulling at his hair and muttering to himself. His story was painted on his face: he had given himself up to the voices.

I started to see a pattern. We were mostly all sitting on our own, all of us on some sort of psychological death row, praying that we could be forgiven, that we still had a life out there. We were all eating just to stay alive for one more day, maybe not even for ourselves – maybe just for the people that loved us. Thinking, *how the hell did I get here?*

I looked back at the table of breakfast clubbers. Why were they all eating together in this organised community when the rest of us were so alone? And then I noticed what they all had in common – they were all thin. Painfully thin. And that's why they had to eat together. They were being monitored.

'See you around,' the ruddy-faced man said and got up to leave. I realised that I'd been staring out to space while he had eaten his whole full English.

46

Whole hours would lapse in this worrying way, until I lost all concept of time. I found it impossible to concentrate and my balance was off. I felt dizzy all the time. I think this was to do with the medication.

My room was soon full with family members again. Mum or Dad, Daisy or Hector, Hugo and Jet, on rotation. Sometimes they all came together.

On the Tuesday, I had an appointment with the therapist.

I knocked on the door, then went in.

Where was the lying-down couch? The tissues? The cushions?

A large man with glasses sat at a computer and asked me lots of questions. He typed in my answers. It was all very matter of fact and unhelpful, more like a trip to the travel agent than a therapy session.

My answers weren't really that straightforward because what was happening to me wasn't either.

'I have . . . *anxiety*,' I felt the need to confess to him, although I knew that he could see all the outlandish scary stuff on my file that

I had said to the J.Lo doctor when I had been admitted. He looked at me as if to say, 'I think that's the least of your worries, girlfriend.'

'OK,' he nodded, pushing his glasses up on his nose. He typed it in.

'Sorry . . . but is this therapy?' I asked.

'I am assigning you to a group, for group therapy. Based on my questions and the answers you've given me.'

'Errrr . . . OK.'

It was all so formal, it felt like I was being enrolled as a space cadet.

'You will be in Group Two. Group sessions run all day, every day, from nine thirty to five with breaks in between. There is no admission for latecomers and no hot drinks are permitted.'

He handed me the paperwork. A small blue ring binder with a timetable and notepaper. I was so baffled and disorientated. *Sorry . . . I've just had a baby – what the fuck is going on?* I couldn't even tell the time. I couldn't read – or write – and all of these times and appointments were overwhelming. It was more than I could manage.

Hugo and Jet came to visit. I didn't know how to touch Jet. It was a strangely cold March and he was wearing his little snowsuit.

Hugo looked like he'd made an effort to see me. He looked too handsome for this hospital. Too beautiful to be knocking on my door. I didn't deserve to know him.

He was in total control of looking after Jet. The beaten-up bag he used to take to his band rehearsals was now full of baby stuff. Milk, nappies, wipes, dummies, swaddles, muslins, a change of clothes. When Jet cried my boobs hurt and swelled but against all my instincts, I couldn't breastfeed him because of the olanzapine. I felt useless. I didn't feel like his mum. I didn't feel like anybody.

I wished they would both just forget about me.

Every fifteen minutes the nurse 'checked' on me, then it was ten o'clock and Hugo and Jet were going home. The Maternity Nurse was there so I knew Hugo would get some sleep.

We said goodbye and Hugo kissed me, but I shied away. *He can't love me still, after all of this. He's leading me on.* I bent down awkwardly to Jet in his car seat and patted him formally on the head. My mannerisms were not mine.

Alone again, the nurse came in to do my vital stats.

Self-Harm – no.

Suicide – yes.

Absconding – no.

Because I answered 'Yes' to having suicidal thoughts, somebody would watch me sleep again.

My medicine arrived in its little paper pot and I swallowed it and waited for sleep to come in the darkness. Because it really was *so* dark. It was thick, the type of darkness that you could imagine shapes coming out of.

Please let me sleep. Take away this pain for just a minute. Let my brain repair and help me find peace of some kind.

My door was left ajar. A nurse watched me. *Just in case.*

Just as I was drifting off, the silhouette of a woman appeared at the crack of my door. There was an amber glow behind her from the lit corridor. She was wringing her hands together and I could tell by her posture that she was not a nurse. She was a petite older lady in baby-pink velour pants, wiry hair and a very well-spoken, almost classic-actressy kind of voice.

'Hello,' she whispered. How she could see me in the dark I don't know.

'She's sleeping, Catherine,' the nurse said.

'Oh ... she's sleeping,' Catherine replied, as disappointed as a child, sad that I couldn't come and play.

She whispered, 'Goodnight.'

'Goodnight,' I whispered back and fell into a sleep that was too deep to even dream.

47

Oh God. I'm here again. Not another day of this. I've lost my whole life. I have to kill myself.

My breasts were giant, painful and swollen with milk. I stood over the sink and squeezed the milk down the drain with my hands. My thighs were sticky, covered in blood. I was constipated too, a side effect of the drugs. And now, I was pretty sure I had cystitis. I had to laugh.

I sat on the toilet, wincing in pain. Top left of the bathroom on the wall tile, way too high to reach, was a single handprint. Too high for a cleaner to notice. The sight of it was chilling. *I have to get out of here.* Somebody had been climbing these walls.

I took my medicine and went down to breakfast, had my 'play it safe Alpen and strawberry yoghurt' and then went back to my room.

A moment later and a nurse knocked on my door.

'Are you not going to group today, Laura?' she asked.

'Yes, I am.'

'You've missed the first session already,' she said.

How? Time is literally rushing through my fingers.

It was too late to go in, so I said I would join the group after the break.

I spoke to my mum who said I should tell someone about my cystitis so I sheepishly headed to the nurses' station, every step an effort, not because I felt drowsy but because I was so scared to even talk. 'I think I have a urine infection,' I mumbled, nervously.

'OK, we'll send the doctor over to see you. Wait in your room.'

This doctor was very different to Dr P. He came in, flustered and intense, with a grumpy face. He was wearing a suit, and was harsh and direct, and very formal. *I really despise him. He wants me to be sick. He's another one of the evil doctors that is experimenting on me.* A nurse joined us, a young Irishwoman with a Walt Disney Princess face, but she was a human too. *Maybe she will help me?* I kept trying to catch her eye. *HELP ME.*

The doctor asked me to wee into a plastic container and said that it would be sent to the lab for 'inspection'.

Can't you just stick a stick in it and tell me if I've got an infection or not? Why does it have to be sent away? I'm an experiment I know I am!

He asked me to lie on the bed so he could check how my Caesarean was healing. The nurse stood by, quietly watching, her big bug eyes locked with mine. He looked into my eyes with a little torch and then looked in my ears. He asked me to stand, to put my arms out and he checked my balance. I fell over and tumbled onto the bed like a clown. *Am I seriously drugged? Why is he doing all these tests? Am I being sold off to somebody? Am I going to be made to have more babies?*

I imagined that I was being 'recruited'. *This can't be real. This isn't legit. This is some initiation to some weird cult. I am in some unlicensed hospital. They are frauds.* I had written a short story about a similar scenario in the past. And in that they ATE the main character. *Oh my God, I wrote about this. And now it's happening to me.*

I'll kill myself before you kill me!

48

G roup Therapy.

I'd never really had therapy before, and now I was suddenly thrust into the thick of it.

Paranoid, I spent ages trying to analyse the different therapy groups and their timetables. Why was I a Group Two candidate? I thought that maybe we'd had that sorting hat from Harry Potter shoved on our heads – it was to do with our most secret 'true' personalities and we were being separated, like battery hens.

I looked at my timetable: CBT, sleep hygiene, managing anxiety, art therapy, salsa? Tai chi. *Sorry, what?*

I headed upstairs at the break time to join my first therapy session. It was upstairs in a small hot room. A small group sat, all sipping water like pill heads. The crying girl that I had seen in the garden was there. She looked cool, like she could have been Jimi Hendrix's daughter, hippyish, wearing tie-dye trousers and an oversized top, but she exuded an angry energy, like she was screaming 'Stay away from me!' There was a thin woman in her mid-forties dressed as though she was on a first date at a wine bar, with a little

204

handbag and dangly earrings. She kept reaching inside her purse and pulling out various pens and tissues and creams or busily tapping away on her mobile phone like she had somewhere to be, mumbling about her busy schedule as if she was trying to impress us. A messy, pale, ghostly-looking boy my brother's age with frantic dark pupils. And a larger man with big dark circles under his eyes, who we learned was being discharged and leaving later that day. I recognised him, like he might have been on TV.

The group all took it in turns to wish him good luck.

We were all invited to 'check in'.

The TV guy spoke like he was reading from a script. His posture and expression didn't match his words: 'So . . . this is it. Thank you everybody. And now it's just moving forward, spending more time with my daughter, losing some of this weight.' He patted his belly and laughed; he was saying *all the right things* to get out.

'But it's really to the future now,' he nodded, proudly. 'I'll miss it here, it's such a safe zone. I'm worried what it will be like out *there.*'

Everybody managed a laugh, which shocked them, and then took an age to recover from.

He actually was scared to leave. He'd been institutionalised.

Oh God. I have to get out before they brainwash me. This is all a part of a bigger plan – right from Jet's birth – to break me down, to turn my brain to mush. What are they going to do with Jet?

We went around the room and said how we were feeling.

The cool-looking girl had nothing to say. 'Pass,' she said. She sounded American.

The pale young guy told us that his name was Ezra. He told us that he had smoked cannabis six months before and had had a serious anxiety attack and had never come back from it. He said he used to be confident and happy. He was popular, smart, with loads of friends. But now he felt like a wreck. He had isolated himself. He couldn't get a job. He couldn't leave the house. He self-harmed. Spent most days in bed. He felt a lot of shame that he had 'whitied', that he was embarrassed that it was cannabis that did this to him and not something stronger. He said everybody was laughing behind his back. He was deeply paranoid and suspicious.

The wine-bar woman was called Sarah. She was a complete contradiction, rapid and intense and very talkative, flitting in and out of conversation with herself. She started every sentence with 'I won't bore you with why—' only then to do exactly that.

She was recently divorced. *But she was fine*, she told the group. She had two children. She was overwhelmed. *But she was fine*, she reassured us. She told us not to worry about her because, you guessed it: *she was fine*. She laughed and then added, 'I don't really like to talk about myself. I'm quite a closed person.'

The group looked like they'd heard this speech quite a few times. I looked at their faces and they all looked distant. Vacant. Numb. Zombies! Even the man that had said how happy he was to be leaving, was staring at the floor, deep in sunken uninterest. He'd thrown the towel in. It was as if they sank back into oblivion the second the spotlight moved off them. Completely switching off. I excused myself.

'You won't be permitted to re-enter,' the therapist warned me.

'That's fine,' I said, but I think the reason I had to get out was because I recognised myself in all of these people and it scared me.

Next up was art therapy. In this group it was Jimi Hendrix's daughter, Ezra, and a new young girl who looked like a pop star. She had dyed pink hair and was wearing an electric-blue fur coat. They all had their water bottles, their croaky mouths, dry lips, dehydrated breaths. Suddenly I felt thirsty too. And I understood why they all had their water bottles. It was the medication.

The therapist was an older lady with a heavy European accent. She told us to help ourselves to materials and express how we felt. I couldn't believe I was there. It was bleeding into stuff I like to do, places where I would normally feel at ease – like being around art material. But I couldn't stand any of it. All I felt was doom.

I watched the others take their materials in silence: clay, paint, charcoal, crayon, pencil. I loved to draw, but I couldn't remember how to do it. My head was blank. I was trembling, my hands shaking. Tears began to form.

COME ON, LAURA!

My drawing 'style' is kind of stick mannish, but that wasn't coming across in this group – it looked like the illustrations of a child victim asked to draw their *experience*. The therapist could really read into this – the depressed mother who had lost the plot was now expressing her loss and sadness through stick people. It was not ironic. It was *worrying*. I even had the audacity to colour in 'my work' with pastel colours.

Before the end of the session, we were asked to 'come together and regroup', meeting in a circle made of school chairs. We were invited to talk about what we'd created. Jimi Hendrix's daughter held up an illustration of a wolf howling at the moon. Her face was so beautiful, with golden skin and kiwi-green eyes. She told us that she was in love with the moon. That she was in pain. Howling. Like a wolf. It was hard to feel that pain because we were all so drugged to keep us safe.

I thought about what we'd all be doing now if we weren't medicated.

Ezra had done an intense almost comic cartoon strip with crayon, full of red and black. He had been pressing HARD with them crayons, boy. He had an illustration of a cannabis leaf. He had a stick-man version of himself with a screwed-up frown. His glasses and dark hair were scratchy. He had red lines and warning signs everywhere saying: 'NO ANXIETY.' He told his story about the spliff again, and said, 'I just hate having anxiety so much.'

He said his whole body was shaking, his heart thumping out of his chest. He said he had wanted to cut himself that morning. He wished he had never smoked the cannabis. He resented his parents for bringing him here. He hated being in hospital. But he hated not being in hospital too.

The pop-star girl was well-spoken. She told us that she was bi-polar. She was also diagnosed with split personality disorder – *maybe I have split personality disorder?* – and an eating disorder. She said she'd been moving around the groups trying to find the right one for her. I can't remember her drawing. She was very sweet.

And then it was my turn. I showed my stupid art. It was an imitation of what I would have normally drawn, but with no personality behind it. I was acting, behaving how 'Laura' would have behaved. And then I burst into tears.

They passed me tissues. They listened. They nodded. The therapist tutted and sighed in empathy. 'How old is your baby?' she asked.

'Just over three weeks.'

'And you're away from him at this precious time,' she said.

I was red-faced and gasping for air, clutching the crinkled tissue to the corner of my eye, and it seemed like these people might become my only friends.

But the reality was, I didn't want to make friends with anyone. And they didn't want to make friends with me either.

49

I was constantly thirsty so I had to find out where the water machine and the kettle were. I became obsessed with camomile tea. Real tea scared me.

I met Catherine properly in the kitchen on our floor. She introduced herself with a bright, brilliant, broad smile. She seemed to have much more of a grasp of this place, like she was a regular. She told me she'd been in and out of this 'fabulous establishment' for years. She told me I had a beautiful smile. That I could light up a room with it. *LIAR!* She asked me what I did. Embarrassed, I said, 'I'm a writer.' I felt like a fraud because I knew I'd never get back to it. She gasped. Gripped my arm. 'A *writer*? Well, why didn't you say so?' She told me she was an actress. She said, 'I've got a wonderful idea! We should *work* together. Wouldn't that be fantastic? We could make a piece about this place! It would be hilarious! It's like a sit-com, isn't it? Why are you here?'

I told her I was suffering from postnatal depression and she looked at me with that look I thought everybody gave me, like, 'That's not real! You're making it up!'

'Oh, so *you're* the one with the baby?' she asked, knowingly.

I went to put the wrapper of my camomile teabag in the bin and she did it for me.

'Did you see my flowers in the living room? They were from my sister. I thought everybody could enjoy them. I've been drawing them. You should come and see my drawings? I could draw *you*?' she said.

The last thing I needed was somebody capturing this disaster.

She narrowed her eyes, suspiciously, and whispered (she whispered a lot), 'My doctor isn't being very clear with me. Who's your doctor?'

After saying his name she gasped again. 'Oh, you lucky girl. How did you pull that one off?'

I looked confused. Was he a celebrity?

'He's the best. Everybody wants Dr P. Oh, *you'll* get better.'

'I hope so.'

'You will.' She grinned. 'I don't go to any of the groups here except for the movement stuff. I don't mind that. Are you going to groups?'

'Yeah, I'm trying to.'

'Good girl.' She came in close. 'Be careful, though,' she whispered. 'There are a *lot* of funny people here.'

My family came with me to the dining room for lunch – I just kept thinking of all the 'terrible' things I'd done. I was picking at some sort of food-based substance with my mum telling me that I should try to eat as much as I could. They told me that it was good news from the doctor: I'd responded to the drugs so well that they almost thought I could be at home by the end of the week. She said I could recover at home with everybody around me. It sounded positive.

But no, I was sicker than I thought . . .

I looked up and saw Hugo's dad, walking through the dining room. I was immediately terrified, it was like a murderer had found my hiding spot. I had to do everything in my power not to scream and run out of the dining room. I decided, in my illness, that he had come to check up on me. To see if I was *really* ill or faking it. I couldn't look him in the eye: I didn't want to be hypnotised again. I was thinking, *how did you find me here?* I was not safe. How could I get my family's attention? *Don't leave me alone with him!*

Why couldn't they pick up the hints that he was the one doing this to me? And now he knew where I was. He knew that I knew, and he had just been able to walk in without even asking anyone's permission! I avoided his glance but from the corner of my eye I saw that he gave me a knowing look.

A cat who had the mouse. *Checkmate.*

I played along. Nicely. I said, 'I'm so sorry you had to see me like that last week.'

'You don't have to apologise.'

Do you think you can come here and play the victim card? You can't hide.

And I got what I deserved. This.

50

Hugo attended my next doctor's meeting with me.

Dr P. sat opposite me.

'You look much better,' he told me. 'How do you feel?'

'Slightly better,' I replied. In front of Hugo, I lied.

'You carry on the way you're going and you'll be out very soon.'

'And go back to normal?'

'You'll go completely back to normal.' He smiled benignly. 'Now, I need to ask you, any suicidal thoughts?'

I thought about it. 'No.'

'That's very good. And I'm sorry but I need to ask you . . . any thoughts of harming Jet?'

'No!' I was alarmed. 'No, not at all.'

'I'm sorry, I just have to ask.'

'I understand.' But the truth was, I was scared of those thoughts, all I needed was a tiny seed planted and I was there – growing a rain-forest of horrendous plans. I had to steer my mind away – *Don't think about Jet. Don't think about Jet . . . but aghhhhhh* – while simultaneously performing a balancing act of focusing all of my attention *on him*, to feel like a 'normal' mum who loved her baby, in order to help me get out of this place.

'I'm going to put you on half-hourly checks instead of fifteen-minute checks, does that sounds OK to you?' I nodded. 'If that goes well over the next couple of days we will reduce you to hourly checks and so on . . .'

And he was gone. Long coat sweeping out into the corridor.

Hugo had Jet's bath stuff with him and we bathed him in my hospital room. I pretended that I wanted to, but I didn't. His naked helpless body was completely trusting in my hands, clenched fists by his head, his big beautiful eyes shining up at me, happy to see me.

I am not good enough for you, Jet.

Hugo knelt beside me and showed me what to do. I hated being supervised in this way. We dried and changed him into a clean baby-grow. We fed him and he fell asleep, leaving just Hugo and I to make awkward conversation.

Every half-hour when the door opened for my check, the nurses were polite and sweet and smiled to see me with my little sleeping baby in my arms. I felt deranged. Pathetic. A failure. I bet the nurses all had kids at home and found it 'a doddle'.

Why was it not 'a doddle' for me? Did I have *any* maternal instinct?

Hugo asked for my phone and typed THIS into my notes*:

Laura – to remember – from Hugo:

    You did not do this to yourself, it's not caused by a problem with your personality or how you live your life.

---

* I have just read it back now for the first time since (I have been too scared to scroll down before now) and am crying at the words.

It is an illness, caused by the trauma of the birth, it includes depression & has a psychotic effect to it. It can and is being treated quickly and effectively. The psychotic side is already gradually going with medication & the depression will go after. They will make sure of that.

Then you'll come home (really soon) and we will have the best possible aftercare & you'll be able to explore every possible thing you can think of to do with yourself and decide how you want to tackle it and also if you even need to! (I don't think you need to do that much – you're an amazing incredible person & mum & we love you as you are.)

Your personality and self will go back to being exactly as you were a year ago as Dr P. promised (except you're a mum for good now.)

The sleeping pills will help here and some proper sleep is right around the corner, that will also help a huge amount.

I'll be here every day & Jet is in the safest hands, I'll be looking after him too & can bring him whenever you want to see him. Your family and friends all love you and think the world of you, all of them are a phone call away. They love you.

I love you.

Thoughts of self-harm? No.
Suicidal thoughts? No.
Thoughts of absconding? No.

51

The next morning there was Alpen, but no strawberry yoghurt. Just vanilla. I freaked out. I really needed to eat the same thing every day. This lack of strawberry yoghurt was upsetting me and sending me into a total spin.

I saw my group pal Ezra across the room; he had his head in his hands. He looked paler than usual, like he'd been awake all night. I smiled. He was so young. I thought of my brother, Hector, and realised that this could happen to him or any one of his friends.

I took the Alpen and the vanilla yoghurt and found a seat. The old me would have sat down next to Ezra.

Sometimes we took therapy with more than one group. I spent the whole time desperately trying to focus my head on what the therapist was saying, but most times I was just sitting there, drowning in my own thoughts, silently spiralling down into a well of rumination and self-loathing, or wondering how I could get out of this situation, or trying not to cry. Other times I would sit staring intensely at the other patients, trying to unpick their life story – why were *they* here?

I was trying to plot them on the graph of madness, placing their 'crazy' score next to mine.

I imagined everybody was thinking 'How can she be here? I would *never* leave my baby', as if I'd decided to dump my baby somewhere so I could do a scuba-diving course in the Maldives.

In my sessions, other than my core Group Two crowd – Jimi Hendrix's daughter, Ezra and Sarah – there was a skeleton-woman in her late thirties with dry straw-blonde hair and a heavy Russian accent. Her face was stretched and shiny and looked like she'd had lots of 'work'. Every day she wore the same oversized blue tracksuit bottoms and a baby-blue turtleneck jumper with raggy tissues jammed up the sleeves like a crap clown midway through a magic trick. It was easy to imagine her in a cocktail dress and expensive designer shoes. She argued a lot with the therapists. Asked them how they could just sit there when there was murder and war and chaos on the television. She talked defensively with her arms crossed. She sometimes posed the questions to the group, asking us if we weren't disturbed by the TV. She sometimes chipped in and commented on other people's issues, questioning their behaviours like she needed convincing that they were actually sick. She often walked out halfway through a session, slamming the door behind her.

There was another giggly and chatty guy, about my age, who was dressed in rude-boy clothes.

There was a woman who was constantly crying. She had big wet, blue globe-eyes and a crinkled tissue constantly pressed against her soggy pink nose and she talked about her boyfriend a lot.

There was a young chatty confident Canadian girl who wore a wig because she had alopecia. Her blood pressure was alarmingly low; she said she passed out a lot, and was terrified of 'ending up in a cave'.

There was a woman who was scared of the radio. Ezra told his cannabis story, again. Wine-bar Sarah told her story, again. And so it went on all day long, but in different rooms with different therapists.

We were all so self-involved and self-obsessed, lost in an abyss of self-hatred and loneliness. We said our bit and then we closed down. Waiting for our next turn to talk about our pain and unhappiness – for somebody to cure us. I was too ill to feel empathy. I was too sick to feel connected. I was too preoccupied to even listen. I was just holding on.

Every morning I picked up the phone, cried to my mum, hauled myself out of bed. I opened the curtains, opened the one-inch of window, breathed in the fresh air. I washed, squeezed the milk out of my boobs into the sink – I figured that when the milk stopped coming I'd be better – I brushed my teeth. I never looked at myself in the mirror.

Within days I began to slip into a sort of routine in this fish-tank world. I recognised the staff. I started to figure out where I was.

But time was a vortex I couldn't seem to get my head around as I mazed my way around the hospital, hopping from group to group like lectures at university, trying desperately not to be late.

Every day at 1 p.m., my dad, scooter helmet under his arm, carrying a rolled-up newspaper, would come and eat lunch with me. Dad was incredibly at ease in places like this, in fact he almost padded around like it was his local pub, getting stuck in with the staff and the 'clients', joking and poking nurses in the ribs with his elbow. He actually made friends. Commenting that the food was 'not bad', he said he didn't mind paying the £5 visitors' charge for a bowl of steaming soup, followed by the day's 'special' and a good go at the salad bar, although sometimes at the till point, he'd ask, without irony, if he could put it on the room.

One day he left an old little rusted metal painted Peter Rabbit by my bedside. He told me that it was his when he was a little boy. It was his good-luck mascot.

'Don't choke on it,' he joked.

That night, my sister came to see me. For the first time it was just us. She told me that she and Hugo spoke all the time, that they all had my back and they were going to get me home and better. I told her that I'd been lying to her. She began to cry.

'That's not true. It's your illness that's lying to you,' she said, and she recorded a voice memo on my phone for me to listen to. She told me that I was brave and strong and this wasn't me. She told me that I had friends and a life. I had Jet and my family. She told me to come back to them.

She asked for my evening meds from the nurse and under the low light of the yellow pineapple she rubbed my feet with arnica cream until I fell asleep. For the first time in my life as a big sister, I was too sick to worry about how she would get home.

Just recently when talking to Daisy about that night, she said, 'That wasn't just it, we hated the idea of leaving you at the hospital alone. That night, after checks, I snuck under the duvet covers and hid.'

'You tried to stay the night in the hospital with me?'

'Yeah.' She said. 'I didn't want to leave you.'

52

Lots of the patients went home for the weekend or had visitors, so then the group sessions weren't as intense. I took part in some strange gong-banging meditation therapy, which basically allowed my brain to go absolutely berserk for a full hour. It was a sit-down dinner date with my depression.

I got a couple of weird text messages from my friends. I didn't know who knew where I was and who didn't. I didn't believe any of the nice things they said in the messages anyway – they were just trying to stop me from killing myself because Hugo had asked them to. I'd spend hours dissecting each message, looking for clues about how much they all hated me. My best friend, who is a singer, sent me the most beautiful song that she'd written for me and it gave me hope.

The Maternity Nurse went home at the weekends, so it was Hugo's first weekend alone with Jet. He was doing the nights by himself. We FaceTimed. I remember waiting for him to answer and changing my facial expression a million times, I was so insecure, so confused by who I was.

I couldn't work out if I was better or not. Sometimes I felt like I was and then at other times it was like I didn't even believe I was sick.

You're making it all up. You're a stupid attention seeker. Every day you're not there is costing you. Jet will forget you. He won't forgive you for this. You've neglected him.

And then my mum or one of the nurses had to remind me that I was ill. Yes, I was getting better, but I was there for a reason.

I'd get photos of Jet from Hugo's family. Jet being bathed, changed, lying naked on the floor, feeding from a bottle. I couldn't decide if I liked getting the photos or not. They made me feel disconnected and sad. It was as if Jet was a baby orangutan whose mother had been shot down in the wild and now he was being raised by vets.

That's my baby.

There were wet circles on my T-shirt from the milk.

Get off! Get off! He's mine! He's my baby!

I saw Catherine in the dining room.

'Oh, it's you, the one with the baby and the smile,' she said.

'Hi,' I said shyly. Yeah me, *with the baby.*

'I'm worrying about the people here. You see her over there?' She pointed to a woman who lived on our floor, 'She's suspicious, don't you think?'

She looked at me with her narrowed paranoid wary eyes, wanting a genuine answer. We were FBI agents thrashing out a plan.

I shrugged, playing along, but I also had to be careful in case it was a set-up. I also started panicking about talking to Catherine too much in case she got me into the wrong crowd. It was like school. Suicide School. There were playground politics. There were cliques.

'It's your first time in a place like this, isn't it? Come to my room and see my art. I'm opposite you. I've been drawing the flowers. And the doorknobs too. Have you seen the doorknobs? Or I can give you a massage? Oh, dear, you're crying, you're crying. Don't cry. Please don't cry.'

She was right. I was crying.

'I know it's a big nasty shock. But it's OK. You get fat here, that's the problem. The medication – *not* what you need after having a baby! And three meals a day – I can't do it! Who are you friends with here?'

'Nobody,' I said.

'Well, you can be friends with me. I don't really go to groups. They know me here. I prefer to talk to the nurses – some of them are all right – if you ask kindly you can go out to the shops but they follow you in their nurses' uniform and it brings a lot of attention,' she laughed. 'I bought the most beautiful notebook so I can take down all the funny things here about this place but listen, we're going to write a book together, aren't we? About *this* place!'

She opened her arms up like she was welcoming me to a show, her eyes twinkled. I thought about her when she was young. She must have been beautiful, the life and soul of the party. I thought about my friends and when we got old and who we would become. 'Could you imagine! Hysterical! Now are you coming to tai chi?'

'I don't think so . . .'

'Come on! What else are you doing?'

And I didn't have an answer to that.

We lined up in the corridor outside. Nobody was talking except for Catherine, who was now talking to the woman who she had called 'suspicious'.

The suspicious woman told Catherine that she had thought she was dead last week.

Could I be dead? Are we all dead?

I wanted to block my ears. I was so frightened of overhearing anything that my brain might superglue itself to and then start believing for itself.

Jimi Hendrix's daughter and the rude boy were there for tai chi too. Sipping our water like addicts, our eyes were all massive. We looked like we were at a rave, but a carpeted-basement-of-a-psychiatric-hospital kind of rave. We were all seriously medicated, feeling nothing and *everything* at the same time, being drip-fed heartbeats to keep in existence.

The instructor was so patronising. I wanted to laugh because it felt like a scene from a comedy but nobody else seemed to get the joke. We were just locked in our own private paranoid picture show. Trying to do the simplest of movements was hugely taxing and close to impossible. Catherine was asking so many questions – 'which foot? What do I do with my hands . . . how should I be breathing?' – it was like she was doing it on purpose to wind the instructor up. A couple of us wobbled over. The instructor said, like we were toddlers. 'Now, don't worry, it's the medication, it can make balancing difficult.'

We didn't know our lefts from our rights and before we knew it we were facing the opposite wall and on the floor like a mound of puppies, bumbling over and taking turns to fall over and roll about on the ground. It was hilarious! But nobody was laughing. We had the most straight dead-pan faces. It was like we were trapped inside some terrible avant-garde play, or a Chemical Brothers' video.

'OK, I'll try and make it a bit simpler,' she said, but she was frustrated. I bet she taught a baby class on Saturday mornings and we were worse than them. The easier moves were no good either.

Catherine was taking it so seriously, eyes closed, smile plastered across her face, pleasantly moving her 'flowing ball of energy' all around her head and into everybody else.

And we were watching, hoping the tai chi had some magical miracle effect, all our marble eyes twinkling like lost stars.

53

I was doing really well. *Apparently.* I didn't feel like it. I was on hourly checks, which was an 'improvement'. But I was just holding on. It was all I was doing.

By now my room was covered with photos of Jet – this interloper, which I couldn't face looking at. Notes and poems and presents from my friends. But I didn't trust or believe any of them. Hugo, Mum and Daisy had stuck them on the wall. Hugo left Jet with the Maternity Nurse and came to visit. He had permission to take me outside (!) for twenty minutes. We walked – well, he walked; I shuffled with my head down – around the corner to the most beautiful old-fashioned second-hand bookshop.

This was the sort of place I would have spent an afternoon indulging in the cracked spines, the browning delicate pages. There was even a wooden ladder that slid along the shelves. I love the smell of dust. The smell of loved things. The hoarder's scent of forgottenness and belonging. Hugo took me downstairs to the basement and said, 'There's something I want to show you.'

Surrounded by newspapers and piles of old books was a piano.

Hugo played a song he wrote for me when we first got together, he didn't sing, just lingered on each note. But I heard the words in my head, and I cried and cried and thought I would never stop crying. I was mourning my life so much. I couldn't take it. I didn't remember who I was.

When Hugo got home he sent me a photograph of our notice-board on the kitchen wall. It was covered in photos of us and our friends. Hugo and I dressed as cavemen for a fancy-dress party; my family at his last gig; us on the boat coming back from the Isle of Wight; Daisy and I drinking beer at a Mel C gig; my birthday party; my friend's baby; me dressed as Beetlejuice; me and Hugo when we were kids, cheek to cheek, arms around each other.

For a minute, I remembered. That was *me*, but then it made me too sad to even look at. I wrote this:

When you've had your fall from grace
Then you know you've found your place
On the
Soft side
> *soft side*
> *soft side of the sun*

she's shown her molten side
And the little heats torn outside
from her
Soft side
> *soft side*
> *soft side of the sun*

Let's play a game of invention
Pack our bags
With old rags
For intervention

Now that all your wires are tied
On the edge with a plastic knife
On the soft side of the sun

Where they watch you sleep at night
Where the chemicals take a bite
Of the soft side of the sun

Let's play a game of invention
Pack our bags
With old rags
For intervention

Let's play a game of invention
Play pretend
With these friends
In no one's bedroom

Soft side
    soft side
    soft side of the sun

54

My dad came to take me out for a walk. We went to WHSmith and I bought a book and chewing gum. As Dad was signing me out, Hugo's dad was there, at the front desk. He'd come to say hello. The colour drained from my face.

I felt guilty because I knew Hugo had had Jet on his own that weekend.

'I think he's quite enjoyed it,' Hugo's dad said.

And that just did something to me. As though none of them ever wanted me to come home. It's so sad, again, it was a nice thing of him to visit but for me, it was a complete trigger . . . and I got worse. Paranoia took hold.

When you are paranoid, believe me when I say that you do not trust *anybody*. It is a full-time job and it is exhausting. You are a watchman, a surveillance camera, an FBI agent. You are bloody Sherlock Holmes; you sleep with one eye open. You are trapped like in that film *Memento*, your head is scrambling at such a speed you make notes to remind yourself of the situation and your 'findings', but then you are paranoid about the notes being found and so then you rip them up or scribble them out. You make new notes – *fake* notes – to make it look like you're well, in case somebody is looking for the notes, but then you decide the fake ones make you look even sicker, so you throw those out too.

Then you wonder if the cleaners are handing your dustbin contents in to the doctors and nurses, so you'd better not throw anything in the bin, and now there is nowhere to dump anything. There is nowhere to hide. So you don't write down anything at all.

You don't know what makes you look mad and what makes you look sane. You don't know what *they* are looking for. They've seen it all before, remember, so there's no point in trying to outsmart them. So, to be safe, you keep it all to yourself, letting the horrible ideas go around and around your horrid little head. You don't want to sleep in case you forget your theories but you have to sleep because now, more than ever, you need your brain to be on *your* side. You have to get better. And there's no denying it – you're very ill. You become obsessed with sleep. With repairing your weary tired overloaded broken head. You know you need to be in hospital, but you don't want to stay there either because they are plying you with medication that is making you sicker. You'll become addicted. And it's eating your brain. It's chewing up your ideas. Your creativity, your imagination, your feelings – erasing your memories.

You feel the need to fight for your life but if you fight, they'll think you're sick. You are powerless. You can't get out. Everybody is calling you mad but *maybe they are the mad ones*! You thought you were deceitful and a bad person but it's *them*! *They* want you to think like this! They want to dismantle you in this way. To disarm you. This is what people do to women. This is what women have had to endure since the dawn of time. It all becomes clear . . .

Oh my God. I see it now . . . I see it . . .

In my sick heartbroken torn-up paranoid head, this is what I came up with:

The medication is going to make me sicker and I'll never get out of here and Hugo and his family are going to steal Jet and win custody of him. They have a plan! That's why they are sending me photos! To show how cooperative they are for when we go into court! That's why Hugo is bringing Jet to see me. To cover his back. They are going to erase me from my life. That's why they are visiting me, to keep an eye on me, to 'groom' me into going along with their sick plan! To keep the nurses sweet. They want to look like the heroes. I've got it all worked out. They are trying to steal the baby!

But nobody will believe me! They all think I'm mad. Who can I talk to when they are all talking to each other! The nurses are telling my family and my family are telling Hugo. It's a complete conspiracy!

How could I be so stupid? The hypnotising. It's a time bomb. I have to get out before the drugs do too much irreversible damage. I have to get out of here to get my son back. But I'm not well enough to come out and I'm not well enough yet to care for him on my own – I have to tell somebody.

Who can I trust?

I tried to keep calm and act normal.

I called my best friend. I didn't speak for long. I was rushing, completely berserk.

'Don't tell Hugo anything that's happening to me. Anything. You are not to tell him anything. Not a single word,' I said.

She was saying, 'OK, OK, what's going on?'

'I don't want him knowing about my medication or my therapy. He is going to take Jet. I know it. I can't tell you now because I have to go to group therapy and I can't miss a class. Just promise me you won't tell him. Promise me?'

'I promise,' she said.

And you know what? She stuck to her word.

55

Things ramped up a gear. I had a plan. I became a 'force' to be reckoned with. (LOLS)

I called my sister. 'Can you bring me some stuff?'

I asked for my running trainers, books to read, a notebook and a pen.

Then I had the Walt Disney Nurse crouching behind the bed with me on all fours so nobody could hear me muttering away my scary epiphany to her.

'I know that everything else I've said is not true, I know that I was highly delusional and extremely paranoid but *this is true*, OK? I know it sounds mad but Hugo and his family, they are trying to steal the baby. I am better now and I can see everything very clearly. You mustn't let him, OK? I want you to take his name off the visitation list. I don't want him to get calls about my medication. Don't tell him anything. I'm not even sure who of my family I can trust at this point, OK?'

She nodded. 'OK.'

'I'm so sorry to put you in this position but thank you. I'm kind of powerless in here so I have to work very quick. But I'm going to get out. And I'm going to get my son back.'

'Whose name would you like us to put as a point of contact?' the Walt Disney nurse asked.

'Just my sister. Only Daisy.'

I decided that my hairy legs were keeping me awake at night and texted my sister to tell her to bring a razor too, adding, 'Don't worry I'm not going to kill myself with it. You can watch me while I use it.'

And then I sent another text. 'And snacks, bring snacks . . . boy, has my appetite kicked in!'

In the space of an hour, I went from confused new mother with a bad case of postnatal depression or postpartum psychosis or whatever the hell this vile thing was, to complete psycho bitch. I found myself strutting down the hospital corridors like I was a badass assassin (rather than just a terrified thirty-one-year-old wearing a baby-pink jumper, bobbly leggings and Adidas sliders on with my sister's cupcake socks). I decided I was the most severe case the hospital had ever seen; I was completely untreatable. Unless I did something about it I would be locked up for life.

I had to get my baby back. But the only way out was the way in; yes, through the heavy, guarded, electronically locked, security-monitored front door. And the only way they'd let me out that way, was to get well. (Whatever 'well' meant.) I went back to my room and worked out my plan.

The Plan

I will take all of my meds.

I will eat every bite of my Alpen and strawberry yoghurt.

I must ATTEND all classes and not be late for ANY. I must have a 100% attendance rate on my records for when I go to court to win custody of Jet.

I will be a perfect A grade student until the hospital release me: I will cry. I will converse. I will laugh.

I will make friends with other patients and sit with people at mealtimes.

I will do all homework sheets and handouts.

I will get physically strong by walking in the outdoor courtyard.

I will stop speaking on the phone and spend any free time revising what I learnt in Group.

Even if I didn't feel like doing any of the above, I would force myself. I could pretend.

I got ready for Hugo's visit.

The best way I can describe this interaction with Hugo is that it was a bit like a scene in a detective film: the characters each have a glass of wine, one with poison in it, and they both keep switching the glasses. One has predicted that the other would try to poison them, but the poisoner has already anticipated that the other (the 'poisonee'), would suspect them, and had already swapped the glasses ahead of the poisonee's switch. I was convinced that everything Hugo said was premeditated, constructed by him and his family. I had to try and de-rail him, catch him off guard, play him at his own game. I was sure that even the Maternity Nurse was in on their plans.

He said that when I got home we should go away with Jet to the Isle of Wight for a week.

Oh, you think I'm so stupid, don't you? You think that will give me an incentive to get out of here quicker because you can't take legal action while I'm in here. You're just trying to seem like a nice boyfriend when really you're a traitor. Besides, AS IF I'm going to let you take me to the Isle of Wight! It's surrounded by water. Do you think I'm an IDIOT? You'll leave me stranded.

Hugo tried to hug me. I stiffened up, but then changed my strategy. I had to humour him, soften him up, so I played along. I made myself sound enthusiastic, said that would be really nice.

Oh, I know your game.

He showed me a photo on his phone of Jet lying on my special silk pillow with the oranges-and-lemons print. His big blue eyes were begging me to love him. Unmoved, I took this opportunity to scroll through Hugo's phone and I found a photograph of a list of names handwritten on a piece of paper.

'What is this?' I asked as though it was a list of candidates that he could have affairs with in the future.

'What?'

'This list.'

'It's the names of the nurses.'

'Why do you have the names of the nurses?'

'Because I want to know who's taking care of you.'

'Why do you have them written down like this? Why do you have a photo of them?'

'I just want to know who they are. To make sure you're being looked after properly.'

He was lying.

'You're talking to the nurses.'

He rubbed his face; he seemed genuine but I smelt a rat.

'Well, yes. I am, we all are, but not behind your back: to get you well.'

You just want me medicated up to my eyeballs so that I never come out. You're going to tell them that I'm sicker than I am so they keep feeding me antipsychotics until I become like that woman that sits in the living room staring into space.

'You're lying.'

'I'm not!'

'YOU ARE.'

'Laura, I'm really not. I swear. Your mum has the list too.'

'Oh, I bet she does.'

She's the mastermind behind all of this. She has Munchausen's by proxy. She's been abusing me my whole life. She was orchestrating this entire saga. Unbelievable. Did they think they could zombify me while they stole my son? And what? I'd be living here eating apple crumble and custard while they got on with their brilliant new life without me?

'I know what you're doing, you know.'

'What am I doing?'

'I know what you're doing, I do. I'm just trying to work out your plan, but I know what you're up to and it's OK. I know *why* you're doing it too. But you won't get away with it.'

Hugo now looked scared and sad.

'Get away with what? Laura. I love you. I don't understand.' He was confused and distraught, but I just laughed, no *guffawed*, I actually guffawed.

He fell back on my bed, exhausted, his head in his hands. For a second, I doubted myself. Perhaps he was doing everything he could to get me well and actually this *was* all just my paranoia?

No, of course it isn't! This is your maternal instinct kicking into gear.

He told me he loved me again, but I didn't respond. Then he left. I took my sleeping aid, zopiclone, and me and my horrid ideas were put to bed – at least for a while.

56

Hugo called me the next day in my break from group to tell me that I might be able to continue breastfeeding when I got home. The Maternity Nurse would help me to get back on track, and I should talk to the nurse and find out if it was safe to take my antipsychotic while feeding.

*Oh, bravo! * shakes head, clapping* (God, psychosis makes you SO smug and punchable it's unreal) *Nice work . . . very, very clever. Well done you, Hugo. Put that extra pressure on me, why don't you?*

It was another test. There was nothing he would love more than for me to give up on the idea of breastfeeding Jet.

Well, ha! I have milk! And plenty of it. And I would show him. I would show them all.

I had completely forgotten about Jet. I was so transfixed by my delusions. It was me vs Hugo. I charged up to the nurses' station and demanded to speak to the Walt Disney nurse about whether I could breastfeed if I was still taking the olanzapine.

No. I couldn't. It wasn't safe.

Ha! He KNEW it wouldn't be safe. He's stitching me up. That way

when we go to court for the custody battle he can say that I selfishly priori-
tised my medication rather than breastfeed Jet. Oh very good. BRAVO!

I rang him back immediately and said how much I would obviously *love* to breastfeed (in case the call was being recorded), but that
I couldn't feed Jet with the olanzapine (of course, no doubt he knew
that already, he'd been googling the hell out of my medication),
however, I would speak to the doctor about alternatives. And in the
meantime would he mind bringing in the breast pump for me to
keep the supply coming so that once I'd come off the drugs I could
start again. I had to show intention and willingness.

I asked trustworthy Walt Disney to get Dr P. for me on the
phone. The minutes were counting down to my next group therapy
session, but there was no way I would miss it. *Hugo would LOVE
that too, wouldn't he?*

Dr P. called me back. I took the phone into the communal living
room and crouched down in a corner so no one could overhear me.
No one could leak my arrangements. I spoke to him like we were
cracking this *case* together.

I asked him if I could come off the olanzapine so I could breastfeed, but Dr P. told me again that that wasn't important: I had to
get well. I told him I didn't trust Hugo, they were going to steal
Jet. That he didn't know Hugo, but *I* knew what he was planning. I
had to get out so I could stop him.

Dr P. calmly said I was wrong. Hugo loved me very much, in fact,
he was going to see Dr P. with my family to discuss how best to
look after me.

This news made me frantic, I begged him not to see them, they
just wanted to spy on me, to find out what drugs I was on, and again
he reassured me. He said I was very loved.

Not true.

'Laura, trust me, you will go completely back to normal. You're doing very well. So well you will not need ECT. You will get better,' he said.

ECT? Electroconvulsive therapy? I practically gagged into the phone. Images of women screaming with leather straps between their teeth. *Oh God. Oh God. Oh God.* I'm in *The Truman Show.* I'm in *Black Mirror.* Nobody had mentioned me having ECT. I was trapped. I would be here forever. I would die here.

'You will get better,' he repeated and I ended the call.

Great. So even my doctor had even been fooled by Hugo! *Why can't anybody see what a snake he is?* He was going to let me have ECT without even telling me! They were going to fry my brain!

I handed the phone back into the nurses' station, not forgetting my *thank you*, and I marched off to group on a serious mission.

I decided to put my custody-battle dilemma to the group. *That was what they were there for, right?* How did they think I should play my next move? Should I switch meds? Should I cut Hugo out completely or keep him sweet? It would be great to thrash out my thoughts, but *obviously* I had to be very careful and play it down so as to not raise suspicions. Everybody gossiped in here, and I didn't want anything to get back to the nurses.

I poured it all out. The group said nothing, they just stared back at me with their massive drugged-up eyeballs. *Great.* Thanks for nothing, guys. The therapists were so impartial and playing devil's advocate that it was frustrating to have them sitting there on the fence with their dangly earrings and silk scarves. I headed back to my room.

I can't even remember what my point is? Or was. What was I . . . Oh yeah I was just . . . hold on, where did I? I was scared of something just then but what was it again?

I paced back and forth, completely indecisive and confused.

If my dad was waiting for me in my room, I didn't know if I should tell him about my suspicions about Hugo or not. What if he told Hugo?

No, I decided, I would say nothing. I had to put on a smile.

That night Hugo came in with Jet. He brought his bath things, some more of Jet's toys and the breast pump. I really didn't want this baby stuff in my room but I knew I needed to bond with Jet and play with him. Also, it was an act so the nurses would think that I was making an effort to be a good mum so that I could GET THE HELL OUT OF THERE!

I wasn't good at playing mind games at the best of times, though, and especially not when I didn't trust my brain and I was being stuffed with meds. It was a catch-22. Being compliant and taking the meds but also not letting my brain turn to mush from what I believed the meds were doing to me.

I shook my head at Hugo and snarled, laughing snidely to myself. 'I know what you're doing,' I said.

'What am I doing?' he replied.

'Oh . . . Don't you worry,' I said, knowingly.

'I really don't know what you mean, Laura.' He looked down at our skinny little son. 'I didn't think you'd turn on *me*.'

Turn on YOU? How about YOU turning on ME?!

He tried to hold me and produced my gold bracelet from his inside pocket. We have one each, two thin chains taken from one long antique necklace. Mine had got broken before I went into labour, which obviously I had read too much into as a bad omen about our bond being broken.

He'd had it repaired. 'I love you,' he said, and smiled. My heart weakened, faltering for a millisecond.

Don't fall for it, Laura! It's a trick! HAH!

I switched, I was so livid I could barely control my rage. The fact he had gone out of his way to get the bracelet repaired, *with a new-born*, just proved to me how far he was willing to go to take Jet away from me. Hugo just wanted to keep me well so that I didn't kill myself, so Jet would know that Hugo had saved me. So Jet didn't resent him when he's older. He was going to pretend that he still loved me so I got better, got discharged and then he was going to screw me over. Disgusting.

My mind was a riot of fury, but I held it together and kept up my defences.

'I think it would be a good idea if I started to see Jet without you,' I said.

'What do you mean?' He was hurt.

Oh, ha-ha, very clever.

'Maybe my dad could bring him? Or Daisy?'

'Why? So you can see Jet without me? Why would you want that?'

'You *know* why.'

'No, Laura, I really don't.'

Oh, yeah, yeah. Poor little Hugo. I know what you're really capable of. Everyone thinks you're soooooo nice and sweet but you're a calculating snake. Off you go, with my little one, back to our home and leave me here. Don't say you love me because I know you don't, Goodnight.

I turn my back. I watch him leave in the reflection of the silver mirrored windows.

Windows so passersby can't look in.

I am an outline.

I should have said, *Please don't leave me, I'm so sorry, I am so sorry. I love you so much. Hugo . . . please . . .*

I hear my door softly close.

The sound of my heart as it breaks.

57

Hugo the Hero Dad.

My 'ex-' friends will pity him. They'll bring him food, start cooking and cleaning for him. They'll bond over how they *all* fell for my nasty tricks, exchanging sick stories of my antics. He'll take Jet to playgroups and the women there will gaze at him, stoical and laden down with formula and water wipes, and whisper, 'Apparently, his girlfriend went cuckoo and is in an asylum getting her brain zapped. Now she's just an apple-crumble-eating zombie.'

'I heard she killed herself by stabbing herself in the stomach.'

'No! She didn't have the *guts* to do that, she overdosed.'

'How could you be selfish enough to leave your precious baby? How could you abandon your family like that? She's disgusting.'

'What a coward.'

'Thank God for formula, poor baby.'

'He's handsome, though, don't you think, that Hugo the Hero Dad?'

They will eye up Jet and Hugo, my beautiful lost property.

They will invite Hugo the Hero Dad over for tea and play dates with the kids and before they know it that four o'clock cup of tea becomes a glass of wine. Or two, or five. And Hugo will play the victim. *Poor, poor Hugo. He really didn't deserve that. Poor Jet. Poor, poor, poor Jet.*

58

After group, I called a meeting with my mum, Daisy and Hector. I got a text from Hector saying, 'Sorry, not going to be able to make it down. Laura's condition has got much worse so we have to go to the hospital.'

Then another message. 'Sorry, Laura, I won't lie, obviously, that wasn't meant for you. See you soon.'

In my state of heightened paranoia, that was really *not* what I needed from my brother. I felt exposed. Talked about. Manic. And that text was a passport to anxiety central.

Poor Hector, we can laugh about that now.

When they had all arrived, I told them all my suspicions about Hugo and the forthcoming custody battle, and that he was telling the nurses I was sicker than I really was, so they upped my medication. The drugs were killing me, but I had to take them to show that I was cooperating.

My mum started to cry. 'You're very sick, Laura, you're very, very poorly.'

And then I turned on her, she just wanted me to be sick with her weird Munchausen disease. Mum was crying, her face covered by her hands, then she said, 'OK, Laura, OK,' and dried her tears.

I broke down and started crying. I said, 'I can't take it any more. I'm so confused. I don't trust anybody. I'm so alone. I'm in a prison in my own head. And the worst thing is that *I've* made the prison. And they just keep giving me all of these drugs and I don't know what they are and they're making me feel worse. I can't deal with it. It's too much. I want to die.'

My mum tried to hug me, but I threw her off. I couldn't stop crying, 'I just want to die, please, just leave me alone. Go away. I can't live like this. It hurts too much.'

My mum and brother left me alone with Daisy. I told her I didn't want anyone to visit or contact me except her. I didn't trust anyone else.

We went down to lunch and joined my mum and brother. I held a meeting: our plan is to win custody of Jet like I was the bloody mafia capo.

'It's Dockrill vs White here, OK?'

They nodded.

The plan, I tell them, was to call Hugo in for an emergency meeting and be straight. I was normally at group at this time, and I caught him off guard. I could hear his friend laughing in the background. *They were all in on it. I bet he was already packing my belongings up in boxes.* 'I need to talk about my medication. Can you come in?' I said.

'With Jet or without Jet?' he asked nervously,

'Whatever's easiest.'

'OK, I'll be there.'

When he got there, I stated my case:

'Look, I know you don't love me any more and you are planning on taking Jet. I understand that. But please can you stop messing with my medication because this is my head we're talking about and it's really scary and really confusing. You don't have to love me or stay with me but please, please stop messing around with my medication.'

He tried to reassure me, but I didn't buy a single word of it. Poor Hugo. We left it again – raw and unresolved. Everything was a mess. The coldness between us was deathly – our fire stamped out – we used to be ablaze.

A nurse came in. Perhaps she'd heard me crying.

'Just doing checks. Is everything OK?'

I nodded. I put on mascara in an attempt to look normal and headed to group. I didn't want the hospital to think I was getting worse.

The nurse saw me and pumped her fist in the air. 'And look at that, you were so upset back then and you still got yourself up to go to group. Well done you!'

On the way down, I saw that the door next to my bedroom near the lift was open. It was usually locked, so I thought nothing of peering in. Inside was something that looked like a dentist's chair, but then I thought, *Is this where they do the electric shock therapy? No. It must be a dentist's chair – would they really put an ECT room by the entrance like that? Next to the lift? Next to the communal kitchen where people make tea?*

In group, a German woman was telling us how she could hear electricity. The buzz of the TV, the fizz of the fridge, the churn of the microwave, even the sound of the Wi-Fi, people sending texts and emails. She could hear it, fluttering through the empty space. It was driving her mad.

I just sat there. A puddle of a person. I was grieving. I loved Hugo so much. I was so sad that it had come to this with him and his family. I thought of Jet. What he'd be doing now. I wondered which friends would stand by me after this – once they found out the truth about me, not many. Not when there was a baby involved.

I felt this warm wet feeling in between my legs. I was bleeding, leaking through my clothes. I had to get up. I excused myself and ran to the nearest toilet, a trail of bloody drips following me to the cubicle. As I pulled down my leggings, there was a violent flash of thick, fresh red blood down my thighs. I looked into the toilet bowl and it was a bloodshed horror show. My knickers were soaked through, my sanitary towel drenched. I couldn't remember when I had last changed it.

Whoever is doing this to me, please just give me a break? You've proved your point but please. Please. NO MORE. I'll do anything. Anything. Just make it stop. I can't take any more.

I stopped. Closed my eyes. Took a deep breath.

Laura, you're in there. You can do this.

I wiped up as best I could, made a makeshift emergency sanitary towel out of scrunched-up tissue paper and walked back to my room. I saw the nurses at the station on my floor.

'Everything OK, Laura?'

Please just let me go somewhere. Just give me space from this head for one second. From this body.

Maybe I had a miscarriage? Maybe this was leftover 'stuff' from the birth? Placenta?

I felt a pulsing in my lower abdomen, like a period pain but not as intense, a kind of throbbing, like a vein, beating, pumping blood. Maybe . . . *a little kick?*

And that is when my brain decided that I was pregnant again, with a phantom baby. It had locked on, fastened itself to the idea. *Oh, good.* Couldn't be more bloody chuffed with that, and no matter how hard I tried to steer the thought away, it wouldn't go. Oh God, it was inevitable: if it wasn't one delusion it would be another. My head was no longer mine. Somebody else was controlling it, like changing channels on a TV – every channel a tailor-made horror, just for me.

I couldn't tell anybody about the phantom baby. They would never let me out.

I bathed. I squeezed more milk out of my boobs and looked up at the ceiling. *How do women cope with this in other parts of the world where there's no healthcare? With no support? Where mental health isn't taken seriously? In the past? In the wild? Where formula doesn't exist?*

Somebody knocked on my door, a nurse. 'You OK, Laura?'

'Yep.'

I was sobbing, NO!

TELL HER ABOUT THE PHANTOM BABY. TELL HER. TELL HER.

Shhh . . .it's our secret.

All I remember is sitting on the bed. Hands plugged onto my knees like I was about to be launched into space. Eyes closed. Doing everything I could not to think of something bad to do with Jet. My brain was teasing me: *Hey, wouldn't it be cool to think of something horrible to do to Jet?* No! No! No! Stop it! Thoughts were smashing around in my head like a pinball so fast and hard that it physically hurt.

I could swallow the metal Peter Rabbit that Dad gave me? But that was ridiculous, it would never work. I'd just choke, be deprived of oxygen and be brain damaged for life. Dad would never forgive himself.

I was meant to be pumping my breasts so that I could stand up in court and say I *tried*. I jumped up and began to furiously express with the hand pump. The nurse checked on me again. Grey milk drizzled into the empty vessel. He looked at me with pity and turned away.

I rang my sister. 'Daisy, my brain is teasing me, it wants to think of something to do with me harming Jet.'

'No. Laura, don't let it.'

'It hurts. My head hurts. I'm tired.'

I have to kill myself.

I rushed to group, believing this imaginary baby was growing inside me. Who was the father? The devil? Or my own twisted thoughts? I once saw an ex-service woman on TV who had lost a leg in a bombing. Whenever there was thunder and lightning it would trigger the trauma of the explosion, and she would feel the pain in her missing limb. A phantom pain.

At some point that day, my dad came to see me. I just remember sitting there in front of him like a zombie, pumping my breasts obsessively, muttering about how I had to do this so I could start feeding Jet again. He must have known I wouldn't be breastfeeding again. How sad and disturbing that must have been for him, watching me, boobs out (nobody wants their dad to see their boobs at the best of times) pumping away for nobody. This is one of the hardest memories to shake.

I couldn't stop thinking about the ECT room that I was sleeping next to.

Hugo arrived unexpectedly to take me out for a walk. I went to the nurses' station to inform them, but I wasn't allowed to leave. I was back on fifteen-minute checks again.

'But why? I'm doing so well!' (Bar the phantom pregnancy, the intense bleeding, severe delusions, racing thoughts, confusion, fear of the ECT dentist chair, overriding paranoia and the possible impregnation of the devil's baby.)

Maybe they'd confused me with the other Laura? Other Laura who never came out of her room. Her head was shaved and covered in nips and scratches like she'd done it herself with a kitchen knife and without a mirror and she had these big black rings around her eyes. If you ever saw her down the corridor it was like a bull charging towards you. *Please do not confuse me with other Laura.*

What if they'd mixed up our medication? What if they'd imprisoned me instead of her and they don't believe anything I say or that it wasn't *me* because I'm schizophrenic. What if somebody handed Jet to her instead of me and she killed him?

I was so embarrassed in front of Hugo. I didn't know why I'd been put down to fifteen-minute checks.

Now I know it was because Hugo told the nurses that he was worried about me and that my mum had told him I was having suicidal thoughts again. But he didn't tell me this at the time. To protect my feelings, he allowed me to believe they'd confused me with other Laura.

At this point, the truth was scarier than my delusion.

59

I wondered about what backed on to my bedroom window.

Who was listening to me? Who could hear me? Who was telling on me? Who was feeding back information to the nurses? Were they filming me? Recording me?

The only place I had freedom was inside my brain. And that was the worst place on earth.

I was chasing the clock, trying to express by pumping in the small break I had in between groups, then pouring the useless miserable milk down the sink. I texted the Maternity Nurse to check in on Jet and say thank you. This was all to make me look like a caring mother and back up my custody case in court.

The door knocked and it was the Walt Disney nurse and the efficient formal male ward doctor. They were upping my olanzapine dose because it had 'been brought to their attention' that I was still 'experiencing heightened emotions and delusion'.

Who had brought it to their 'attention'? I was like Julius Caesar! Who was Brutus? I was shouting. I wanted answers. I looked at Walt Disney, she couldn't help me. *What if this zapped me into complete oblivion? The ECT machine. It was going to happen. They were going to electrocute me and burn my brain and . . . my head, convulsing. Bbbbbbbrrrrrrrrrrrr . . . .*

'Laura, don't make a fuss,' the ward doctor said.

'Have you spoken to my family? Who made you do this?' I knew full well who was behind this. Hugo. 'Can you please speak to my partner?'

'There's nothing to say. We are upping your drug to the maximum dose; you will notice some weight gain and possible dizziness.'

Maximum dose? If that didn't work then the next step would be ECT, wouldn't it? This had gone too far.

'Please speak to my partner,' I said.

'OK. Very quickly,' he agreed, but it was like I was taking up his time.

I took my phone, fingers rapidly sliding across the screen trying to unlock it, I scrambled for Hugo's name on the recently dialled call list . . . *No more games. No more drugs. They'd kill me. My brain would turn to porridge. I would never get out.*

Hugo answered. 'Hugo, Hugo, the doctor is here, the floor GP, they want to up my antipsychotics! Why? Why would they do this? Can you speak to the doctor? Does Dr P. know about this?'

Hugo said, 'Laura, it was Dr P. who instructed it.'

60

Recently, I talked to my sister's boyfriend Ramsay about all of this. He said, 'It was a strange paradox because you were so paranoid and suspicious of us all talking about you behind your back but at the same time you were right. We had to. You were saying different things to all of us. We had to communicate. The difference is you thought we were conspiring against you, but we were keeping you safe.'

I understood. It's like a surprise party. You think all of your friends are leaving you out and talking behind your back. They are but it's for your benefit.

61

That night, after the conversation with the doctor, Hugo came to see me with Jet. I just fell to my knees in tears and said, 'Hugo. I know you don't love me any more. I know you're going to leave me and I understand why, but please don't take my baby from me. Please.'

Hugo knelt down beside me and he looked me right in the eyes. It was the most real experience I'd ever had. His eyes were big and bloodshot, with exhaustion and confusion and loss, his pupils focused on me. I know now what people mean when they say that eyes are windows to the soul – I felt like I actually *saw* Hugo.

He held my hands and said, 'I'm not. I'm not going to take him. I'm not going to leave you. I promise. You can do this.'

'I can't. It's all my fault,' I cried.

Hugo began to cry; he sucked back his tears. I clung to Jet.

'You *can*. This is not your fault. You didn't *ask* to get ill. Laura, you thinking this is your fault is like anybody with any illness saying they asked for it. It would be like saying my mum asked to get MS. You didn't ask for it. And you will fight it. You will. I'm not going anywhere. I'm not. I'm staying with you. I'm sticking with you.'

We held each other and cried and cried. Love proved to be the medicine that fixed me.

62

I felt delirious and heavy from the stronger dosage of the anti-psychotic. Just getting through my day was like trying to solve a murder mystery. My appetite was roaring. I snacked all day long on stuff my sister had brought for me – yoghurt-covered cranberries, dried mango, dark chocolate, nuts and smoothies and then at lunch I scoffed my face on a jacket potato and fruit salad, and had spaghetti Bolognese for dinner. I honestly couldn't tell you if it was a loyal vegetarian or not. It was simply food.

Throughout the day I picked at toast that I made in the little kitchen on our floor. Yes, next to the ECT room. Mostly the door was locked. Sometimes you could hear a drilling noise from inside.

It MUST be a dentist.

I went to group therapy. Ezra told us all he was going home for dinner that night and how excited he was. We wished him luck.

My family got permission to take me out to Pizza Express. With Jet. I bloody love Pizza Express and now it was tainted with *this*. (Hugo actually tells me we went to Pizza Express twice but I don't remember the first time.) It was nice to be out with everyone but it felt forced. Everybody was trying to be upbeat but I felt so ashamed. I was, however, so very happy to eat a whole pizza.

I thought of Ezra from my group. At home with his family. Trying to be normal too. I could imagine how he was feeling, like his family were watching and interpreting his every move. We were on probation.

Weirdly, as though life couldn't play any more mean games with me, a tall woman burst into the restaurant and tried to steal something. A member of staff caught her and held her up against the door, her face squashed onto the glass like a slug. She threw something at the wall and screamed. I remember that I instinctively launched myself over Jet, who was asleep in his car seat, to protect him.

But I couldn't tell if it was a genuine reaction or if I had done it for show.

After they upped my dosage of the drugs, I no longer really trusted the nurses any more. I felt like the Walt Disney Nurse didn't like me as much, like she was keeping a distance. (Later I found out that was because Mum told her off about a lack of communication about my urine infection results – the least of my worries.) I felt that Hugo was only with me because I was Jet's mum; that Daisy and Hector were terrified of me and I was no longer their big sister. That Dad thought I was gross, a drama queen. He'd seen my boobs, which embarrassed me. That Mum liked me being poorly and she'd have me in here for ever if she could.

That Jet didn't know who I was.

Back in group therapy, wine-bar Sarah was 'checking in'. Or rather, she was checking out. She was leaving later that day and was very nervous about it. She said she was excited to see her kids and go home, but was anxious about sleep. She'd been prescribed zopiclone but she'd heard they were very addictive.

Oh God, I'm on zopiclone. I'm going to become an addict. I won't be able to sleep again without it. Wait . . . what if I go mad again?

Ezra was back from his stay at home. He told us it went really well, but then said that that wasn't exactly true. He'd broken down over a family dinner and burst into tears and had spent the whole evening under the duvet in his bedroom. He had had to resist cutting himself.

'You will get better,' the therapist reassured him.

He says he knows he will *get better* but it had been months. *How long will it take?* It was eating up his life.

In break time, I accidentally got caught up in a conversation about suicide – who had made arrangements with their money and if we had 'plans'. It became a competition. Who was the most suicidal? Who actually went *there*? It was a horrible conversation to be part of, because I understood it.

But I didn't feel 'mad' enough to fit in, not 'suicidal' enough to legitimately earn a place in their gang. I wanted to live too much.

Did I have to make friends here? Could we bond over suicide?

We were *all* constantly being told that we would 'get better'. That *all* of us would recover from this, on repeat. It was like some strange delusional mantra that the therapists and psychologists drilled into our heads to keep us alive and un-suicidal. A sick catchphrase that we would cling to until our dying day, to make us hold on. We just walked around like sponge-headed muppets, repeating, 'We will get better.' But I wouldn't get better, would I? None of us would, would we?

Over lunch I made an effort and sat with my group in case I never got better and I was in there for the rest of my days. Wine-bar Sarah diverted the conversation to life on the outside. It was her last meal in the canteen and she couldn't wait for a glass of wine. She talked about her ex and how much she was looking forward to seeing him now that she was well, and she started to cry. Then she said, 'It's just . . . he's so happy. And I'm not. I'll never get better.'

That sentence will always stick with me. She properly broke down. I held her hand, which was a lot for me at this point.

And then just like everybody else I said, 'You will get better.'

Because it felt like the right thing to do.

63

Over a year after I left the psychiatric hospital, I went back to visit it. I took Hugo and Jet with me for moral support.

I'd arranged to talk to the Walt Disney nurse. She had taken really good care of me when I was ill, so I'd called to tell her about this book and asked if she would be happy to talk to me about those two weeks I'd spent on the ward.

I dressed like myself, in a pink velvet leotard and leopard-print flares. I put on pink lipstick, and my wooden hand-painted cat-and-fish earrings that Hugo bought me.

The hospital looked exactly the same as it had a year before, with its waiting area where I had sat in the middle of the night, not knowing what was around the corner for me. I had a flashback of the Walt Disney nurse standing over my bed in her off-duty clothes, telling me she wasn't going to be working at the weekend but to look out for another really nice nurse who would care for me. I remembered how nice that was of her. How she had gone out of her way to make me feel safe.

I walked past the 'locked' ECT room. And there she was. We hugged.

'I remember you so well, but you're much more glamorous now!' the Walt Disney Nurse said. (Hardly an achievement when she'd only ever seen me before in my grubby bobbly leggings.) 'When you called I felt a bit emotional. It's so brilliant to know you're well and you've recovered. Many people never want to come back here.'

'You know, you were the first person I've ever cared for with postpartum psychosis,' she confessed. 'It was so scary for you. I could see the fear in your face.'

I said that although it was only for two weeks – 'Ha! *Only*!' she joked – it felt like forever at the time. Even now it all felt so raw and fresh in my mind. Being back here had stirred up so many memories and emotions.

I said that I knew how fortunate I'd been to have such great care and treatment. I understood that some women had so much longer experiences of postpartum psychosis and were hospitalised for much longer periods.

'You know, what made you recover so quickly though was your amazing family. They were here non-stop. They made your room so cosy and homely,' she told me. (To me, my room hadn't felt like that at all!)

'Not all families are like yours. People just don't have the support. That's a big part of the problem with mental illness. You feel like you've called all your favours in. And it's often not true,' Nurse Disney sighed.

A couple of patients walked by the nurses' station. I felt connected to them somehow. They didn't look scary, or manic, or even drugged up and sedated as I remembered us looking. They looked like any healthy human you'd see anywhere. Like people you'd chat to at the supermarket, or give directions to on the street. Teachers. Police officers. Box office workers. Politicians. Musicians. Chefs. Which just goes to show how invisible mental illness is.

I put Jet down on the carpet and he crawled around in his croissant leggings, giggling, making people laugh with his ridiculous hippo teeth. The last time he was here he was just weeks old.

I feel protective of the hospital, of the people inside. The rooms. I feel oddly safe.

I asked her why I was assigned to Group Two. She said that there was no hidden message, there were several groups and I just happened to be put in that one. I asked about the therapists, if they kept a file of everything we said in group. She said, no, they only reported back if there was something of concern.

It was funny how, when I was trapped inside my psychosis, all of these minor things had seemed such a massive deal and had fed my paranoia. It goes to show how hyper-alert and suspicious I was when I was in hospital. How hard my brain must have been working. Now, the fear was dialled down, the trauma was relieved.

Jet crawled down the corridor and into somebody's room. *Oh God.* I thought about how much that would have set me off a year ago. Could you imagine being in psychosis and a baby crawling into your room?! Hugo chased after him.

'The good thing about having this when he was so young is that he won't remember any of it,' Nurse Disney reassured me.

'Yes, but I'll make sure to remind him!' I joked. 'Every single Mother's Day!'

We laughed.

We went to look at the canteen and the therapy rooms. As we were walking to the lift, we went past my old room, and I saw the locked 'ECT' door with a sign saying 'occupied' and then Hugo and I heard it – a bone-tinglingly loud, overpowering drilling noise. I'd almost forgotten to ask about what I'd seen in that room.

'Is that where the shock therapy is carried out?' I asked.

'Yes,' but she explained that it wasn't ECT or 'shock treatment'. They used a treatment called RTMS which has a similar effect. She said that it was like a chair with a light over the top.

'It looks like a dentist's chair,' I said.

As we walked past the door, the drilling sound started up again.

'No wonder you were so terrified!' Hugo said. 'That would have scared anyone. Having that happening next to your bedroom.'

We looked into the canteen, the staff's faces felt familiar. It felt warm, human, welcoming. I felt safe there. People have visions of *One Flew Over the Cuckoo's Nest*. But no.

I saw the groups of smokers out in the rain. The therapy rooms busy with patients in group sessions, where I had sat, stripped of my personality. I thought of the countless times I'd paced up and down these corridors thinking I'd 'worked it all out', only to destroy my next theory like a sandcastle being washed away by the tide.

My memories were so sharp and potent. I felt like I was here yesterday.

It makes me feel happy to know that a place like this exists. Where mental health is taken seriously but also is normalised. Where it's understood. And it's comforting to know it's there for me should it happen again . . .

I am so thankful to the nurses and therapists that took care of me here. I am *almost* grateful for the experience.

But today I am also *so* pleased to sign out my name and say goodbye.

64

At one of my last group therapy sessions, one I'll never forget, a very young girl was telling us that she was having shock therapy the next morning. She was leaving the hospital to be treated. It would be the first time she had left the ward for months. I felt nervous for her, of the outside world. Oddly protective.

She was in so much pain that I felt her energy radiate across the room. The only way to truly describe her mood was disturbed. She had long black curly hair and pale translucent skin, she looked like a porcelain doll. I just remember how long it took for her to speak, to even string a sentence together. The voices in her head were so loud they were almost audible. Her hands were gripped around her head like her skull was blowing open. I felt the reaction of the therapist – *shock* – trying to remain composed. It was sobering. It felt like I'd been whipped.

It was one of the most intense moments of my life. How can mental health and well-being still not be taken as seriously as physical health? It's all *health*. This young girl couldn't even communicate because she was so unwell – how could she be expected to get a job?

Go to college? Make friends when her brain was clearly broken? No yoga or colouring-in books or mindfulness or positive thinking could remedy her. Just like with my own illness, this was not something she could 'snap out of', the same way as one cannot simply 'snap out of' cancer.

It also proved to be a big turning point for me in my treatment. That's when I thought, *I have to get out of here. I have a life out there.*

I wrote in massive letters in my notebook: THE ONLY PERSON I WANT TO SEE IS JET.

And for the first time, it was true.

Towards the end of my second week I had a meeting with Dr P. who said I could go home tomorrow morning for the weekend. I would come back to the ward on Sunday night and, if all went well, I would be discharged the following day. But there was a condition: I couldn't be left on my own with Jet.

'I know that's hard,' he said. 'But I don't want you alone with him for at least a week.'

I said that I understood.

Dr P. asked if I was having any dark thoughts, so I told him about my worries about the phantom pregnancy. When he asked if there was any chance that I might be pregnant again, I was horrified. My fanny was shut down for business. I didn't say that though, I just said that no, I didn't think there was any possibility.

'So you know you're not pregnant then, *don't* you?' he said.

'Oh yeah. Yeah course,' I batted it off. 'Course I'm not.'

'OK, let's see how you go. You can leave this place but I'm afraid you're going to be seeing me for the rest of the year,' he said, and he shook my hand in goodbye.

Later that day, Catherine invited me into her room to give me a back massage. I couldn't really think of an excuse not to say yes. It had been a rough few weeks to say the least (LOL), and it wasn't like I had anywhere else to be. It was actually a really good massage. As she worked at my knotted shoulders, she told me about her life.

We were interrupted by a visit from the ward doctor. 'Catherine, I've spoken to your psychiatrist and I've got some information for you regarding your medication,' he said.

'Go ahead, there's nothing you can say to me that you can't say in front of Laura,' she snapped.

He told Catherine – in that lovely nonchalant formal tone of his – that she wouldn't be coming off her drugs anytime soon. Catherine became angry, and started karate-chopping my back.

'NO! NO! NO!' she shouted, getting angrier and angrier until she was actually whacking me, winding me with her hefty Hulk-like hacks. Oddly, the ward doctor said nothing about 'the massage'. It was almost as though this behaviour was nothing out of the ordinary to him. And, secretly, I was glad that it wasn't interrupted because it was SO good to *feel* something that wasn't *just* my own sense of dread. A pain that wasn't inflicted by me, in my head. That was real and not clouded or numbed by drugs. It was as if the desire to live was physically thumped into me by Catherine.

I wanted to live so badly.

The weekend at home passed peacefully. The Maternity Nurse was with her family so we were on our own. I don't really remember much about it. I suppose that's a good thing. I can taste the *feeling*, though, the sense of that time back at home again spent mostly pretending to be happy to be there, wrapped in shame and guilt and apologetically, *desperately* trying to find my way around Jet. To catch up, to learn the ropes. Trying to understand him, trying to love him – it was like an arranged baby–parent-matching scheme and we were trying to make it work, to bond – like somebody had paired us together but there was no *spark*.

I *do* remember Hugo opening up the front door and just being hit with that smell of new baby and the stupid, annoying scented-bamboo sticks I had bought for my 'nest' that always made me gag.

I knew now that I had the will to get home and stay home.

There is a state called 'hysterical strength'. The most common example is that of a woman being able to lift a car that is crushing her child. In any usual scenario, a woman would never be able to lift a car, but in some cases of extreme urgency or terror or survival, humans can employ an almost superhero quality that makes them furiously powerful and strong. In a way, psychosis can induce a similar state. It turns you into a machine, removing the need to sleep or eat, or even feel physical pain. Perhaps it's the excess of adrenalin.

I really do believe I was visited then with some form of *psychological* hysterical strength. I'm not sure if it's close to psychic brainpower, but I *mentally* drove myself out of that hospital in order to get back home to my son.

65

After this 'successful' weekend, on the Monday I was discharged from the hospital. Mum picked me up on a snowy March morning. I had so much stuff to take home. My letters and photos and presents from my friends, books, my blanket, my lamp. I couldn't wait to see the back of that room. But I was scared of leaving too.

On the way home, Mum took me to the garage and I bought a rose plant for the Maternity Nurse. And some honey-roasted cashews for Hugo.

It felt weird using my bank card.

'OK?' Mum asked.

I nodded.

I was coming home.

66

I'd like to say I came home and I was all better: ta-da! the end.

But, no. It was a crash landing. My expectations were high: I was trying to be positive and I was 'meant' to be better, but I just wasn't.

For that first week, I was never on my own with Jet and this made it a horrible transition. The Maternity Nurse was there to ease us back in but the house was boiling with tension. I understood why it was for the best, but it didn't make it any less uncomfortable and awkward for all of us with our bumbling embarrassing handovers and jilted exchanges.

To be fair to my family and the Maternity Nurse, they were never dicks about it. No one supervised me constantly but I knew that every time they trusted me with Jet they were essentially putting both of us 'at risk'. I felt sick the whole time, nervous in case I accidentally made Jet cry, or if it was too quiet, and Jet didn't cry, and the sound of silence would make them think that something terrible had happened and they'd rush in panicking. So I would just sit there and opt out, not taking the opportunity to mess up.

I constantly ran through catastrophic thoughts in my mind: *What if I throw him out the window? What if I suffocate him? What if I strangle him? What if I drown him?*

And I'd be pulling the plug out of the bath I'd only just run for him.

I decided that the intrusive negative thoughts meant I must still be unwell ... and almost instantly I was thrust into a deep depression.

This was not the 'I'm a bit depressed after watching a vet documentary' kind of depressed: it was a deep and awful *clinical* depression, a debilitating emptiness, a deadening dread and, surrounded by the baby stuff, the white noise needed to make him sleep, the creepy lullabies, the white vests, my home now filled me with terror.

It was paralysing. (How people live with this illness for long periods of time, I will never know.) Mental illness is often associated with 'weakness' but it's the opposite – every day was like lifting weights in my mind. It was living hell.

I waded through the slow hours (and if you've ever taken care of a newborn you'll know the days are treading-through-treacle slow enough as they are) praying that it would get better. I felt like I'd been trapped in a house of horrors all by myself and nobody could understand where I'd been.

I made my own skin crawl. I had no self-esteem, below zero confidence. I couldn't stand myself. I put my personality on mute and I pushed through.

I wanted to go back to hospital. Run away. Or die.

Friends and family would support me by saying, 'It's all over now, put it behind you.'

There was such a pressure to be happy because I was home, I was better! I had a lovely baby. HOORAY! WELCOME HOME!

Time was of the essence – because of Jet. I had a responsibility. I needed to take care of an underweight two-month-old that I didn't feel worthy enough to love.

67

D r P.'s Harley Street office was grand and posh with a big old wooden door and a shiny marble floor. A wide staircase that curved around the corner of the entrance. Slim black umbrellas sat in an actual umbrella stand – *that* kind of place.

At each appointment, Dr P., in rose-pink shirt and striped braces, would be standing at the top of the stairs ready for a warm welcoming handshake. Happy to see me but always acting with caution, like he was trying to *work me out*. His room was how you would envisage an old-fashioned lawyer's office: a gorgeous chunky big mantle above a bright yellow open fire. Artwork (yes, even a self-portrait), a proper dark-wood desk best suited for spreading blueprint maps of places your fleet is about to invade or writing crime novels. He used an excellent fountain pen and his letters were like music notes.

He would make small talk with Hugo, always warm. Funny. Polite. Understanding. Always asked Hugo how he was and asked after Jet, but I could tell it was me he was looking to for the answers: watching me, looking for signs of *it*. I felt like I was trying to impress a headmaster of an all-boys' boarding school and he'd nod and write things down.

What are you writing down there, Dr P.?

Then he would record his prognosis on the most old-school Dictaphone you have ever seen in your life, like a reporter. *Where would this be going? To his assistant to type up?*

He would stare me in the eye as he spoke into his brick-sized walkie talkie, as if to double check that that was *exactly* how *we* felt about the situation, to see how I'd respond to his opinion, but I also liked to think it was a look of kindness, it was reassuring, touching, as if to say, 'It's going to be OK. I'm here with you. You are not going to have to do this on your own.'

I'd always leave Dr P. feeling a bit better. Like my illness was somehow legitimised. Like it wasn't something I just invented in my head. His handwritten prescriptions in my pocket made me feel safe. He was the sort of person you could imagine measuring you up for your first proper suit, representing you in court, writing you a cheque, or quite possibly selling you a wand.

68

I found out pretty quickly that if I didn't take care of Jet, I felt even worse. I wanted the dirty nappies and baby sick clogging up my hair; I wanted to be the one moaning about how *tired* I was, because to me, that was being a 'real' parent. I didn't have any of the normal things to moan about: I didn't give birth normally; I couldn't breast-feed properly. I wasn't *even* present. I was a zombie mum.

I wanted to be Jet's mum so badly but I felt like I didn't qualify. I'd say to Hugo over and over again, 'He doesn't know I'm his mum', 'Does he know I'm his mum?' and he'd reassure me, 'Of course he does.'

Jet had been passed around like some little homeless abandoned kitten waiting for somebody to take him in. But there were times when I wanted him to disappear; I was surreptitiously looking up nurseries and full-time care. *How soon could you put your baby in full-time day care?*

Had I already scarred him for life? Had I already provided him with the material for his angsty teenage poetry?

Hugo was incredible at allowing me to lean on him. He took the lead but was never bossy or overbearing. He let me go to Jet when he was crying. He let me have all the cuddles, but deep down I knew that Jet thought of Hugo as his *parent*. He would follow Hugo around with his eyes. I wanted him to look at *me* like that. He wanted Hugo to pick him up. He wanted Hugo to burp him. To change him.

Now, I think it's so cool that Hugo and Jet had that special time to bond. So many fathers feel like that's something they don't get in those first few months. Many new dads feel redundant in this time, whereas Hugo and Jet are a watertight unit. So that was a real positive. And I'm just so grateful that Jet had Hugo – it isn't always the case in some families.

We decided it was time we tried to get things back to some normality and we should let the Maternity Nurse go. We could get Jet's bedroom back, at least, and make the house feel like ours again.

During the days I ached. I pretended that I was OK. But I was drowning. I'd run off to corners of the flat to silently cry or scream into a blanket. I bit my nails off. I chewed the flesh around my fingernails like a crazed cannibal until I bled. I bit my lip. I didn't fit in any of my clothes – the drugs were making me gain weight rapidly – as if I didn't have enough of a complex about my body after spending the best part of a year growing a human. I felt like I took up too much space as a person. I still couldn't look at my scar, and my milk was still leaking (to feed my phantom baby, obviously). I didn't want Jet or Hugo to look at me.

On the walks around the park, I thought about throwing myself in the Thames. I considered jumping in front of a car. One time, Hugo and I went for a drive with Jet and I was looking out of the window thinking about rolling out of the passenger door like a stuntwoman and running away, but I know I'd never pull that off. Then I looked over to see tears silently streaming down Hugo's cheeks.

It was like he knew.

At night, I took my antipsychotic drug and two zopiclone – for the sleep – but I refused to let Hugo do the night feeds because I wanted so badly to keep up with my responsibilities. Getting out of bed to go to a screaming baby in the middle of the night is tough at the best of times but on a maximum dose of antipsychotics and two strong sleeping pills, I was a walking corpse. Slumped in a chair in the bedroom, dropping in and out of sleep and misery, bottle feeding my baby.

In the morning, Hugo would let me sleep, as the pills would be so hard-hitting that they'd knock me out and left me with a hangover that made me feel even more lethargic, slow, tired, heavy, useless, drained and irritable. Once upon a time, I had always been the first to wake up, full of energy, singing along to the radio and making eggs. Now I hated dragging myself into the living room to see Hugo and Jet watching breakfast TV.

I believed that everything Hugo organised for us – a week in the Isle of Wight, Kew Gardens, a restaurant meal – was because he felt sorry for me, something he *should* do for his conscience. How a grandson might take their grandma for a walk to the beach, to 'get me out'. I'd drag me and my miserable body to wherever Hugo suggested, but it was always there and it came with me – like a stone in my shoe – my depression, stalking me, and tainting everything. Yes, it *is* a 'black dog' – if we're talking about the three-headed Greek monster Cerberus . . .

Everything scared me. From that ghastly human-sized bear (don't worry, he's gone now– apparently he's the main feature in a window display in a children's charity shop) to Jet's clothes – he had a pair of leggings with colourful monsters on them and I would gulp in fear every time I saw them. The clang of a dropped spoon – terrified. Hugo leaving me to go to a meeting – terrified. Going to the supermarket on my own – terrified.

I couldn't go beyond my postcode. I couldn't get on public transport. I didn't even go to my mum's. I couldn't hear birthing stories without breaking down, or watch documentaries about mental illness without feeling a shudder. I'd see mums in the park with prams and I wanted to gag behind a bush.

Certain words acted as triggers, and if I heard them, that could ruin my day. I would sit there and look at every person on TV and think, *Have they had any mental health issues? Do they sleep normally? Are they scared of everything*?

Or is it just me?

I would hear any story *anywhere* about *anybody* (but mostly women) losing their minds and I would spiral, internalising it mostly, but physically feeling symptoms of anxiety too.

With my friends, I was numb and slow. I was highly anxious and on edge. I was suspicious and cold. I was shy and really weird. Subdued and confused. Defensive and guarded. I felt like everything I wanted to say was stupid and pointless. My voice was quieter, my body language was smaller. I felt humiliated. Judged. As if I was under the microscope and everybody was second-guessing if I was still unwell or not, testing the water. I was still paranoid that everybody was talking about me; that everyone thought I 'deserved' this 'reality check'; that it was inevitable that I would eventually one day 'go mad'; that I was a drama queen going the extra 'Laura Dockrill mile'.

At one point I experienced depersonalisation, a form of disassociation (I didn't actually know what *that* was either, but Dr P. told me). It's basically where you feel like you are not inside yourself.

Like you're in a dream. Like you're disconnected or detached from your body. It's hideous and can often follow trauma. There is a 'you' inside, screaming, but you are unable to surface. Now I understand that all of these frightening symptoms are the body's way of reacting to fear. It's a way of protecting us and is actually really clever – but that doesn't really help at the time, does it? No. Thought not.

Everybody seemed to be better with Jet than I was. He'd get passed around a room, taken from me, ushered and changed and dressed and kissed and tickled and cuddled and fed and rocked to sleep and I'd just sit there thinking, *Hey, wait. That's my baby. Please don't touch my baby.*

But I didn't. I was 'locked in'. I couldn't say a word.

69

The psychotherapist is blonde and bright and pretty with impressive white teeth and sparkly eyes. There is a fire. The smell of candles and plush velvet sofas. A little white dog looks up at me – *I wish I could swap lives with that dog.* The therapist sits opposite me. She asks me how I feel and I break.

It feels like the first time for almost a year when I wasn't being prodded by nurses, monitored, stretched and swept, blood taken, blood pressure monitored, swabbed and probed, prodded and weighed, fingers in me, cameras up me, scans, having a baby cramped inside me – kicking my ribs, pressing my organs, slowing me down, making me itch, keeping me awake, making me constipated. When my fanny wasn't out in front of everyone, urinating into cups, waters manually broken, injected in the spine with a 10ft needle and then being cut open, bent over, bleeding, being fed, feeding non-stop, tubes up my nose, weeing into a bag, scratching until I bled, doctors, nurses, midwives, surgeons, visitors, other mums, other babies screaming, Jet sucking from my breasts, midwives squeezing my breasts, being injected every morning, crying, Hugo by my side, then GP after GP, family, being on suicide watch, somebody sleeping with me, bathing me, standing by while I went to the toilet, people in our home sharing our bathroom, turning over our TV, the psychiatric ward, nurse after nurse watching me every fifteen minutes – even while I slept – visitors, group therapy, psychiatrist, patients and then home to where it all began – Jet, Hugo, the Maternity Nurse, family, health visitors and it was just all too much.

And now somebody was sitting opposite me actually asking me, 'How do you *feel*?'

And she wasn't going to report it back, or log it down, or change my meds, or tell my mum or my sister or Hugo. It wasn't going to be recorded or used against me. It was safe to speak.

70

The weeks rolled round. I'd wipe off my brave face at night only to smear it back on again the next day. Hugo was so patient and supportive. He'd put his arms around me, kiss me, tell me that he loved me. And I just don't understand how he could love me, let alone *fancy* me. I felt totally unlovable. It was too much to ask, I was too in debt. I was grieving our relationship. *I'll never know happiness like that again.*

I went to my favourite vintage shop and got some dresses in bigger sizes but I just got distressed at going anywhere that reminded me of *me.*

Every time anybody mentioned something about Jet in the future – 'He'll be walking before you know it' – the Voice replied, *Ha! You'll be dead before that.*

The Voice was with me when I was washing up. When I was boiling a kettle. When I was hanging out the washing: *You'll be dead before he has his first tooth. You'll be dead before he starts school. You won't live to see him grow up. It's all a waste of time. Just do it now. Just end it now. Stop pretending to be better. He hates you. Your own son.*

NO! COME ON, LAURA!

I started to think that I'd become addicted to the zopiclone and then it wouldn't work any more, then I'd have to take even MORE sleeping tablets, and by the time I was fifty, I'd need a bottle of sleeping tablets and a strong jab of the old heroin to get me to sleep each night.

Oh, great. So you're a heroin addict as well now.

I decided to start weaning myself off the sleeping tablets. Within two weeks I was off the zopiclone and sleeping with just the knock of olanzapine.

I maybe could imagine myself getting better?

Once again, I became absolutely totally obsessed with sleep. It was *all* I thought about. Counterproductive, I know.

The trail in my head began to go like this:

If I don't sleep

I'll go mad again and then

I'll go back to hospital or commit suicide

I had to, *had to* sleep. I used to pride myself on my ability to fall asleep anywhere at any time. I once fell asleep on my friend's shoulder standing up at Glastonbury.

I had the constant irrational negative Voice that would interrupt my every move throughout every day, poking me in the back and whispering, *Hey, what if you don't sleep tonight?*

The more I thought about it, the more anxious I became about thinking about it. Why couldn't I just STOP thinking about sleep? It was driving me mad.

No matter how many people told me that they didn't sleep well either, I didn't listen. I believed that sleeplessness was the root of all of my illness and that was my first clue that I was getting unwell again. My brain had to repair from all those nights without sleep. The brain damage would come back. If I was sleeping – all was well. If I wasn't – off to madness town I'd go.

It was quite a lot of pressure to put on myself. Of course the very act of worrying about not sleeping only makes you, errr . . . not sleep, and time once again began to chase me.

Next came my 'magical thinking'. I began to think superstitiously, *If I use this glass to drink from I'll sleep well tonight. If I put Jet in that babygrow tonight, I get to sleep tonight. If I read* Where the Wild Things Are *to him before bed I won't get ill again. If I wear this dress today I won't get ill again.* These thoughts built up to the point that I felt like I was in some horrendous game show.

Traps, more traps.

I remember as I child I used to 'dare' myself. It started off with silly things like, 'If I don't get down the stairs before the toilet stops flushing I'll get eaten by a monster.' To 'If I don't drink this glass of water by the time this song on the radio gets to the chorus, I'm going to die tomorrow.' Before I knew it I'd be speeding up on the pavement to get past cars before they passed me, tapping spoons and dodging bits of the road, hopping over drains and missing out certain cracks in pavements. If I didn't, I'd fail an exam, my brother would get murdered, my cat would die.

I remember crying to my mum once that I physically couldn't STOP myself, like being stuck in one long everlasting game of 'he loves me, he loves me not' that seemed to never stop. I'd eternally dare myself until something landed in my favour. So that nobody had to die. No one failed their exams. No monsters ate anybody.

I don't remember how that bad habit left me. But it just did, it was one of those things you grow out of I suppose.

I didn't realise this was actually anxious behaviour, which can translate into OCD tendencies and now it was coming back. In full force. There were certain clothes Jet couldn't wear; I'd have to finish washing all the bottles before the kettle boiled; hang clothes out on the rail to the drumbeat of every song. I'd be living the first dare / challenge while already lining up the next one ahead. It was exhausting.

And there was another thing: I was drinking. It was self-medication. To soften the shock, to cope, to drown out the weirdness, for Hugo and I to re-kindle what we'd lost, to feel light and carefree, and to calm my anxiety. You feel like you *need* a reward, something once you put the baby down to bed. A symbol of another day conquered. But also, I was *taking* alcohol to help me sleep, because at night my mind would rattle and race around like a tin-can in a twister, trying to *work it all out*. I wanted to shut the noise in my head up.

I was waking up feeling gloomy and slow and lethargic, plus the wearing effects of alcohol made me have even more of a lapse in time memory: to know what was real or a dream, more lost time unaccounted for, more delirium and dizziness and confusion. My head became scrambled eggs – fragments of a handwritten diary lost in a storm.

We didn't all know people on antipsychotics – but we all knew people who drank a bit too much. It was joked about by other mothers at the playgroups I dragged myself to.

'Can't wait for my glass of wine,' one would say. 'I mean it's five p.m. somewhere in the world, right?'

'Please say there's vodka in that?' they'd chuckle as I glugged back my bottled water.

'I might as well just become an alcoholic,' one mum friend

giggled and I remember thinking, 'What a good idea.' Like it was an option.

At one of my appointments, I told Dr P. that I thought I was drinking too much. The look he gave me was far more concerned than the look he gave me when we were discussing any of my other prescribed meds, or even when he had listened to my deranged thoughts during my psychosis.

'Why are you drinking?' he asked.

And I said, 'To sleep.'

Dr P. said that's what I had the zopiclone for, but I told him I was scared of being addicted or reliant on the sleeping tablets.

'I would much rather you became addicted to sleeping pills than alcohol. I'm more concerned about the alcohol than anything else,' was his response.

It's so hard to admit and it's even harder to stop. Like Julian Casablancas from The Strokes wrote, 'I wish two drinks were always in me.'

But alcohol doesn't help. It fuels the fire. And when my mum – who bloody loves a drink – said, 'Lolly, this isn't you,' I just stopped.

71

The recovery process can be long and difficult for the mother and all of the family involved. I spent a long time ruminating and rationalising after my illness. Lying in bed at night tossing and turning trying to 'work it all out'. My thoughts were confused and muddled. I'd settle on a theory, run it past Daisy or Hugo only for them to dismantle it. I realised that when I had been unwell, my actions didn't necessarily always correlate with what was going on inside my head. I had covered my tracks, hidden my suspicions and told people different versions of how I was feeling and then got these all confused. There was no single *real* truth behind any of it, which made it tough to process.

I was seeing my psychotherapist weekly. Dr P. was seeing me monthly and he began to slowly wean me off the antipsychotic, olanzapine.

I felt the benefits with every smaller dose. I had more energy and felt lighter. My clothes were starting to fit slightly better. And as Jet was getting older and more alert we began bonding. I was settling back home.

By the summer, Jet was five months old and I took my last dose of olanzapine. My best mate, Hugo and I went out for a massive meal. We got these mad crazy ice creams with candyfloss halos around them.

I decided to organise a big 'off the drugs not being crazy any more' party to celebrate my return from 'Psychosis' like it was a country I visited on my gap year. I had recovered!

THE POSTPARTUM-PARTY.

But I did tell my friend that I had lied on the form at Dr P.'s saying I wasn't having 'negative' thoughts, when I sort of *was*. I was still feeling 'kicks' from my phantom baby. I was still experiencing suicidal thoughts. I put that trusty old brave face on again and then it happened – I had a sleepless night. This completely threw my confidence off track. I thought, *Oh my God. It's coming back. I'm getting sick again.* The fear roared back.

It's OK. Take a zopiclone and you'll fall asleep.

I lay there waiting for sleep to come, but it didn't, and the longer I lay awake, the more tense I became and the less chance I had of ever getting to sleep. The sound of Hugo and Jet's breathing, the noise of my own heart beating, disturbed me. I began listening to the world outside, wondering who else was awake at that hour. Doors shutting. Cars driving. The sound of my neighbours' footsteps, a toilet flushing, a television, or a washing machine . . . until everything stopped and all was silent.

Everybody in the universe was asleep, except for me. Two a.m., three a.m . . .

I can't get ill again. Everybody has helped me so much. It's up to me to get better. I'll let everyone down. I can't get sick. There's so much resting on my recovery. Come on, Laura. Go to sleep. Go to sleep. Go to sleep.

Four a.m . . .

I took another zopiclone. And I slept.

The next day I felt like a failure. Jittery, distracted, unable to focus on Jet, paranoid, highly anxious, disturbed and on high alert, plus with the hangover after-effect of a very strong sedative.

One sleepless night turned into three. I found it impossible not to count the days. The zopiclone had lost its magical effect and I'd lie there, thoughts racing, soaring, while I tossed and turned. I'd go from bed to couch to couch, to bed, to floor, to other end of bed. My forehead cramped, my jaw clenched, dehydrated, needing a wee every five minutes, my legs throbbing, too hot, too cold, I'd flip my pillow, get up, have a drink of water, or milk, wee again, avoid all eye contact with the clock, knowing that I'd have to get up again any time soon to tend to a wild little baby who needed my full attention.

I was going mad again. I couldn't take it. I had to kill myself. I couldn't do this being alive business any more. I wasn't cut out for it. I was too scared to see what came next.

And so, I was put back on my antipsychotics. I felt so sad. At home we were deflated. In my head, Hugo was off with me, cold. I felt like I'd let him down, like it was all my fault. The party of 'my life' (in every sense of the meaning) was cancelled.

I'd relapsed. Recovery isn't always linear; and I admitted to myself that I was probably going to be recovering from this forever.

72

In August 2018, I got the guts to share my experience on Clemmie Telford's Mother of All Lists blog. I wrote it like this, on my phone. I wanted to write an honest account of this terrible illness. I wanted to end the silence and blow the whistle.

Overnight the blog went viral and the next morning I was swamped with media requests, messages and phone calls from close friends, old friends, school friends, my parents' friends, neighbours, teachers and responses from strangers. It was intense.

I was overwhelmed by the reaction and immediately regretted sharing the post. The reaction was too much. I'd let my guard down and now everybody knew I was ill. People would use this against me. I felt vulnerable and scared. I'd never get better. *Just make it all be over. Just make it all stop.* I went quiet. I didn't see my friends. I avoided social media.

It was so ironic – the illness had got me again – *oh, ha ha, bravo, well done.* For years, I had wanted my writing to make an impact and when it finally did I was unable to even leave the house.

Lavender baths. Camomile tea. Hot milk. Yoga. Exercise. Meditation. Reading before bed. Tincture after tincture. Nothing was working. I couldn't take care of my baby. I was never going to sleep again.

Stop. Stop. Stop.

And eventually . . . it did. It stopped. I got better. Medication and time (and of course the wonder that is Jet) helped my recovery, but it wasn't simply a case of lying back and waiting for the medication to do the work. It takes more than that.

Support, therapy and talking were crucial, but as my therapist said, 'Laura, you can do it but you're gonna have to put some bumwork into this.'

And *that* is exactly what I did. If I worked as hard at anything else as I did for my recovery, I could I be anything I wanted in the world. An athlete. A prime minister. Anything.

I tried all sorts of things to get better (Hugo got on board with every single one of the below and supported me entirely – especially the cigarettes and alcohol, obviously). These are just a few:

A stupid ridiculous starvation cleanse juice diet, which made me highly anxious and lightheaded and even more tired.

Acupuncture, which was awkward because I was wearing a dress and she wanted to put the needles in my thighs and stomach and after a Caesarean, I felt even more exposed and prodded and probed and it did the opposite of relaxing me.

Bought a running buggy (it lives in the cupboard and hasn't moved for months).

Bought new running trainers, a new running bra and wait for it, a running cap. WTF?

Cigarettes – OK, like six, but that's a lot for me.

Vaping? Not even joking. My friend got me a rainbow one with candyfloss vape juice.

A really weird 'thank you' breakfast for my family at a stupid hour in the morning.

Some strange skullcap herbal remedy tincture thing.

Travel sickness tablets.

Boxing.

1000–piece jigsaw puzzles.

This coloured light that makes you sleep when you look at it (it's terrifying and doesn't work).

Bought a PlayStation– what the actual hell?! Seriously! I mean the signs were there – I was a woman on the edge!

A breathing CD (yes, a CD: a present from Dr P. Hugo went to every shop in south London to find me a disc-man to play it on).

Meditation (oh God, no: not ME alone with my THOUGHTS).

And do you know what? All along the one thing that actually PROPERLY helped me was right under my nose, the whole entire time.

Books.

I don't mean this in an annoying kids' educational morning TV show way, like 'Books are allllllll youuuuuu neeeeeeedddd!', but I devoured so many people's stories of their experience of depression, anxiety and psychosis, and read every book my psychotherapist and psychiatrist recommended to me.

Books are a conversation. A silent companion. And if I'm honest – I think that's maybe why I'm writing this one.

I am particularly grateful to have read Dr Claire Weeks' *Self-Help* *for Your Nerve*s. I ate this book up in one greedy sitting and slept with it under my pillow for a week.

The most important passage for me in this book, which has become my mantra and phone screensaver (and also since, a couple of my friends' screensaver too) is this:

Float past tension and fear
Float past unwelcome suggestions
Float, don't fight
Accept and let more time pass

I now have Post-it notes reminding me to 'float' dotted all over my house. When I couldn't get up in the morning, I would *float* out of bed. When I didn't want to leave the house, I would *float* towards the front door. *Float* through the park with the pram. Not committing. Not setting myself up for a fall. Taking *my* time.

I spent a long time going, 'I can't believe that this has happened to us.' It left me with a bitterness, a sense of self-pity, I felt truly sorry for us. I felt like we didn't 'deserve' it.

I remember saying to my therapist, 'I don't actually know what to do with these thoughts. I don't know what's healthier – do I ignore them? Do I tell them to go away? Or do I go with them? Allowing my brain to *live* through the disturbing memory or thought?'

And she said, 'Why do you need to do anything with them? Why don't you do as Claire Weeks suggested and just *float* past them? Let them drift past you. They will go, and then come less and less.'

And it works. Experiencing an anxious *thought* does not have to make you anxious.

In moments of illness we have been taught to 'fight' our way out.

From terminal illness to a common cold, doctors and friends say, 'You'll have to *fight* this thing.'

But 'fighting' is *not* the right approach to recovery from a mental illness such as postnatal depression. We don't need to 'fight' anything. The very word invites tension and anxiety, rapidly flooding the body with adrenalin and fight or flight responses, the very feelings we ought to avoid.

It is a worry (and I get it, I worried about this too) that if you are not 'fighting' the illness then you are *encouraging* it, that you've given up, that you are the victim. Quite the reverse is true: you cannot change events that are out of your control, but it *is* in your control *how to respond* to those events, and to your illness: calmly, and with grace and acceptance.

73

None of us are immune from bad things happening to us. There is no law in the universe which states that I – or anybody else – 'must not suffer'. I do not 'deserve' anything – good or bad.

This realisation really helped me overcome my trauma. Yes, it was really horrible and uncomfortable and sad, but it has happened now. It is a part of my life now and I am left with anxiety and grief in its wake, but when I consider that I nearly lost my life to the illness, that is a small price to pay. So, I accept it and am thankful to have got so much better and stronger now.

Time heals. It's a cliché, but guess what, guys? It actually does. If you are ill, I know it doesn't feel like that right now but . . . Wait it out. Be patient. You can feel short-changed not having 'an answer' to your illness, but *let it go*. Let your blood pump around your body. Trust that your body knows how to repair itself. Master the skill of doing nothing at all.

The truth is – if you are suffering, what actually helps you is *you*, along with, and in no particular order:

Family.

Friends.

Air.

Space.

Food.

Sleep.

Sun.

Water.

Warmth.

Love.

Time.

Anything on top of that, quite frankly, is a frigging bonus.

You were built to survive. You were designed to cope and endure. And you will. You are. You are helping yourself by reading this bloody book, even if that's all you've done today. Well done you.

In the words of Nick Cave, 'And if you want to bleed, just bleed.'

Bleed until you have nothing left to give. And break and fall and cry and lose and scream and run and rage and do all the things that YOU need to do to *feel* but do NOT give in. Do NOT see that as an option.

At the psychiatric ward they said to us, 'The only way out of hell is through the path of misery.' And I remember thinking, WHAT THE FUCK? HOW IS THAT HELPFUL . . . it's uncomfortable – but it's true.

It is a painfully long waiting game. *You will not feel like this forever.*

You will be happy again. You will love again.

You will throw your head back and crack up laughing again. You will hold hands again. You will sleep again.

You will cry at a film again. You will go for a drink with your friends in a sunny beer garden again.

You will go on holiday. You will enjoy the seasons. You will get your hair cut. You will go shopping. You will see your friends. You will have a party. You will go to work. You will kiss. You will have ideas. You will run. You will be able to buy a sandwich from a shop. You will be able to fill out a form. You will be able to enjoy a meal at a restaurant. You will feel happy for no reason. You will feel safe. You will be able to think of other things besides your illness and your fears. You will get your relationships back. You will feel like you.

You ARE just around the corner.

I know you don't believe it. I know you don't believe me. But you are. You're waiting.

Stuff that Scares Me Since Recovering from Postpartum Psychosis

Nothing.

Because what's the point in worrying about something that hasn't even happened yet? (Gosh, does that maybe mean I'm rational these days? I suppose it does.)

I am a mother lion. Fearless.

Give me a ramp to roll down. A slope to slide down. A Go Ape course. Monsters to fight. Zombies to massacre. Spirits to exorcise.

I am not afraid.

Afterword

Jet has turned one. It's a milestone for any parent and it feels quite miraculous. They are alive. And so are you.

In the days leading up to his birthday, I felt anxious, worried that the date would trigger something, that I'd fall off course. It wasn't just his birthday but it also marked the day I left myself behind. I found myself crying at the drop of a hat at anything to do with motherhood or babies on TV, and not just sniffling – I'm talking big, deep, animal, hyperventilating, wailing, dribble and rivers of snot . . .

And I'm a really great mum. No, I'm an *amazing* mum. I haven't failed. Not in the slightest. I've *aced* it. As the comic and activist Hannah Gadsby said, 'There's nothing stronger than a broken woman who has rebuilt herself.' I've proven to myself that I am the strong and ferocious brave woman I always wanted to be. Look at what I just pulled myself through for my little boy. There still is and always will be more work to do, until I am old and grey. But it's amazing to know that I'm not going to die of suicide. I am just not – so *that's* exciting. We are all eternally searching for some final point of eventual happiness . . . but what even is that? When do we know when we've arrived at it anyway?

I can't believe I'm writing this and how much it helps to do so. Every chapter I have written to the soundtrack of *Toy Story*, while trying to duck wee and juice and milk, with Jet crawling across my legs, while I've been interrupted by naps and nappy changes, my toes covered in smushed banana, and the writing has made me feel lighter and lighter. As I got closer to writing the painful stuff, I knew I could stop and scoop Jet up for a cuddle at any moment. Now that he's one, he might even cuddle me back, rather than just sit there like a splodge of mashed potato, a bag of sand.

As Jet grew up, so did I. Having a chubby adorable hilarious face peeping up at you all day long is something to live for. He needs me and I need him.

The bleeding stopped. Then, no sooner had it stopped, than my periods started again, like, '*Hey there girlfriend. Fancy doing it all over again?*'

I treated myself to a massage and silently cried into the massage table. I could not believe how loyal my body has been to me, what it's been through to get here. From pregnancy, to bringing Jet into the world and everything that happened after it, it has not let me down. I have never loved my body more.

I was scared of knives for a while, but now I can chop onions. Like anybody else.

Walking in the park, I spotted the first GP I went to see. She was having a coffee with a friend, and I tapped her on the shoulder, apologising for interrupting. Straight away her face fell, her eyes widened.

'I don't know if you remember me but . . .' I said.

'Remember you? I couldn't forget you. I'll never forget that day. Gosh, yes. How *are* you? You look so well,' she replied.

'I'm doing good. I just wanted to say thank you for calling and checking up on me and for being so good at your job.'

Another day, I had to get some medicine for Jet and I decided to be brave and 'float' to the chemist that I'd become so scared of. I nervously pushed open the door and all of the memories rushed back to me. The plastic smell of aniseed and sickness and terror clogging up my nostrils. *What if that judgemental chemist lady was there?*

But she wasn't. It was a new chemist woman. And this chemist woman was so nice and gave me a discount for no reason whatsoever.

We went on holiday to Paris. The sun was shining. We walked through a fabulous square with people sitting around drinking little coffees and glasses of wine. We got to our ridiculously beautiful hotel and for no reason at all the hotel upgraded us to a suite. Hugo, Jet and I jumped up and down on the bed. We went out to a perfect local restaurant with crumbling wonky walls with the menu scribbled down on a chalk board. That evening the maître d' spoiled us rotten, took Jet into the kitchen to meet the chef, cooked him up a whole plate of sautéed potatoes and squished his cheeks. We ate like kings.

I had all my hair cut off – which I've wanted to do for a while but you don't really want to do anything too sudden like chop all your locks off when you're recovering from psychosis in case people think you're mad again. The hairdresser said, 'You're very brave. The haircut suits your personality.'

Suddenly a haircut – on the scale of things – is a completely minor ordeal.

And my maternal instinct kicked in. Jet and I are a complete team. We understand one another. I look at Jet, right in the eye, and I say, 'I'm so sorry, for everything. I didn't before but I can honestly say, I love you. I really, really do. Getting to know you was like meeting a stranger. I'm sorry I took my time, but I'm here now.'

Jet's first word was *Mama*.

One day, he bumped his head, and it was me he wanted. And now, he's pretty much totally obsessed with me.

Daisy is pregnant. So I *didn't* put her off babies for life and even though there's not much chance of me having another baby – there's a 50 per cent chance of me getting postpartum psychosis again – I can love hers just as much. I know now how to support my sister through everything. Postpartum psychosis or not!

And if you're reading this, it means I've had the guts to float this over to my publishers. Writing this book has actually been the best therapy that could ever happen. It has made this a story.

People kept asking Hugo, 'When are you going back to work?' Nobody asked me! I work just as hard and earn just as much as Hugo does. In fact, we both still earned and provided for our family when I was sick!

Dads are entitled to parental leave and should take it. It's the father's time too and, thank God, it's no longer the 1950s. It's OK for mums to go to work. To *want* to. It's OK to want to earn money for your family. It's OK to be ambitious and want to feel good about yourself, to feed your brain and have your independence. And it's also OK not to stay at home too. You do exactly what's right for you and your family.

There needs to be more support for and conversation about parental health in general. Men also suffer from depression, postnatal and post-traumatic stress too. Having a baby can be a trigger. It's one thing a woman going to the GP to say she thinks she has postnatal depression, only to be met with, 'It's just the baby blues, why not try and sit it out and give yourself time to adjust?' But can you even imagine the reaction a man would get if he said, 'I think I've got postnatal depression?'

Hugo read every book I read, came to every doctor's meeting with me, let me be exactly how I needed to be. He let me blame him. Accuse him. Need him. He's watched me attack this illness from every direction like a moth at a lightbulb and picked me up every time. He's run in the rain with me, cried with me, stayed up all night with me, thrown out stuff that reminded me of being ill, listened to me over and over again. He's let me wake him up in the middle of the night crying. He's given me so much time, space, love and care.

For a long time, every time he went for a run I thought, 'Wow, he might never return again. He might just actually literally run *away*. Imagine if that was how he left me?' But he came home every time. And never doubted me for a moment. He's incredible.

If it was the other way round, I'm really not sure I would be as amazing as Hugo was with me. I was a threat to Jet, but he has never made me feel bad about that. He has confidently waved us off on our days together, knowing we'd all be at home together, safe and sound.

As I am editing this book, Hugo has just recovered from post-traumatic stress disorder, which came in the form of twenty-four-hour panic attacks. I guess he had been our guard dog, protecting us all throughout my postpartum psychosis and now that I was better he could settle – but his mind and body were on some frantic adrenalin overdrive from what we've been through. Suddenly, it was my turn to take care of him.

'Hey . . .' Hugo said, as he was reading this while eating a packet of Jet's crisps, 'make sure you tell them that I'm all better now.'

FYI: He's all better now.

In fact, no, he's better than ever – he's making music and being a stupidly brilliant dad and is signed up to run the bloody London Marathon. I remember him saying to me when he was unwell, 'What if I feel like *this* forever?' as though he hadn't only just seen me gold-fishing my way around the flat asking him the same questions a million times over myself – the depression/ anxiety tricks you into thinking this is your new self for the rest of your life, remember?

My therapist has given me a journal with eleven questions, which I answer every day. Question number nine is, 'What is your most cherished wish in the current situation?'

When I first started this journal, every day I'd answer that 'I didn't have anxiety' or 'I wish I wasn't unwell' or 'I wish that this never happened to me.'

Today my wish is that Hugo, Jet and I are healthy, safe and happy. Which we are. In other words, my most cherished wish has come true. And I couldn't really ask for anything more than that.

If You Need Help

SOME TRUTHS ABOUT POSTPARTUM ILLNESS

A lot of people, when they hear you have become unwell after your pregnancy, respond with, 'Was it your first baby?' As if you were *just so* overwhelmed with your new role that you just simply couldn't manage and lost the plot. Postpartum illness is *not* the result of not being able to cope with a newborn or new motherhood. I know mothers who have experienced maternal mental illness on their second, third or even their fifth child.

Postpartum illness is *not* triggered because the reality of life with a new baby didn't meet your rose-tinted Hollywood expectations. Nor is it caused by being envious of 'social media' mums. Yes, social media can exacerbate the anxiety, stress and feelings of inferiority but you don't develop a serious and rare mental illness because you are *jealous*.

Postpartum illness is *not* caused by being stressed and busy during pregnancy. A postpartum illness can happen to *anybody* for *any reason*. Yes, stress doesn't help but when does added stress help *anybody* at *any* time ever?

It does not mean you've failed.

It does not make you a bad mum.

If we talk and support each other, normalise these strange feelings, prepare ourselves in some way by educating expectant families, we can shine a light on the horror of postpartum depression and psychosis, and help to demystify this unexplained shadow, to no longer be so afraid and ashamed of its stigma.

My GP gave me a referral to Professor Ian Jones, a psychiatrist at the University of Cardiff, who specialises in research into bipolar spectrum disorders and in particular the relationship of mood disorders to childbirth. I was keen to talk to him in more depth about my case and what happened to me.

Very little is known about postpartum psychosis. This severe and debilitating psychiatric illness can develop immediately – during labour, moments after childbirth or any time after – but we don't know why it afflicts some women. (Some women experience psychosis during pregnancy.) For many women, the illness occurs completely out of the blue, with no previous history of psychiatric illness, although women who have previously suffered from bipolar disorder have a higher risk of experiencing it. Some women can look back over their life and see previous 'episodes' or examples of similar behaviour when undergoing stress, while many, like me, cannot.

There has been some suggestion that certain factors, such as a traumatic delivery, may contribute to the chances of suffering from postpartum psychosis, but many women experience extremely traumatic births without any adverse mental illness effect. Conversely, women who have had 'normal' births can go on to develop the condition.

Another suggested factor is that many postpartum psychosis

sufferers learned of there being something 'wrong' with their baby, during or after labour. But again, many more women with a similar experience *do not* go on to have psychosis.

Stress during pregnancy or labour is another possible common thread, as is a lack of sleep, but sleeplessness does not *give* you psychosis, otherwise people would be running around all over the place with psychosis. Likewise, many women report a lack of *need* or *desire* to sleep as a symptom of the illness.

It's not cause and effect, there are no definite answers. It's a mysterious enigma of an illness.

Before I talked to Dr Jones, I wondered whether I was suppressing some deep internal stored-up pain or trauma from childhood that I hadn't dealt with. Had I *always* been on the cusp of having a breakdown? Would I have a psychotic episode regardless of having a baby? Was Jet's birth simply just the trigger? Could I have experienced psychosis if I experienced a different trauma such as bereavement? Would I have had postpartum psychosis if I hadn't had a traumatic delivery? Could I have done anything to prevent it?

I asked Dr Ian Jones, 'Why me?'

And he gave me the best answer ever: 'It just wasn't your day.'

And I can live with that.

Writing all this down helped me to file the order of events, and see it as something that *happened* rather than something that is still *happening*. I've also realised that the best thing for me to do is to move forward and stop analysing my breakdown altogether, because I'll never get to the bottom of it.

I told my psychotherapist that now the whole thing felt like a bad dream, and she suggested that that wasn't really such a bad thing. Perhaps I *could* just see it as a bad dream? And that helped, a lot.

There is a new anxiety too: that it will come back. And just like shoving my tongue in a mouth ulcer to check if it still hurts, I run a series of self-sabotaging troubleshooting experiments to make sure that I'm definitely not going mad again: Can I hear the Voice? If I listen *really* hard can I make it reappear? If I think about it hard enough will I hallucinate? You think you are conjuring up a spirit. Summoning up the devil. Playing with fire. But it's not that: you're processing it. You're recovering.

I've heard stories of women having to move house because they are so overwhelmed by the shame of their illness. A lot of women have to deal with traumatic, sometimes tragic, moments that are difficult to live with. It's not easy to admit that you tried to harm yourself or your baby. It's tempting to isolate yourself. Your confidence is so shattered it takes so long to come back to who you were *before*, especially while trying to find yourself in the role of being a new mother too.

I have found it very helpful to alleviate shame, guilt and embarrassment entirely. They are wasted emotions. They don't serve me and they certainly don't serve Jet.

I've also found that opening up, talking about it, laughing about it and sharing my experience of postpartum psychosis is a very effective antidote too. Once you start talking about it, you quickly find out that you are not alone, in any way. People love you. And you don't need to ask for forgiveness. You've done nothing wrong. You have a new outlook on life. It's called insight.

And I realised that at the hospital they were telling the truth, you *do* get better, and you will.

The truth is, if you were to ask *any* new mum about her emotions after childbirth most women would say they felt *weird* (good or bad). So it's really difficult to diagnose somebody with something more serious.

Ha! And they said I'd be *glowing*. (Some women are – some women feel total euphoria and joy – the DREAM! – but some of us don't.)

When you ask older women about it, many of them say, 'It just wasn't something we spoke about.' Well, boy, are we speaking about it now.

This is the text I received from my neighbour on the snowy spring morning she bumped into me when I was first back home after the birth:

'Hey Sweetie,

I think I know what you are going through.

I remember feeling as though I had 'post-traumatic stress disorder' after Eleanor's birth.

The lack of sleep, the shock of this baby's effect on my life and the overwhelming fear took me into a horrible space.

My advice is get help with the feeding overnight. Step back . . . Jet will be well cared for and unscarred.

AND if you need meds, take them!

I resisted and suffered for almost a year!

If I am over-reacting forgive me. Text me if you would like to pop over for a chat.

Love ya so much. Jude x'

She didn't have to tell me that but she did. Now it's my job to do the same.

See, it really does take a village.

And there really aren't three trimesters to pregnancy. There are four. *And this is it.*

Depression

It's agonising but you feel too numb to feel the pain properly.

You believe you are a terrible person, worthless, hideous, unlovable, you are a burden.

You can't even find the energy or care enough to get out of bed, get dressed, take a bath, change your clothes, clean your teeth, wash your hair, or eat.

You lose your appetite and nothing tastes of anything anyway. Food is wasted on you.

You know you should 'write', 'read', 'see your friends', 'go for a date', 'run', 'do yoga', 'buy some new clothes', 'listen to music', 'bake', 'put your make-up on', do all the things that remind you of *you*, and that are meant to make you feel better but those exact things have the opposite effect on your state of mind because you *cannot* access them. Your pleasures have lost their magic. They don't make you feel better like they usually do. And that, in turn, makes you only feel worse. It's a Catch 22.

Yes, you know you should 'help yourself' but you can't think of anybody you'd like to help less.

You want to be by yourself but the idea of being alone is petrifying.

You've used up all of your friendship 'tokens' and cannot possibly ask for help from anybody.

You believe everybody is talking about you, is bored of you.

You only remember the bad things in your life, the people who have left you rather than the people who have stayed, the things you did wrong rather than the things you did right.

You compare your devastatingly hopeless life to everybody else's wonderful existence to the point that you would give anything to swap lives with anybody. You are selfish, self-absorbed. Full of resentment, you, again, feel worse for feeling that way.

You sit there thinking of any time you've been unwell in your life and how much you would swap that feeling ten times over to not feel like this any more.

You believe nobody on the planet in the history of the world has ever felt this bad ever, ever, ever, nobody understands and nobody ever will.

In fact, you feel so bad that you are almost certain that this thing will kill you.

You might have been prescribed medication but you decide that taking medication might make you sicker, might numb you, dull you, stop you feeling joy as well as pain, destroy your creativity, your wit, might make you seem weaker, that people will talk about you, gossip about the fact you're 'on meds', because taking medication will prove you're really mad, or sad, or unstable. Meds will rob you of your spark (cos, oh yeah, that old shiny personality of yours is on total fire right now, boy), that people will lose faith in you once you've turned to medication, that you can't do your job, nobody will want to snog you. You've heard that meds can cause side effects like weight gain so you don't take them because you're afraid it will make you feel worse. So you plough on, the hard way.

You care what everyone thinks about you.

You don't give a fuck what people think about you.

You feel nothing.

You feel everything. And it's TOO loud, TOO close, TOO much.

You only live in regret of the past. Or fear of the future. And the present is spent mulling over one or the other, or wasting time thinking of how you can avoid mulling over either one.

You withdraw. You screen your calls and then stop answering your phone.

You start to just want to stay in bed all day, in the hope of blanking everything out, even if only for a moment, in blissful sleep.

But you cannot sleep. You cannot find peace.

You feel the depression as physical pain. Your poor sick brain hurts so much that sometimes you think you can't bear another second of this mental pain. It can literally floor you. It can paralyse you, disable you, bind you to your bed. It hurts.

You start to drink too much, or take drugs, anything to make the pain go away just for a while.

You might self-harm or contemplate suicide.

You don't ask for help.

Other unpleasant symptoms include: paranoia, suspiciousness, fatigue, delusions, low self-esteem, loss of interest, self-doubt, anger, self-pity, annoyance, jealousy, negative thinking, catastrophising, rumination, insomnia, mania, chronic fatigue, severe anxiety and panic attacks . . . Just to name a few.

But, I promise you, like everything, depression *has* its weaknesses.

I fell for every single one of depression and anxiety's stunts.

You can get better. You will get better. It will take time, and medication will help speed the process, but it won't last forever. Nothing lasts forever. I promise, it will get better.

You are capable. You are strong. You can tolerate it. You can do it. Just look at you, you already are . . .

ANXIETY

We had a school nurse at my secondary school called Sister Webb who was perfectly nice, but we used to joke about her because no matter what your symptoms were, your prescription would always be a Strepsil, and then she would send you skipping back to class. We would joke that you could go and see Sister Webb with your arm sawed off and she'd still dole out one of her trusty honey and lemon throat lozenges.

But, like some short-acting psychosomatic cure, the Strepsil mostly worked. We did feel better. Maybe that's why she gave them to us? Because most of us were just experiencing teenage anxiety?

I can now remember, as a child, waking up on any normal day and deciding that I was going to die that day. I'd just *decided.* I would feel *doom* on Sunday night before school. I would be scared of driving over London's bridges in the car with my dad in case the bridge crumbled into the river Thames. I would fret about us running out of money. I would be up at night panicking how we were going to afford a parking ticket *if* we got one. Our family would crumble. Daisy, Hector and I would go into care.

I would get a present for my birthday and my first thought would be, 'Oh God, I love it so much. What if I lose it?' Ridiculous.

From small worries: What if we didn't have enough milk for cereal the next day? To big ones: What will Geri do for her job now that she's left the Spice Girls?

Perhaps it's my slightly chaotic upbringing? My parents' self-employment? The fact they didn't have 'normal' jobs and regular income. That I knew they didn't have pensions. Or back-up plans. I worried so they didn't have to.

To be fair to my parents they both had highly anxious childhoods with anxious parents from God-fearing backgrounds. There is a lot to be said for passed-down anxiety, inherited trauma and the true core cause of anxiety being within our DNA and genetics. It's nobody's fault.

(It always stems from childhood, doesn't it?)

Like many kids – without even thinking about it – I'd bite my nails through school assembly, chew the edges around my nails in maths, and when I tried to conquer that bad habit, I'd go for something a little more secretive and sinister: I chewed the inside of my mouth, my lip, picked the soles of my feet, or scratched my head until there were little scabs and sores. I'd grind my teeth to the point of needing rubber gum shields. More recently, when I had serious anxiety about not sleeping, I'd scratch my joints until I drew blood.

I never thought of any of this as anxious behaviour. Now I would even go so far as to call it self-harm.

Since my head cracked, to survive my anxiety attacks, I had to take the goblins and ghouls, and horror out of it. I had to understand it as chemicals, hormones, emotions, feelings. I had to see it as science and not let my imagination do the dirty work.

316

I had to learn and accept that we are not disturbed by events themselves but instead how we *perceive* these events. I had to learn *my* anxiety. What it does to me, how it makes me feel, what triggers me and, most importantly, how I can cope with it.

Later, on page 339, I'll detail where you can seek help. But first:

If you suffer from anxiety, it doesn't mean that you are a 'worrier'. That you're a control freak. A nervous person. Jumpy. Shy. Scared to meet new people. It is not a weakness. It does not make you weird. You can be the loudest, most confident, exuberant, courageous, sociable person in the world and suffer from paralysing, life-wrecking anxiety.

Anything can be a symptom of anxiety. An anxiety attack *can* make you feel like you are about to die, that you're having a coronary, when in fact there is nothing *physically* wrong with your healthy heart. Ironically, however, the effects of anxiety on the body and the soul *can* be drastic.

Just like the invention of the wasp, it's easy to ask yourself, what is the point of severe anxiety? It's unpleasant and debilitating. As a species we are built for survival; our instinct is to protect ourselves. Anxiety is basically the brain's alarm system, causing the body to react to fear. It activates our 'fight or flight' responses in order to defend ourselves if under severe attack; it shuts down our body so that the primary organs can act quickly and effectively and thus avoid harm.

That's why when people are in shock they often don't know that they are injured because they don't feel the pain in that moment. The brain has spared them the pain so that they can complete their getaway and tend to their wounds later.

You might have noticed that when you do feel the symptoms of anxiety you feel the need to be sick or poo. This actually traces back to our lizard days (yes, I just said 'lizard days' – sorry about me). When a lizard is in danger, it evacuates its bowels making it as light as possible, thus speeding its escape. Very clever. Hmmm, not so clever when you're about to give a presentation at work or just trying to maybe even buy your sweet self a sandwich.

HOW TO COPE WITH DEPRESSION AND ANXIETY

I know people who refer to their depression or anxiety like a friend. Some even choose names for theirs. I think the idea of this is really nice as it can humanise your negative feelings and diminish the terror, but as my fears stem from the characterisation of my thoughts – hearing voices, split personality disorder, schizophrenia and hallucination – I prefer not to. I feel it gives the anxiety too much power.

Others suggest giving their 'anxious/ depressive voice' the tone of somebody they love rather than a bully – one girl at the hospital chose Barack Obama. If it is helpful for you to think in that way, great. (Although personally, again for the reasons above, I just don't want Barack Obama – or anybody – muttering away in my head.)

You cannot treat *your* anxiety until you understand it. Because it is so personal and individual to everybody but here is what worked for me and my brain:

CBT (Cognitive Behavioural Therapy) /
REBT (Rational Emotional Behavioural Therapy)

CBT is a philosophy and way of thinking created by Aaron Beck. REBT was developed and modified by Albert Ellis in the 1950s – I have used both techniques to get well.

The therapy is based on stoic philosophy. Eliminating unreasonable and irrational possibilities, keeping things real, present and in the moment. It's practical and can be applied to every scenario. And, luckily for us, it works particularly well at treating anxiety.

You can do a course; the NHS offers a referral service but I taught myself through podcasts and books (Dr Windy Dryden's *Ten Steps to Positive Living, Overcoming Anxiety* and *How to Stubbornly Refuse to Make Yourself Miserable about Anything: Yes, Anything!* by Dr Albert Ellis were most helpful and I found Derren Brown's *Happy* useful too. Integrating CBT into my life has *changed* my life. I couldn't imagine a life without it. I'm not even joking: as geeky as it sounds, my friends and I actually have dinner, wine and CBT evenings now. And it is great. We are taking care of ourselves and each other.

Through CBT/ REBT I now behave – would you believe it – like a scientist, *not* a storytelling, exaggerating, drama queen.

Both therapies at first will seem like a lot of work but it is very much like creating a new path in your head and the old one, with time, will become overgrown with disuse. It's like learning a new language: yes, it takes practice, discipline and time, but one day it just connects, and the new path is created.

For example, one superstition I had was: 'If I don't put Jet in this babygrow I won't sleep tonight and I'll go mad again.' And before I knew it I could visualise myself in a padded cell for the rest of my days . . .

But with cognitive behavioural therapy, this became: 'Jet's baby-grow does not determine in *any* way if I have a sleepless night or not. That is *magical thinking* and counts as an *irrational anxious* thought. *If* I do have a sleepless night, which is highly unlikely as I've been sleeping very well, that does not indicate that I will go mad again because that is *not* how sleeplessness works and I am not under the same circumstances I was when I got sick previously. And even if I was to get sick again, I can tolerate it, I can cope, look at what I've tolerated up until now.'

Yes, it starts off a bit pedantic in this way but you will get used to it.

You can exist perfectly happily alongside your fears. It won't happen overnight but it will happen.

How to Help a New Mum

People want to help out but they aren't sure how. I was enormously fortunate to have so many friends and family close by, but even still, sometimes people, even loved ones, can end up getting in the way and making life more difficult: it can seem like there's *another* person in the house that is going to want a cup of tea, and making you feel like you can't be naked and cry.

Before stepping in, please understand that this is *Mum's* time with her baby. She's trying to find her feet. Get *herself* back. She's trying to establish a bond. To fall in love with her baby, intimately, immediately, and it might be taking a while for those love feelings to come. She's trying to acclimatise to this new dynamic in her home. She's overwhelmed and daunted. Excited and exhausted. She's vulnerable. Her body may be in pain. She's spinning plates. She's trying to adjust, to understand herself as a woman and now a mother too. She might even shout, snap or cry. But that's because it's A LOT.

First of all, it is unhelpful to invite yourself round unless you are INVITED.

Next, it is unhelpful chipping in with anxiety-inducing, patron-ising, unnecessary, judgemental, unwanted advice/ comments/ anecdotes about previous, personal experiences with raising a child unless ASKED. For instance:

'When I had *my* baby I didn't do it like *that*, I did it like *this*.'

Yes, OK, but *that* was *your* baby and *this* is *my* baby and *you* are *you* and *I* am *me*. Oh, and if I need your advice, I'll ask for it.

If you've done it all before (which you haven't because it's always different) and know everything there is to know about motherhood (which is impossible) then you should know how bloody hard work it is.

But you can help. You are important. So recruit yourself as being this mum's best supporter ever by going with *her* instinct and let-ting *her* let you know how *you* can help *her*. Remember, she is following baby's needs and *you* can follow hers.

She needs space. She needs support. She needs to breathe. She needs to eat. She needs to stay hydrated. She needs to wash. She needs to rest.

So, go to the supermarket for her. Make a cup of tea. Put a wash on. Charge her phone. Hoover the living room. Make a shepherd's pie. Take the bins out. Remind Mum how much she's *smashing* this motherhood thing, boy!

But do not run the show. Do not do it for her. Do not make her doubt herself. Stand back.

You might find it frustrating watching somebody doing some-thing for the first time that you've done a thousand times over – I find it basically unbearable standing behind Hugo while he's making dinner and not telling him what to do is very hard to resist. But I don't. I walk out of the kitchen. I get on with something else. I'm nearby but not hovering over his shoulder like a bad smell. And what happens? He becomes a better cook for it!

Support her, check in on her BUT do not overwhelm her; she knows your telephone number, be on hand to answer questions but *let her breathe.*

HOW TO LOOK AFTER YOUR BABY

Trust your own instinct. You do not have to listen to anybody's unsolicited advice. And when you ask for advice, even then, you do not have to follow it.

HOW TO TAKE CARE OF SOMEBODY WHO IS SUFFERING

Mental illness is often invisible and might be difficult to identify or even sympathise with – the best way you can understand somebody suffering is to sit with them and hold their hand and tell them that THIS WILL PASS.

- Encourage them to see a GP if needed
- Listen. Validate. Reassure
- Do not ask anything of them
- Be patient – treat them as you would like to be treated if you were to get unwell, encourage them, *gently* without patronizing to wash, get fresh air, eat and drink. Keep things simple and done with little fuss

- Make decision making easy – do not overwhelm them
- Take over admin roles and domestic roles wherever possible
- Change bedding, let fresh air in
- Explain *gently* to friends and family what is going on
- Do not let them (or make them) feel guilty
- Do not say 'cheer up'
- Do not tell them *how* to feel
- Remind them that they are doing well
- Tell them you love them – remind them that they are loved
- Remind them to avoid crowded places/ difficult people/ intense TV/ the news
- Remind them that they can take as long as they need to get better, and that they are not letting anybody down
- Celebrate mini victories
- Ask them to tell you how they are feeling, and if you are worried do not hesitate to get professional help and support

An A – Z of Self-Care

Acceptance – Not getting frustrated by things that are out of my control. Not being annoyed at myself. Accepting my illness.

Acknowledging that certain things can make me anxious: hangovers and caffeine and dehydration; hunger. Even holding in a wee for too long. My period; watching horror films or weird reality TV shows; Internet trawling; social media crap; certain newspaper articles; tax; bills; and some people. I steer clear of those (that I can) and thus prevent the bad feelings. This is not avoidance, this is just protecting yourself. Likewise, the timer on the oven, the beep of the washing machine: I just turn them off rather than feel distressed by them.

Alcohol-free beer at the time, was very useful and made me feel sociable and 'like myself' whilst also retaining a level of control over my fear. Alcohol is to be avoided with antipsychotics anyway and can be extremely dangerous to take with sleeping aids.

APP (Action on Postpartum Psychosis). Seeing an actual real-life leaflet, listing the symptoms of my illness. I DIDN'T make it up. It wasn't 'in my head'. It is REAL. Hearing other survivors' stories, being supported by other women and then supporting other women once I was able to. Learning that you are NOT alone with this cruel illness and recovery. We are a rare species but we are out there.

Books on CBT, on mental health, on recovery, stories of survival, biographies too – learning that yes, *even* your heroes are not immune from getting unwell either!

CBT (cognitive behavioural therapy) – see pages 319–20.

Changing my viewpoint, not trying to be the hero by not taking medication. Learning that I'm being responsible as a person and a parent by taking care of myself and listening to the doctors and professionals. I wouldn't tell anybody to have four teeth taken out at the dentist's without drugs – why would I try and get through this without pain relief? That's why it's been invented.

Compassion – focusing your attention and care to other people can help you heal yourself, it gives you purpose and value. You only have to stand at a bus-stop and feel the stories and scars of everybody surrounding you, where they have come from, where they will go. Most of us are just ordinary people trying our best. Be kind.

Connecting with others that have been through similar things to me. Trauma of any kind. That said, yes, read recovery stories, but

I try not to compare my own recovery process with anybody else's. There is no right way to get better.

Confronting the universe – I have gone 'beyond the veil' and it's OK, I made it back. I know I am a small dot on this big earth, nothing is as *heavy* or as *awful* as it once seemed.

Cooking – I found great comfort in recipe books, flicking through them before bed. Eventually, cooking gave me purpose: to introduce Jet to food. Hugo and I ate well and were nutritiously strong and healthy *and* eventually I started to invite friends over and I would cook for them. It built my confidence up, endorsed my creativity and encouraged me to be sociable. It remedied my overthinking and reminded me of myself.

Courage – finding it to do something fearless, like write this story down and share it. I never thought I'd have a 'memoir'. And look . . . here we are.

Crying – allowing myself to *feel* all emotions come and go, not blocking or avoiding. And being proud of my sensitivity.

Doing nice things for other people for no reason whatsoever. Being at the other end of the phone, making the effort to check in on all of my friends (yes, even the ones that always seem to be 'all right'), listening, sharing and being generous with what I have.

Eating three good meals a day to avoid getting anxiously 'hangry'.

Educating myself and Jet on the importance of taking care of ourselves.

Empathy – that grumpy person that's always been a dick for no reason? . . . I now try to think twice; *why* are they like that? Life can be cruel and sometimes, it changes people *and* their view of the world. Instead of dismissing them, why not get to know them more?

Exercise – feeling my heart race and pound and it not be from an anxiety attack. Hearing myself grow breathless makes me feel so alive. I felt like I was hearing *me*. Wanting to live. And lifting weights! Feeling physically strong helps me feel mentally strong, and to my gorgeous eighty-two-year-old neighbour who caught me coming out of the gym the other day and said, 'Laura, it isn't *good* for a woman to lift,' she obviously doesn't know we are lifting every day; heavy toddlers and possibly a mental illness! (But do *not* force yourself to exercise because you *think* you should. I know how hard it is to get your bum to the gym in the first place, especially after you've just had a baby and/or if you are taking medication with weight gain and lethargy symptoms . . . gently does it – walking COUNTS as exercise. You WILL feel better if you move and get outside.)

Family – they are amazing. Rely on them, a time will come when you can take care of them and return the kindness.

Floating. Float to work, float to sleep, float to your sofa, float to the beach, float to a restaurant . . .

Forgiveness – for all that went wrong, to my illness and to myself.

Friends – the ones who stick to you. Who show up. Who stay up. Who don't judge. Who never give up. And love you regardless.

Growing up – and growing out of my fears. Is this how one stops becoming afraid of monsters under the bed . . . by meeting *real* monsters? By *becoming* a monster yourself?

Humour – I had to give myself permission to laugh. Finding the humour in my story has helped me greatly. It doesn't dilute what I went through, but it does make it easier to swallow. When I think back to some of the wild stuff I was doing when I was unwell I *have* to see the funny side. I don't want the first year of my son's life to be remembered as this terrifying dark painful year that I can't talk about. Laughter is infectious, laughter releases tension, laughter can ease anxiety. My friends can talk about it too and ask questions about it. It humanises it. Laughter is the best medicine of all!

Kindness to yourself. Be patient and easy on yourself. Put yourself first. Do not beat yourself up for cancelling plans. For getting drunk. For needing help. For crying. For not going to work. For doing things that make you feel good. For eating what you want. For not going to the gym. For going to the gym. For behaving how you want. For staying in bed. For being yourself. For taking your time.

Meditation – it works really well for some but for me it felt unnatural – my heart rate would increase and my breath would tighten and I'd feel worse after. It might work for you, it might not, so don't be worried or think it says something about your mental health if you don't get on with it. My meditation is definitely just watching cooking shows and weight lifting and that still counts.

Mindfulness – I think my 'forced' approach to mindfulness (apps, audio and books – which really do work for some people and that's fantastic) stunted my recovery, I got a bit caught up in trying to find a solution to my illness and it wasn't until I learnt that mindfulness does not have to be found inside a breathing app or the pages of an adult colouring – in book that it began to sink in. Mindfulness really just means being present and in the moment.

Music – it's times like this when music can be a real friend. Eventually my love for music came back and even stronger than before. Suddenly I understood the lyrics to songs, I listened and related properly. I also enjoy singing my heart out, it's a wonderful treat for both Hugo *and* the neigbours, I love it and don't care one bit how incredibly alike I sound to a drowning cat. And watching Jet find music has been amazing to see.

Negative Automatic Thoughts (NATs) – these are habitual automatic behaviours that our brain slips into when we are faced with an 'activating event' or 'trigger'. (I was guilty of so many of these behaviours without even realising.)

You can catch your behaviours and emotions the second you experience them, acknowledge them and challenge them. You test your 'beliefs' against reality. The behaviours below are all common examples of NATs:

- **Catastrophising**

'What if'/ creating imaginary scenarios/ negative thought rabbit holes/ tricking your brain into believing the worst possible outcomes and future reality, e.g., losing your loved ones and family; ending up in an asylum in isolation; losing *everything*; dying.

Instead of 'What IF', challenge the thought with 'What IS?'

What IS? Is everything OK right now? As in RIGHT now? Yes, it is.

In other words, instead of fearing and dwelling obsessively on the worst, deal with the now and that event or obstacle when and *if* it even ever occurs. Chances are the worst-case scenario you've built in your head is *extremely* unlikely, if not impossible . . . and in that case you are simply putting yourself through the hell of imagining it for nothing.

Basically, if it is NOT a fact, dismiss.

- **Asking for reassurance**

Asking friends, family and professionals for reassurance is exhausting for you and those around you, and is pointless: how do *they* know?

The person reassuring you is not only compromised but will never be able to give you the answer you really want to hear. They *cannot* give you the reassurance you need because they *don't know*, so any answer, either way, is never enough, and you will then be unsatisfied, unconvinced and consequently more anxious.

Asking for reassurance might relive you short term but it is not the solution. If you find yourself doing it, here's what you can do: simply do

NOT ask for reassurance, and eventually you will lose the habit! Plus, you do not need reassurance anyway – you can reassure yourself.

- **Superstition/ magical thinking**

This is a weird one and one of the harder ones to shake, but basically *stop it* – no 'touching' of any wood will help anything. If you are suffering from OCD, seek advice from a psychiatrist (CBT can also help with OCD).

- **Negative analysis and self-blame**

This includes unpicking the past, constantly unpacking your personality and coming up with the conclusion that you are somehow to blame.

Instead, dispute the findings: where is the evidence to support or back this up? Why are you forgetting about all the good, honest and healthy ways you've thought, reacted and behaved in your life? What about all the times bad stuff has happened and it's not resulted in psychosis and disaster?

- **Black-and-white thinking**

If you fall off track or have a bad day, don't go down the trail of thinking that all your hard work for recovery was for nothing. Instead, dispute black-and-white thinking. It's OK to have a bad day and be fine with that. Life has good bits and bad bits but it doesn't mean life is either good or bad. And you are neither good nor bad.

- **Low frustration/tolerance**

Trouble comes when we overestimate the size of the 'threat' and underestimate our ability to cope. With anything. Remind yourself you are a robust resilient human being and you can cope.

- **Self-pity**

See what a total badass you are!

See your story as one of survival rather than what the illness has robbed you of. What have you gained from it? Learnt from it? (In fact, this way of thinking has been so positive for me it actually dries up my tears.)

- **Positive thinking**

Positive thinking can amplify anxious behaviours. Just because you 'tell yourself' that everything will be OK does not ensure that everything will actually be OK; it is more likely to set yourself up for a fall and think you are 'jinxing' something. Instead, try to be rational, do what is within your OWN control, the best you can. Try to be flexible and open minded.

No – and saying it! Removing all extra stress, deadlines, tension, strains, commitments, unnecessary responsibilities. Delegating admin. Refusing to take on extra projects unless you have to or want to. Knowing it's OK to be late, to cancel or rain check. Having no shame of putting everything off except what was right for Hugo, Jet and me. And that means being slow, taking it easy, sticking to my area geographically.

That was enough. You need to work out what is enough for you, and say no to anything that's too much. Know your limits and stick to them. Everything can wait.

Owning my illness. Owning my recovery.

Oxygen masking – it is NOT selfish to put your health first, it does not make you a bad parent. Think of the oxygen masks on aeroplanes – you are asked to put yours on first before assisting your child, because how can you help them if you are not fit to help yourself?

Patience – recovery is not a race, it's a process, it isn't linear. Go slow and steady . . .

Perspective – everything has changed, for the better. I am a better mum, a better girlfriend, a better friend, daughter, sister. I'm better at my job. I can cope with daily life. All *because of* and *with ginormous thanks to* my illness. I am informed and have a new intelligence in appreciation and gratitude. I am grateful to life. It could always be better but it could be a hell of a lot worse . . . I only want what I already have. And, I believe, that is a real gift to learn so early on in life and parenthood.

P. J. Harvey – 'We Float'

Playing with my baby! Not many people get to come out of trauma with a fantastic silly little person there waiting to have fun with. I played and played and played.

Podcasts – listening to people's lives and realising that *everybody* has, is or will go through something in their life that changes them and to find comfort and hope in that. Blind Boy's podcast on CBT was so useful to me, it's honest, funny and frank talking and was a great companion to have in my headphones to get me back into running around the park at night on my own.

Pottering – it's OK to just exist for a day. Not every day has to be busy, stuffed with activities, emails and To-Do Lists. We love being at home, all three of us, doing our own thing in one another's company. It is grounding and peaceful.

Prioritise – when you prioritise properly, you realise what is actually important. Do I care if the house is a mess? No.

Reaching out to others. I've made some new friends during this experience, friends that are willing to go there and talk about this actual stuff.

Sharing my illness. Sharing my recovery.

Simplifying – I used to have a real habit of making things more complicated than they needed to be. I don't need to be a superwoman. I just need to be myself and do what I can do, when I can. And it's OK if I can't.

Slowing down – At points, I have had to physically stop walking in the street just to *breathe* because I have found myself pounding to the supermarket like a serial killer with an axe just to get Jet a sodding apple.

Talking – when you talk about your mental illness, you expose it for what it really is – chemicals, nerves, emotions, thoughts, feelings, habits, behaviours, patterns, cycles, hormones. Do you know how much closer it's made my bonds and relationships with my friends and family? I can talk about *stuff.* People talk to me. My life has flourished. It's informed me. It's enriched me. I have *no more boring* conversations at parties. I have *no more* small talk. I go there. I live *out loud.* This is how you make friendships . . . and you never know . . . you might talk about it *so* much you might even bore yourself – naturally, you will want to move on and life will whisk you off onto something else as it always does. Also, depression hates being bitched about! So bitch, bitch, bitch.

Taking my time. Coming off my meds as slowly as possible. D*o not* rush. There is no *end* to recovery. Take your time. Bit by bit.

TV – my secret night-time friend in the dark.

Tea – yes, real tea!

Understanding my illness and what happened to me the best I can and not being afraid of it.

Writing – words have been there for me since I was a little girl. How a musician has a piano, I have a pen and with it, I have been able to have a go at digesting this big old ugly mess that I believe *is a* love story. And now that I am working again, as a writer, I am finding my identity. It is a privilege to trust my head and my instinct. My imagination is a happy and safe place to be inside once again, I enjoy spending time there, daydreaming and thinking and making up new stories. And I embrace it all, the dark bits too. The very act of writing *this* has saved my life and I believe is what has made my recovery so swift and stable. Years ago would a woman have been able to write about this stuff without being called a witch or thrown into an asylum? Probably not. I'm doing it for them too!

Yes to new stuff, exciting stuff, stuff that used to scare me, that's the plus side of nearly dying – it's so liberating – I enjoy my life so much more than I ever did. I have so much gratitude for my spot on the earth.

ZZZZZ – sleep and lots of it.

As I write this, Hugo is making tea. Jet wakes up from his nap and looks at me with his big blue eyes and I look back at him. One day, maybe you'll read this book, Jet. Maybe you'll say, 'I love you,' maybe you'll say, 'And I don't blame you for what happened, Mum, it's not your fault.'

Jet. This is for you. I can't believe I *made* you. And actually, when I think about it, I realise, no, I didn't make you at all.

Turns out it is *you* who has made me.

Where to Seek Help

Postpartum Psychosis is considered a medical emergency. In that case you should not hesitate to go to A&E or call NHS 111/999 if there is imminent danger.

If not urgent but you/ someone you love is struggling contact your GP. If your GP is not immediately (the same day) available and you need help call **NHS 111**, your local out of hours service or A&E. If you are in an emergency or there is high risk imminent danger, **call 999** and ask for an ambulance.

If you have been told by a health professional you don't have postpartum Psychosis or 'something more serious' and yet your symptoms still persist or worsen, go back to the GP or get a second opinion from a trusted medical professional. It is OK to go back. The symptoms can be hard to spot. Looking back, I probably masked mine!

There is still little understanding of the illness but there are places that can help.

Action on Postpartum Psychosis are here to support you, your family and friends.

https://www.app-network.org/

APP are also available on socials. They are *so* helpful. Many of the team are made up of people that have suffered with the illness or know it up close. They WANT to help. I have pointed many parents in their direction. They also have a page of 'useful links' on their website (not just for postpartum illnesses but many helplines and associations.)

If you or somebody close to you can identify with the symptoms inside this book and they aren't birth related you may also want to look at

www.mind.org.uk

You are not wasting anybody's time.
Yes, it 'could just be nothing' but it is better to be safe than sorry.
It is not your fault.
You did not *ask for it*.
You are not a failure.
Nobody is sick of you.
No shame. No guilt. It can happen to anyone.
Asking for help is not a weakness, it is the bravest thing a person can do.
One day, you might be able to help somebody else in the same way somebody has helped you.

Acknowledgements

Thank you to my village:

Ariella. Rowan. Thank you. Jodie. Molly. Emily. Dan. All at United. Lucie. Kate. Rosie. Mireille. Rosemary. Justine. The team at square peg. Vintage. Issy. Action on Postpartum Psychosis; Ellie. Jess. Jessie. Helen. Kathryn. Fiona. Thank you. Ruth. Azerou. Rashieda. Karen. Jeremy. Chi Chi. Henri. Emma. Ian. Caroline. Bryony. Jude. Shereen. Maria.

Thank you to Hugo's family.

Thank you to my friends. You know who you are, one of you is probably sitting next to me right now eating me out of house and home- exactly how I like it – I LOVE you. Thank you for not letting me close the door.

Thank you to my neighbours. Yes, my actual next-door neighbours.

Thank you to the women and mums who helped me in the early days; Pamela, Leah, India, Jenny, Charlotte, Paloma, Lucy, Jessie.

Thank you to all the people who sent us cards and presents when Jet was born. I was probably too unwell at the time to say thank you properly.

Thank you to all the NHS midwives who took care of us.

Thank you to the staff at both hospitals who cooked and cleaned and talked to me.

Thank you to all the professionals who helped me and thank you for letting me tell this story with your permission.

Thank you to all the women who have shared their stories with me.

Thank you, Clemmie.

Thank you to ALL the people who have cornered me at various times from events to parties, supermarket trips to the playground, the pub, playgroup, the gym – even at a Spice Girl gig and shared their own experiences or encounters with mental health, illness or trauma. From new mums to giant Security guards at gigs. It doesn't discriminate.

Thank you to my family (yes Ramsay that includes you.) I love you ALL so much. I'm sorry this was so scary for everybody.

Daisy, you are the greatest sister, friend, daughter and mum anybody could ever ask for. I am so proud of you.

Thank you, mum. I remember you saying, 'Laura, you're the biggest scaredy-cat in the world, you get scared of ramps! of the dark! of crap ghost trains but I've never seen anybody braver or stronger than you trying to get better. It was like watching the best athlete in the world.'

And I didn't know how to reply . . . but now I do.

Mum – everyday with you is like watching an athlete. You were the one who taught me how to lift.

Adele – I don't even know what to say. My one-woman army Spider-Woman. Thank you. I love you. I wouldn't want to be a boiling hot mess with anybody else.

Thank you also to Laura, sorry about all the mess!

Thank you, Hugo. Thank you Jet. I love you both so much. Thank you for giving me so many reasons to live.

Lastly, I want to say sorry to anybody whose mental health I never understood before. I apologise for my ignorance and if I said or did the wrong thing. I didn't know what I do now. And I am so sorry you had to suffer. I'm so sorry it was in silence and that it was invisible.

I'm sorry if I wasn't there for you.

But I'm here now.